NATURAL DISASTER REDUCTION

NATURAL DISASTER REDUCTION

Girish K. Misra
G. C Mathur
Editors

RELIANCE PUBLISHING HOUSE

and

THE INDIAN INSTITUTE OF PUBLIC ADMINISTRATION
(Centre for Urban Studies)
NEW DELHI

1995

ISBN : 81-85972-15-X

Published by
Dr. S.K. Bhatia (Life member ILA & INSA)
for **RELIANCE PUBLISHING HOUSE**
3026/7H, Ranjit Nagar,
New Delhi-110 008 Ph : 5722605, 5737377.

Laser Typesetting by
STAR LASER TYPESETTERS
1A/3, NPL Colony, New Rajendra Nagar,
New Delhi. Ph : 5754404

Printed at Excellent Printers, B-85 Naraina Industrial Area,

New Delhi.

Foreword

Several parts of India are vulnerable to natural disasters of one kind or the other, like flood, heavy rainfall, cyclone, strong wind, earthquake, avalanche, landslide, fire, volcanic erruption, etc. Since the beginning of humanity, natural disasters have been causing heavy losses of life and property forcing man to 'learn to live' with natural disasters. However, due to advances in science and technology, the phenomenon of occurrence of natural disasters and their characteristics as well as the nature of damage and destruction caused, it is now possible to determine these more precisely. As a result, occurrence of natural disasters, identifying locations of possible damage and destruction can be forecasted with a greater degree of accuracy. Availability of such crucial information in advance can greatly help in avoiding or minimising loss of life and property. Therefore,, armed with this information, today, we are required to cope with natural disaster through taking effective measures that are neccessary for prevention and mitigation of losses and sufferings.

It needs to be realised that though, generally speaking, the frequency of natural disasters has not changed much, loss of life and property and losses due to dislocation of developmental activities have gone up alarmingly because of all-round growth in human activities resulting from the pressure of demands of our fast-growing population. Besides, deterioration in ecological balance is also enhancing vulnerability of a larger number of people to natural disasters.

The effects of natural disasters must be fully analysed as these pose a major problem in some developing countries which have deleterious effect on economic growth in real terms. Awareness on the need to give greater attention to disaster mitigation, preparedness and management has been growing in governmental quarters. Pre-disaster planning is now being considered as an integral part of national development planning.

At the international level also, the United Nations have announced to observe the present decade as the 'International Decade for Natural Disaster Reduction (IDNDR) 1990-2000 AD', which aims at reducing, through concerted action, the loss of life, property damage and social and economic disruptions caused by natural disasters.

Papers authored by eminent specialists, who have considerable experience of dealing with natural disasters, have been included in this volume. Indicating measures that have been devised to mitigate natural disasters as well as suggestions for further work, these papers cover a wide range of subjects having technological, economic and social ramifications. It is expected that the contents of this volume would be found useful by all concerned with mitigation of, preparedness for, and management of natural disasters. Needless to emphasise that much more material needs to be presented on its different aspects to help avert the tragedies that are caused by natural disasters. Advance planning and implementation of programme can greatly reduce the misery caused by natural disasters.

B. C. Mathur

Director

Indian Institute of

Public Administration,

New Delhi.

Contents

Introduction

Natural disasters have been causing a heavy toll of death and suffering. At least 17 major disasters have occurred during the past four decades, where more than 10,000 people were killed in each incident. Earthquakes, landslides, floods, cyclones, hurricanes, volcanic erruptions, wild fires and such other natural calamities have claimed more than 2.8 million lives all over the world in the past 20 years, adversely affecting 820 million people. Damage caused by natural disasters during the last two decades is estimated at 25-100 billion dollars.

The scenario in India is not different, as it has been hit by at least one major disaster every year. The loss of life is invariably accompanied by devastating economic loss and hardship for the survivors. Floods have caused the biggest havoc in the country and the average annual damage is of the order of Rs. 768 crores and the average area affected being around eight million hectares. The coastal areas are greatly exposed to the tropical cyclones inflicting extensive devastation. The unprecedented tidal wave and severe cyclonic storm of 1977, 1979 and 1984 in Andhra Pradesh are recent incidents whose ghastly pictures are still fresh in our memory. Earthquakes have been the cause of sorrow to many. The 1991 earthquake in Uttarkashi had caused untold miseries to several people. The loss of life and property suffered by other natural disasters like landslides, avalanches, etc., has also been substantial.

By taking anti-disaster preparedness measures in advance and thereafter by undertaking systematic post-disaster rehabilitations, the effect of most of the dreadful natural calamities can be considerably mitigated and valuable work in this direction is being done in our country.

In an attempt to alter attitudes and change reactions to natural disasters, the International Disaster Reduction (IDNDR) was launched by the United Nations on 1 January 1990 as the first globally concerted effort to reduce the impact of natural hazards. The decade plans to achieve these aims by instituting an integrated approach to disasters, by stimulating data acquisition for their application in more widespread forecasting and warning system, by making improvements in disaster preparedness and by changing the sometimes fatalistic attitudes to disasters. Increased community participation and more and better education and training will be very important components of the decade. Achievements of these aims will cause a change in the basic approach to disasters, from the present concentration on post-disaster relief to a future emphasis on pre-disaster preparedness.

The World Health Organisation (WHO) has urged that prevention or mitigation measures should be seen as prudent long-term investments that will weather the sudden down-turn that natural disasters create.

Incorporating preparedness planning into long term developmental strategies is, therefore, not a luxury but an essential need. An estimated two-thirds of the countries most vulnerable to disasters are still without adequate disaster planning.

A study prepared by WHO points out that war and degradation of the environment in combination with the over-crowded cities and the overthrow of those populations into high risk areas, make the task on hand increasingly difficult. Difficult or not, disaster reduction is now a human imperative. Further delay will simply result into more deaths and destruction.

It is when human population moves into vulnerable areas, or themselves create conditions of vulnerability that natural disasters become human tragedies. Poverty and population pressures have pushed people into increasingly unsafe grounds, hillsides prone to landslides, undefended coastal plains and islands, river water sheds, and areas of great seismic risk.

According to U. S. Overseas Development Council, six out of every 10 of the World's poor are being pushed by agricultural modernisation and high population growth into marginal lands that are more vulnerable to disasters. Many are driven by slow man-made calamities such as overpopulation, economic inequalities, personal and national debt burdens and civil war.

The degradation of the environment by the pollution of

fossil fuels is a calamity. The deforestation poses a great hazard. The global warning and rising sea-levels represent cataclysms in the making. Water scarcity is an acute problem for over 60 per cent of the world's population. Water pollution clearly combines health problems.

The restoration of health infrastructure is one of the most important tasks facing governments and the people following a disaster. Rehabilitation that is slowed or prevented due to lack of funds can lead to health hazards. Cost of rehabilitating shattered infrastructure and economy are enormous particularly where, as in many developing countries, property is uninsured. Therefore, measures taken before disaster can pay off handsomely after it.

Disaster relief, reconstruction and rehabilitation as well as prevention, mitigation and management including disaster preparedness are the major responsibilities of public administration. Methods and procedures have to be devised so that the relief is provided in full measures, as intended without leakages, to the beneficiaries. The urging and speed become the hall mark of relief operation, reconstruction and rehabilitation.

An overall view of natural disaster management is required encompassing disaster mitigation and preparedness so that over a period of time the consequences of natural disasters are reduced minimising loss of life and property and disruption in economic and social activities.

The public administration should be oriented to the advances in the science and technology and their impact on disaster mitigation and management which requires considerable studies. Education and public awareness of all citizens beginning with school-going children are neccessary for disaster preparedness.

In the present volume, there are select papers written by eminent scholars in this field which throw light on various aspects of natural disasters mitigation, including the technological advances that have been accomplished. Meaningful suggestions have also been given in these papers to reduce the ill-effects of these diasasters. After all the preparedness for disaster is a prudent investment.

G. C. Mathur, in the first paper of this volume, suggests various planning and management methods for the prevention and mitigation of natural disasters in metropolises of India in which there is a large concentration of population which is exposed to disaster risk. According to him, the most important aspect of strategy of disaster preparedness comprises : the development of contingency plans, establishment of a centre for training and linkage between the relief and schemes for providing work and employment. He suggests a regular forum for exchange of information on designing major projects in various zones vulnerable to natural disasters; appropriate planning regulations and building bye-laws, a net-work of Research and Development (R&D) institutions for undertaking joint surveys, investigations and research and preparation of specific case studies.

Y. P. Pathak and M. A. Sinare mention about the major role of Armed Forces in handling the natural calamities and assisting the civil authorities in hours of need. The Defence Research and Development Organisation is in a unique position to undertake the design and development of equipment, materials, processes and systems required for disaster management. A variety of bridging equipment and boats for disaster management which have been developed and dealt with in their papers are : (i) portable fixed bridges, (ii) portable floating bridges, (iii) mechanically launched bridges and (iv) boats for flood relief. These devices have been extensively used by Army for rescue and relief work.

G. C. Mathur in his second paper, in this volume, has presented the recommendations of the Task Force on Housing in areas prone to natural disasters constituted by Government of India and suggested strategy for implementation of various technical and siting and control measures and research for housing in areas prone to natural disasters.

J. C. Pant deals with several issues connected with disaster relief in the wake of natural calamities and outlines the genesis of disaster relief in the country. He underlines factors responsible for the shortcomings in the relief system in the pre-independence era. Prior to 1878, he points out that no special financial provision was made to meet the obligations imposed by periodic recurrences of famines. After independence the primary responsibility for providing relief measures was entrusted to the state governments. In the present time, natural disaster management approach has moved from crisis manageement to risk management. This has provided timely relief to affected people.

J. S. Mani describes natural features responsible for coastal erosion. He also describes types of coastal protection works that are usually carried out either to protect the existing beaches or to build-up the beaches lost due to erosion. He also suggests various measures to protect them.

G. S. Mandal makes an effort to provide a 'bird's eye' view of tropical cyclones. While doing so, the exceptional nature of the problem in the Bay of Bengal and the Arabian Sea has been brought out. At the end, one of the important short-term mitigation measures against tropical cyclone disaster, the cyclone warning systems in India, has been discussed.

J. Shanmugasundaram, T.V.S.R. Appa Rao and B. Venkateswarlu illustrate typical damage caused to different types of building and structures during cyclonic storms. Mitigation of damage to structure is of prime concern to engineers, designers and administrators. The paper presents a critical assessment of the problem and complexities involved in R and D work. The investigations carried out by the Structural Engineering Research Centre (SERC), Madras on risk analysis of cyclonic wind speeds in different coastal regions of India have been highlighted in their paper.

S. Ponnuswamy and C. T. Sriramulu examine the impact of cyclones on transport in Madras and describe the measures to mitigate the losses which include : expansion of storm water drains and river outlets, better road designs, relocation of some transport facilities, improving water ways, etc.

Tushaar Shah states that in many areas conditions of over-exploitation of ground water acquifers have resulted in serious ecological consequences. In such areas, first the ground water balance is to be snapped for the farming system to slide down to a new equilibrium at lower levels of output and incomes. Secondly, some system of rules is to be accepted by ground water users for a sustainable community-based management of the resource.

P. Jagannatha Rao says that landslides are caused primarily by natural phenomena and also by human activities. These can be controlled and damages minimised by taking precautionary measures in the shape of proper surveys, sampling and testing, designing and evaluation of slopes, so that adequate stability of slopes is maintained and no adverse effects arise.

B. Ganguly states that with the growth of science and technology, it is possible to minimise the result of natural disasters. For this purpose, it is essential to have a well thought-out pre-disaster and post-disaster planning in which education constitutes an important component. He brings out the necessity to educate the citizens, specially the school-going children.

D. P. Singh shows the significance of training and education in managing natural disasters. In fact, training is a means to improve performance and problem solving capabilities of people in difficult situations. Hence it is very important to develop a trained human resource in India which can be utilised in preventing and mitigating the disasters. He also emphasises the need for public education and awareness programmes.

GIRISH K. MISRA

1

Planning and Management for the Prevention and Mitigation of Natural Disasters in Metropolises of India

*G.C. Mathur**

Asia is the continent most prone to natural disasters. It is followed by Latin America, Africa, Europe and Australia. Human settlements in India have been subject of vagaries of natural disasters caused by floods that pereniaIiy occur; cyclones and duststorms which are a seasonal feature; and earthquakes which occur frequently. Being a vast country, India has been prone to recurrent natural calamities from time to time which have debilitated the agricultural and industrial economy and posed grave problems of relief and rehabilitation.

Floods pose a serious problem in thickly populated states like Uttar Pradesh, Bihar, West Bengal and Assam. On an average, 8.2 million hectares of land are annually affected by floods in the country. The number of houses damaged is colossal.

Cyclonic storms from the Bay of Bengal severely affect the coastal districts of Tamil Nadu, Andhra Pradesh and Orissa. The worst cyclone in which about 10,000 people perished, hit Andhra Pradesh Coast on 19th November, 1977.

Earthquakes have been occurring frequently as more than 55 per cent of land area in India, particularly in the Northern Belt falls under a seismic zone of moderate to severe intensity. The Himalayan range from Kashmir to Assam, Indo-gangetic plains and the Kutch and the Kathiawar region of western India are geologically the most unstable parts prone to earthquakes. Some of the most destructive earthquakes have occurred in towns along the Himalayan Belt like Shillong (1897), Kangra (1905), Bihar (1934) and Assam (1959).

---

* Former Director, National Buildings Organisation, New Delhi.

Other forms of natural disasters which occur in India include *avalanche* in the snow-bound northern region, *tornado* in different parts of the country and *landslides* in the north-eastern region.

In the planning and developement of human settlements, particularly the metropolitan centres, therefore, high priority is being given to disaster prevention and mitigation.

Growth of Population and Metropolitan Centres

India is the most populous country in the world, next only to China. With a population of 770 million in 1986, the country experienced unprecedented rate of urbanisation, resulting in massive increase in urban population. The proportion of urban to total population has increased from 11 per cent in 1901 to about 23 per cent in 1981. There were only 25.6 million people living in urban areas in 1901 which increased to 156 million by 1981. By the turn of the century, the urban population is expected to be about one-third of the total population of the country.

Growth of Metropolitan Centres

There was an increase of 19 million in urban population during the last census decade 1971-81 and a few large cities had become still larger. The growth of population in 12 metropolitan centres in India, having a population of one million plus, since 1951 and projected to 2001 A.D. is given in Table 1.

Disaster Risk

The process of rapid urbanisation has significantly contributed to risk exposure to larger sections of population in the event of occurences of natural disasters. Besides almost a quarter of the urban population which is about one-third of the country's total population is living in 12 metropolitan centres whose population is one million plus. Due to heavy concentration of population in large cities like Calcutta, Bombay and Delhi, the density of population in some parts of the metropolises is as high as 1,000 persons per hectare. The Indian metropolises are exposed to a large scale damage and destruction at times from more than one type of natural disaster.

Moreover, for rapid economic and social progress development activities have been taking place in metropolises involving large magnitude of construction of different types of buildings and other structures as well as provision of infrastructural services. It is, therefore, incubent to ensure the safety of these in the event of natural disasters to minimise loss of life and property.

Table 1

Growth of Population in Metropolitan Cities, (1951-2001)

(in '000)

Metropolitan Cities	1951	1961	1971	1981	2001 (Projected)
1	2	3	4	5	6
1. Calcutta	4,589	5,736	7,031	9,194	11,932
2. Greater Bombay	2,967	4,152	5,971	8,243	14,965
3. Delhi	1,437	2,359	3,647	5,729	13,400
4. Madras	1,542	1,945	3,170	4,289	7,463
5. Hyderabad	1,128	1,249	1,796	2,545	8,640
6. Ahmedabad	877	1,206	1,742	2,548	5,216
7. Bangalore	7,790	1,200	1,654	2,921	4,760
8. Kanpur	705	971	1,275	1,639	2,673
9. Poona	606	791	1,135	1,686	2,445
10. Jaipur	304	410	637	1,015	2,478
11. Nagpur	485	690	930	1,302	--------
12. Lucknow	496	656	814	1,008	1,272

Poverty Syndrome

Generally, it is found that in developing countries there is a steep rise in mortality with decreasing income. There are more deaths per disaster in low income countries. The poor countries which suffer natural disasters are the same countries in which environmental degradation is proceeding most rapidly. Countries with severe deforestation, erosion, over cultivation over overgrazing tend to be hardest hit by disasters. In many cities, the poor live on land prone to natural disasters. They live in self-built shelters unable to stand up to strong winds, rain or tremours. They also did not know how to protect themselves from natural disasters.

The size of the urban population in India and its unabated growth pose a major challenge to Indian policy makers and planners in the task of natural disaster prevention and mitigation. The urgency of formulation of comprehensive national policies for disaster mitigation is being increasingly realised by national government to minimise the heavy loss of life and property which has been taking place from time to time and also to avoid abrupt disruption of industrial and agricultural developement activities and sufferings of the millions who are victims of natural disasters.

Disaster Preparedness and Management

Recognising that with the increase in population and the expansion of human settlements, the Seventh Five Year Plan (1985-1990) aims at building-up an effective system of disaster preparedness and management taking an advantage of technologies available for weather forcasting. For this purpose, the approach will be mainly based on the following measures :

(a) Zoning and mapping of vulnerable areas;
(b) Land use regulations;
(c) Early warning and communication;
(d) Community preparedness; and
(e) Contingency planning.

More purposive public policies for natural disaster mitigation are being formulated and steps are being taken to strengthen the existing legislative frame work at national and state level for effective implementation of the policy measures. These include policy shift from disaster relief to management; financial grant by Union Government to state government for relief and rehabilitation; formulation of national policy for environmental protection and ecological balance; support to science and technology for disaster mitigation; assessment of new development projects from the point of view of natural disaster mitigation; strengthening of legislative framework for effective implementation of policies; stress on regional and spatial planning of human settlements; people's participation and preparedness, etc.

Prevention and Mitigation of Disasters

With the fast increase in population and the expansion of human settlements, the threat to life and property has increased on account of natural disasters. To appreciate the gravity of the problem, the extent of occurrence of major natural disasters and damage and destruction caused in recent decades in India are briefly indicated in the following paras along with the measures being taken for planning and management for prevention and mitigation of natural disasters with special reference to metropolitan centres.

Floods

The seriousness of the flood problem in India can be judged from the extent of damage it causes. Available data for a period of 25 years from 1954-76 reveal that the average annual direct damage is of the order of Rs. 2,474 million. The details of losses are :

(i)	Total area affected	8.2 million hectares
(ii)	Cropped area affected	3.5 million hectares
(iii)	Number of houses damaged	9.25 lakhs
(iv)	Population affected	24.6 million
(v)	Number of human lives lost	1,240
(vi)	Number of cattle lives lost	77,000

In addition to the direct damages, there are indirect losses resulting from the disruption of rail, road traffic and dislocation of normal life.

Flood Forecasting and Warning : Flood forecasting and timely warning are the essential pre-requisites for preparedness to meet the disaster when it strikes. The Central Flood Forecasting Organisation of the Central Water Commission is discharging the function of flood forecasting. It has set forecast sites at 120 locations and observations are recorded from 320 gauge/discharge sites. The meteorological department has opened flood meteorological offices at important cities like Patna, Bhubaneswar, Guwahati, Jalpaiguri, Lucknow, Delhi and Surat. They provide information to the forecasting centres regarding weather, rainfall and quantitative forecasts of preparation for the next 24 hours for the river basin.

The multi-purpose Indian National Satellite (INSAT) launched recently is being utilized for warning purposes and it is possible to have a reliable and complementary warning system *via* the satellite. Through this system, it is possible to reach officials lower than district level authorities directly when all other land link systems of communications are affected due to disaster.

Flood Preparedness and Preventive Operations· During the flood season every year, control rooms are opened in all the vulnerable districts as also in the state headquarters, which operate round the clock for reception and dissemination of messages relating to floods, etc., to all concerned. District level flood relief coordination committees are set up in each district with officers of various departments as also non-officials, for the purpose of undertaking necesary precautionary measures well in advance. The people of the disaster prone areas are being made aware of the disaster management and education as to how to react to it.

All flood-prone villages, blocks, etc., are properly identified and steps are taken to see that all such areas can be reached over telephones/WT sets in the event of occurrence of disaster. Foodgrains, clothing, tents, tarpaulins, medicines, dry food, etc., are kept ready in all vulnerable areas well in advance to avoid any dislocation of relief operations after occurrence of calamities. Suitable lands are also selected in advance for air dropping of food grains and relief materials.

The Government of India have, as a part of the disaster preparedness, formulated a Model Action Plan for disaster preparedness for floods and circulated it to all State Governments and Union Territories.

Rescue and Relief Operations· Rescue operations are undertaken by the local authorities, Police force, Air force, Local volunteers, etc. During the floods in West Bengal and

Delhi in 1978, local volunteers, philantropists and certain agencies played a very useful role. Most of them were either students or young men. Educational institutions and charitable organisations also came forword with food supplies, clothing and other necessities. The Panchayats and local leaders were also involved in this work. They helped select proper sites, brought more volunteers, helped with publicity and offered local hospitality.

Flood Control: It is estimated that the area liable to be affected by floods is about 40 million hectares. According to National Flood Commission, out of this, 32 million hectares may be considered as protectable. Accordingly reasonable protection has been provided to about 10 million hectares. Hence the residual area to be protected would be about 72 million hectare.

At the time of attaining independence in 1947, India had 5,280 kms of embankments along different rivers giving protection against flood to about three million hectares. During the first plan, the technique of flood protection by moderation through multi-purpose reservoirs was adopted for the first time, in addition to the traditional method of embankment. Inadequacy of flood protection measures taken in the past were brought during the severe floods of 1954.

A national policy regarding the problems of floods and remedies in a comprehensive manner was enunciated in 1954. In brief this policy envisages that floods in the country can be contained and managed and that the problem is capable of solution. It is also called upon the administration and the people to share the responsibility and undertake this task of huge magnitude in order that the country may be rid of menace of floods. Since then, considerable work has been done for providing flood protection in the most vulnerable areas.

National Commission on Floods To develop a long-term strategy for control and management of floods, the Government of India set up the National Commission on Flood in 1976. The Flood Commission has submitted its report containing important recommendations, covering methodology, flood damage assessment, areas needing urgent attention, land use and regulations, cost and benefit criteria, future approach, planning and administration, financing research, education and training, etc.

Special River Commissions have been set up in some of the States where flood problem is serious. The Brahmaputra Flood Control Commission for the planning and implementation of works in the Brahmaputra Valley, and Flood Control Commission in Patna for Ganga basin have been set up. These Commissions will prepare comprehensive plans and ensure their implementation in a phas-d manner.

Cyclones

Every year some part or the other of India's vast sea coast is affected by violent storms, which lies in their erratic paths. The east coast of India stretched over a length of 3,000 km from Rameshwaram to Calcutta is prone to severe cyclone wit wind pressure intensify about 200 km /hour (Fig. 1)

The fury of the cyclone that struck Andhra Pradesh and Tamil Nadu on the night of November, 19, 1977 was unprecedent in over a century. Approximately 7.1 million people in 2,302 villages were affected by loss of life, property, crop and other damages. In Krishna district alone the death toll was estimated over 10,000 besides loss of 2,31,000 cattle and 45,000 live-stock. About 36,000 huts were completely washed away. In all property worth Rs. 450 crores was lost. Communications, railways, roadways, telephones, electrical installations, canals and storage buildings suffered substantial damages.

Disaster Preparedness, Contingency planning has been evolved by the state governments, to deal with any situation on the basis of advance preparedness and planning done. In Andhra Pradesh there is a Standing Committee under the Chief Secretary of the State government for overall responsibility for disaster preparedness. Operational responsibility is given to a relief section in the Revenue Department. Government plan generally involves identification of the villages within a specified distance from the coast or within the specified distance along the disaster prone belt; location of suitable pucca buildings likely to be outside the reach of major disaster; establishing contact with the local people by the various levels of government administration; location of free kitchen facilities; likely government vehicles available, possible evacuation routes,

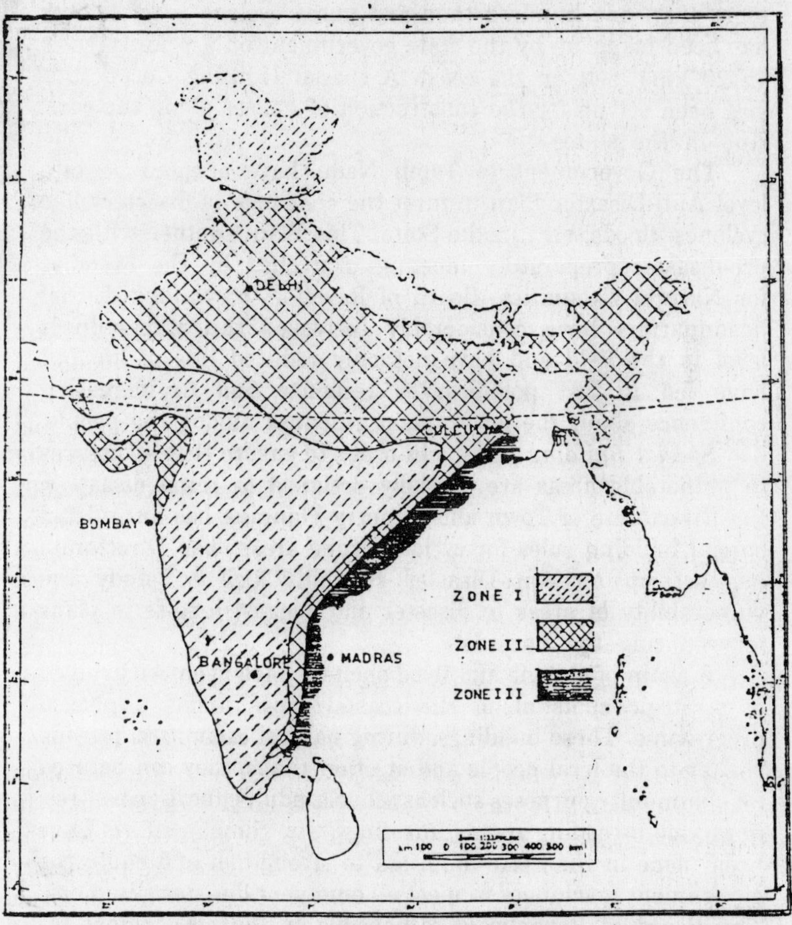

Fig. 1 : Basic maximum wind pressure including winds of short duration

location of suitable markets for various needs of the evacuee people, etc.

As a permanent rehabilitation measure, construction of more than one hundred thousand pucca cyclone proof houses has been taken up by the state government on a priority basis in 20 kms belt on the coast. A special Housing Corporation has been set up for the construction of houses along the coast line in the states.

The Government of Tamil Nadu have adopted a state level Anti-Disaster Plan to meet the challange of disasters like cyclones, floods, etc., in the State. This Plan together with the pre-disaster preparatory meetings convened by the Member for Natural Calamities, Board of Revenue, at various district headquarters have considerably increased the preparedness level in the field and have not only reduced loss of life but have led to fast post-disaster response and to increasing confidence about the government response among the people.

Special Building Rules : In order to ensure that structures in vulnerable areas are specially designed to resist disasters, the Directorate of Town and Country Planning has formulated special building rules for cyclone prone areas. The Directorate has set up an Anti-Disaster Planning Cell to study the vulnerability of areas to disaster and suggest long-term plans for reducing the hazards.

A chain of cyclone and flood shelters have been constructed at strategic spots along the coastal areas under a phased programme. These buildings, during natural calamities, provide shelter to the local people and at other times, they can be used for community purposes such as schools, adult education centres, library-cum-reading rooms, meetings, etc. Similar efforts have been made in the State of Orissa to strengthen and equip the government machinery to meet all emergent disaster situations. The Board of Revenue is responsible to the government for all kinds of relief operations and the Member, Board of Revenue functions as the special Relief Commissioner. Special Committees called Natural Calamities Committee have been constituted each at the state and the district levels to consider the situations arising out of natural disasters and take all necessary decisions and relief measures with promptitude.

Earthquakes

About two-third of India lies in the seismic zones of moderate to severe intensity. The loss of life in the case of earthquakes has been of the order of about 1,00,000 persons in just two centuries. An earthquake occurring near Calcutta in 1737 had claimed 3,00,000 lives.

Earthquake is the most disastrous of all national calamities which catches people mostly unaware and unprepared. While the possibility about the occurrence of earthquake can be predicted in a region but the prediction precisely in terms of place and time is still a difficult task despite the availability of modern technology. Areas around the globe which are earthquake-prone have been identified and demarcated. India too has been divided into various seismic zones as per IS code 1893-1975. These are shown in Fig. 2 considering the varying nature of intensity of earthquake occurring in different parts of the country.

As precise time of occurrence of earthquake is generally not known, people are required to be educated to take steps to meet the situation. The key to minimising the impact of such incidents is earthquake preparedness. The problems that are generally faced after disastrous effects of earthquake include: damages to buildings and other structures; occurrence of fire; blocking of roads; landslide or rock fall causing damages or blockade, devastating floods; tidal waves, etc.; damage of communication facility; failure of drinking water pipe lines; maintenance of law and order; protection of public and private properties; emergency shelter for population; first aid treatment to the injured; and prevention of spread of disease and epidemic.

Relief and Rehabilitation: During the earthquake of 1934 in Bihar, an international team of Services Civil International (SCI) came to India at the invitation of Bihar Central Relief Committee for carrying out relief operations in the affected areas. Until late sixties, most operations in natural disaster situations were of relief type. There was hardly any consciousness about the disaster management. United Nations has of late been increasingly concerned about Disaster Mitigation and Prevention. A world body named United Nations Disaster Relief Organisation (UNDRO) was set up in March, 1972 at

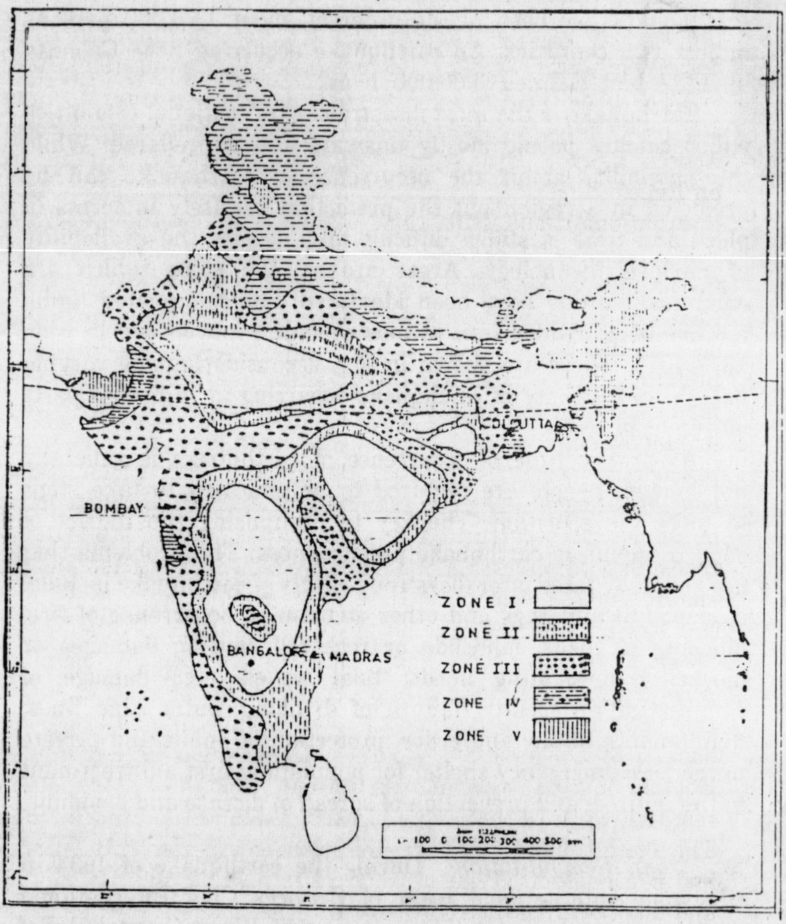

Fig. 2 : Seismic Zones of India

Geneva. It helps mobilize and coordinate relief, develop contingency plans at national levels and promotes disaster preparedness.

Some voluntary agencies have contributed significantly to the work of relief and rehabilitation. These include Red Cross Society of India, Village Re-construction Organisation, India (VRO), CARTITAS-India, Appropriate Reconstruction Training and Information Centre (ARTIC), Church's Auxillary for Social Action (CASA), Evangelical Fellowship of India Commission on Relief (EFICOR); Ramkrishna Mission (RKM), Service Civil International India (SCI) and National Services Scheme (NSS).

Preventive Measures : Based on the research work done in the country and elsewhere, the Indian Standard Institution (ISI) has formulated standards for design and construction of seismic resistant buildings and other types of structures to be built in different parts of India. These are being followed by major construction departments and other agencies, particularly in metropolitan centres which lie in seismic zones of moderate to severe intensity as in Delhi and Calcutta. Special considerations are given in the planning design and construction of important structures like high-rise buildings, large dams, transmission towers, atomic energy power stations, etc., to ensure their safety in the event of earthquakes.

Research in seismic design of buildings and other types of structures is being given due importance. A chain of seismological stations has been set up in the country to record the occurrence of earthquake and to develop a proper data base. The University of Roorkee, Department of Earthquake Engineering is the premier institution which has done notable research work in the design of earthquake resistant structures. The National Buildings Organisation is promoting the design and construction of earthquake resistant buildings and houses and had bearing masonry buildings which are the principal modes of construction. (Figs. 3 and 4)

Other Types of Natural Disasters :

Other types of natural disasters which occur in India include landslides and avalanche in the northern high mountainous region of the Himalayas and fires which occur accidentally, particularly in and around villages, and in large human

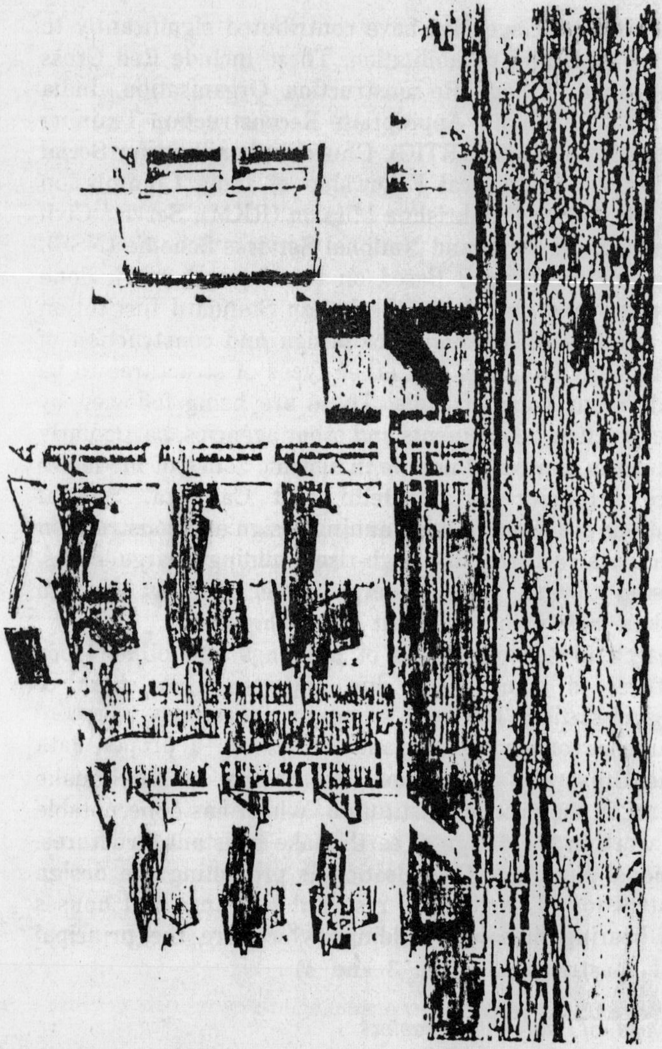

Fig. 3 : SEISMIC DESIGN OF FOUR STOREYED RESIDENTIAL BUILDING IN DELHI PUT UP BY C.P.W.D. UNDER NBO EXPERIMENTAL SCHEME

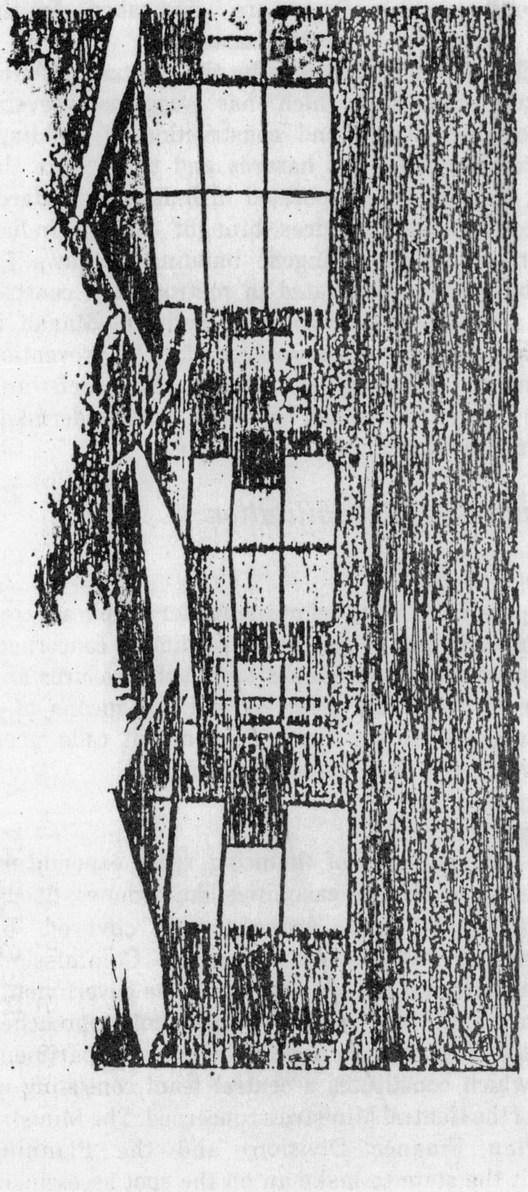

Fig. 4: EARTHQUAKE RESISTANT LOW COST HOUSES IN ASSAM (SEISMIC ZONE V) WITH ECRA WALLING, PUT UP BY NBO

settlements particularly in high-rise buildings. Depending on the local situations several measures are being taken for the prevention and mitigation of such disasters.

Fire research is being undertaken by the Central Building Research Institute, Roorkee which has suggested several measures in planning, design and construction of buildings and houses to minimize the fire hazards and to mitigate the disasters. These have been incorporated in building standards and codes of construction practices brought out by Indian Standards Institution. More stringent building bye-laws for the fire safety have been formulated in metropolitan centres.

The Snow and Avelanche Research Institute, Manali is studying the various aspects of the problem for the prevention and mitigation of disasters therefrom. Research and investigations to prevent landslides have also been undertaken by some research institutions in the country.

Disaster Relief and Rehabilitation

Responsibility of States

The primary responsibility for relief measures for people affected by natural calamities is that of the state government concerned. If the seriousness of the calamity calls for relief measures and consequent expenditure is an order beyond the means of a state in a particular year, the State Government calls upon the Central government for financial assistance.

Central Assistance

The policy and arrangements of financing relief expenditure in the states affected by natural calamities like cyclones, floods, hail-storms, landslides and drought are covered by recommendations of the seventh Finance Commission, constituted by the Government of India. The state governments needing assistance from the central government approaches the Union Ministry of Agriculture and Cooperation (Department of Agriculture) which constitutes a central team consisting of representatives of the Central Ministries concerned. The Ministry of Finance (Plan Finance Division) and the Planning Commission visit the state to make an on the spot assessment of the damage caused and requirement of additional expenditure.

Under the present policy of financing relief expenditure in the states, financial ceilings are determined every five years by the Finance Commission. The expenditure on relief for the period 1974-80 was Rs. 6878.8 million. Emergency relief is provided for people accommodated in temporary shelters and also for people whose life has been dislocated in the disaster affected areas as per the guidelines and norms stipulated by the Central government from time to time.

Rehabilitation and Reconstruction

Rehabilitation refers to the process of restoring the public and community assets as well as private assets to the pre-flood conditions. Reconstruction goes beyond rehabilitation and aims at improving upon the conditions prevailing before the occurrence of the disaster.

Immediate repair and restoration of public assets are undertaken by the respective government departments. Restoration of communication, water supply, electricity is done with the maximum speed and expertise.

The persons rescued are provided with temporary shelters like tents or structures put up with bamboo or bamboo mats. The houses are constructed in case they are washed away and repairs made to the damaged houses.

If the lands are damaged, steps are taken for reclaiming them. The damaged roads, culverts, bridges, etc., are repaired immediatly. Financial help to recover the loss is given to the affected people either in the form of subsidy or loan. Health and education measures are taken besides cultural programmes to boost the morale of depressed victims to recover from shock.

In India most of the low income families do not have proper housing facilities which can withstand natural disasters. Therefore, measures are being taken to improve the housing conditions by way of better planning and safe house designs. For low cost and durable houses/buildings improved use of local materials and innovative techniques suggested by the institutions like National Buildings Organisation are being increasingly adopted in areas prone to natural disasters.

International Cooperation

Besides the Central and State Government agencies the

role played by voluntary organisations in a disaster situation has now been acknowledged as very important and significant. A number of international organisations like OXFAM, UNICEF, CARE, RED CROSS undertake relief operations in the case of a large scale disaster.

Disaster Preparedness in Urban Centres

The most important aspect of the strategy of disaster preparedness comprises :

(i) First, the development of contingency plans in disaster prone areas to meet different probabilities;

(ii) Secondly, establishment of a Centre for training in disaster preparedness; and

(iii) Thirdly, the foregiving of adequate linkage between the relief and other schemes for providing work and employment.

The important measures for disaster preparedness which have been taken in India for planning and management for prevention and mitigation of natural disasters which have special significance for metropolitan centres are briefly mentioned below.

Mapping of Areas Prone to Natural Disasters

The specific areas prone to natural disasters like flood, cyclone, earthquake, etc., are required to be identified. In India such mapping has been done specially in respect of cyclones and earthquakes and such maps have been published in the National Buildings Code of India. The Central Water Commission has also prepared a map zoning out areas prone to floods.

City Planning : While evolving development plans, specially for the Development of Metropolitan Centres and large cities these maps should be taken into consideration. Although Master Plans for the development of Metropolitan Centres and many large cities in the country have been prepared, the zoning regulations, which form an integral part of the Master Plan, do not include provision for treatment of areas vulnerable to natural disasters.

Model Laws : A Model Regional and Town Planning and

Development Law has been formulated by the Central Town and Country Planning Organisation which is to be adopted by all States and Union Territories. Suitable provisions in the Model Law should also be incorporated to cater to the areas prone to natural disasters. The City Planning and Development Authorities should, at the plan preparation stage, identify such areas by carrying out surveys and studies. Expert advice of concerned institutions and experts should be availed of to include suitable provisions in the zoning regulations which form part of the Master Plan, to cater the specific types of natural disasters in vulnerable areas. A detailed development plan for different metropolitan areas should then be prepared.

National Buildings Code

The National Buildings Code of India formulated in 1969 by the Indian Standards Institution, provide suitable guidance for design and construction of buildings and other structures to resist different types of natural disasters to which the specific area may be prone to. The revised 1983 edition of the National Code contains more detailed provisions with regard to structural safety, construction safety, fire safety and health safety for prevention and mitigation of natural disasters.

The existing local building bye-laws in many metropolitan centres and large cities, which are out moded, are being revised in conformity with the National Buildings Code. As a result more stringent building bye-laws for fire safety, specially in high-rise buildings have been adopted in metropolitan centres like Bombay, Delhi and Madras.

Greater attention is also being given to modifications of the existing building bye-laws in respect of safety of building and other types of structures from earthquake force in metropolitan centres like Delhi, which lies in seismic zone of severe to medium intensity.

In metropolitan centres which are in coastal regions as is the case of Madras, appropriate measures for protection of buildings and other structures from cyclonic effects are being increasingly adopted. To ensure safety of buildings and other types of structures as well as the people, particularly in densely populated metropolitan centres and large cities which lie in areas prone to natural disasters, on the basis of latest advances in science and technology, the provisions in the National Buildings Code of India need to be further reviewed from time to time.

Mandatory Provisions

The psychological impact on the population of the area where a major structure is to be built in an area prone to disaster is a matter of common concern. The fear of failure of the structure in the event of natural disaster need to be dispelled as in India, where major river valley projects lie in severe seismic zone along the Himalayas and large atomic power plants, satellite launching stations, major ports and harbours are located in coastal areas prone to tropical cyclones. To alleviate fears all possible measures for disaster prevention and mitigation have to be undertaken.

In metropolitan centres it should be mandatory to design and construct all important buildings which include multi-occupancy buildings, hospitals, cinema halls, offices and also important structures like water tanks, power stations, etc., so as to make these disaster resistant to the possible extent.

In the case of government funded constructions, a minimum set of provisions for importing these structures against natural disasters should be formulated and made known to all concerned.

In the case of low cost houses and other types of buildings, the disaster resistant features should be incorporated in stages on an increamental basis, so that when the buildings and houses are finally completed over a period of time, they have the necessary disaster resistant features incorporated in them. Such low cost techniques for imparting disaster resistant features to houses and buildings should be formulated and widely publicised particularly through audio visual media for the benefit of common man.

Meteorological Forecasting

For official management of floods and cyclones due attention should be given to strengthening of arrangements for forecasting warning and communication systems, purchase of equipments for rescue and relief operations, construction of cyclone shelters and training of personnel in disaster management measures.

The Government of India have approved a national

technological mission for improving the Weather Forecasting and Meteorological Services in the country during the Seventh Five Year Plan (1985-90) which will greatly help in issuing warnings well in advance of the impending cyclones, floods, heavy rainfall, hailstorm, snowfall, avalanche, etc. Taking advantage of the advances in science and technology, the following are the meteorological forecasting services which are being provided:

Rainfall Forecast : Meteorological services have been organised in India on countrywide basis. Short-range weather forecasts which include monthly and seasonal forecasts regarding rain and monsoon, are regularly issued by the Indian Meteorological Department (IMD), Government of India. Radio medium is effectively utilised for the dissemination of the forecast data.

Flood Forecast : The Central Water Commission (CWC), Government of India have their Water Resources and Flood Forecasting Division Stations at 22 places in the country and eight more such stations are being set up for issuing of timely flood warning to protect the life and property from devastating floods.

IMD has established 10 Flood Meteorological Offices (FMD) at Delhi, Hyderabad, Ahmedābad and other large cities to provide active support to CWC in flood forecasting and regulation of medium/large dams and reservoirs.

Cyclone Forecast Cyclone warning system is one of the most important factors in cyclone preparedness. The four essentials of an effective warning system are accurate detecting facilities, reliable forecasting techniques, fast communication channels for disseminating information and clearly worded warnings and advice on precautions. The IMD is using latest technology for cyclone warning system. INSAT-1B is used for continuous monitoring and tracking of cyclones which provides cloud pictures every hour to half-an-hour during all day and night during cyclones.

Cyclone Detection Radars have been installed at Calcutta, Madras, Bombay and five other stations with 400 km range each to track the cyclone continuously. Area Cyclone Warning Centres have also been established at Calcutta, Madras and Bombay. Modern telecommunication facilities like telephone, teleprinters, telex and WT facilities exist at these centres. Computers are being used for data processing, prepartion of forecasts and exchange of meteorological data.

A cyclone alert is issued 36-48 hours before the expected commencement of adverse weather by the cyclone warning centre to Chief Secretaries of the states, Coastal Collectors and All India Radio for repeated broadcast and to other user agencies. Numbered cyclone warning bulletins are commenced nearly 24 hours before the expected landfall of the cyclone.

Earthquake Forecast: So far, no reliable technique has been developed for forecasting the earthquakes. Some earthquake precursors have nevertheless been identified which show promise in achieving the ends. Of these, mention may be made of decrease of seismic activity before major events, change in random content in well water, changes in electrical and magnetic properties and deformation in the earth's rod. For detecting these, specialised instruments have been developed. Under the programme of the Department of Science and Technology in the north eastern region, which is prone to severe earthquake, instrumentation for recording strong ground motion are being installed for recording of different types of measurements. The data so obtained would enable to understand the behaviour of severe tectonic forces prevailing in the region.

Ecological Balance: Although natural calamities cannot be averted, their destructive impact in terms of loss of human and animal life and the upset of ecological balance can, no doubt, be considerably mitigated. India's Sixth National Five Year Plan (1980-85), therefore, had listed protection and improvement of ecological and environmental assets as one of its basic objectives. Further the national policy for science and technology states that development should not upset the ecological balance for short as well as for long term considerations. Poorly planned efforts to achieve apparantly rapid development, ignoring the long term effect of many technologies on the environment, have resulted into serious ecological damages. It is, therefore, essential to analyse the environmental impact of the application of each technology with due regard to the preservation and enhancement of the environment in the choice of technologies.

Emergency Shelters: Instant shelters are required to be

put up in disaster prone areas for the potection and well being of the people. Generally emergency shelters, particularly in areas where the weather is incliment, have to be put up in less than 24 hours using materials that are readily available at hand. In metropolitan centres and large cities for putting up temporary shelters in large numbers as quickly as possible, a variety of new materials and construction techniques are being employed which include : asphaltic sheets, ferrocement sheets, precast reinforced concrete products for roofing and masonary walls made of stabilised soil blocks, burnt clay bricks, concrete blocks, etc., steel structures, such as tubular sections, cold form light gauge sections, etc.

Use of prefabricated buildings components and housing elements such as prefabricated timber huts, portable cabins, fibre glass, shelters and prefab houses have also been developed which can be adopted in large cities and metropolitan centres with economy and speed. For construction of emergency shelters and temporary houses at as low cost as possible in as short time as possible, research and development work should be undertaken to evolve appropriate techniques and packages of building materials and component kits.

Suggested Action Programmes

Planning and management for prevention and mitigation of natural disasters are matters of vital significance for the safety and well-being of millions of people who inhabit the globe in disaster prone areas. In addition to national action, international and regional cooperation should be promoted for their prevention and mitigation. Following proposals may be considered in this regard with particular reference to metropolitan centres.

Forum for Exchange of Information

A regular forum should be established to exchange information on the decisions and decision process for design of major projects in various zones vulnerable to natural disasters in different countries. Appropriate planning regulations and building bye-laws can greatly help in prevention and mitigation of disasters in metropolitan centres.

Case Studies

On account of vast similarity of situation arising out of geographical factors, social and economic conditions, it will be advantageous to undertake specific case studies of work done for natural disaster prevention and mitigation in metropolitan centres in different countries of Asian and Pacific region in particular, which are most prone to frequent disasters as compared to other continents. This will bring out typical features common to many countries, which can be considered by the countries concerned in natural disaster mitigation and prevention work.

Network of R and D Institutions

A network of R and D institutions should be developed, particularly in the Asian and Pacific region, to undertake joint surveys, studies, investigation and research to understand the various phenomena of the occurrence of natural disaster and to make collaborative efforts for devising ways and means for prevention and mitigation of natural calamities. Some international reputed R and D organisations in the Asian region have done pioneering work in disaster prevention and mitigation. The two U.N. Regional Housing Centre of ESCAP-- one located in National Buildings Organisation, New Delhi and the other in Buildings Research Centre at Bandung, can help in coordinating the activities of the network and disseminate the work done.

Regional Action Programme

As the phenomenon of natural disasters often transgrand national boundaries, an international and regional cooperation is called for in natural disaster mitigation and prevention work. The suggested Regional Action Programme for disaster mitigation in housing and human settlement is briefly outlined in Fig. 5. International and Regional agencies like UNCRD should consider taking up follow up action which will be of great consequence in mitigation of natural disasters, particularly in large urban centres in many Asian countries which are thickly populated.

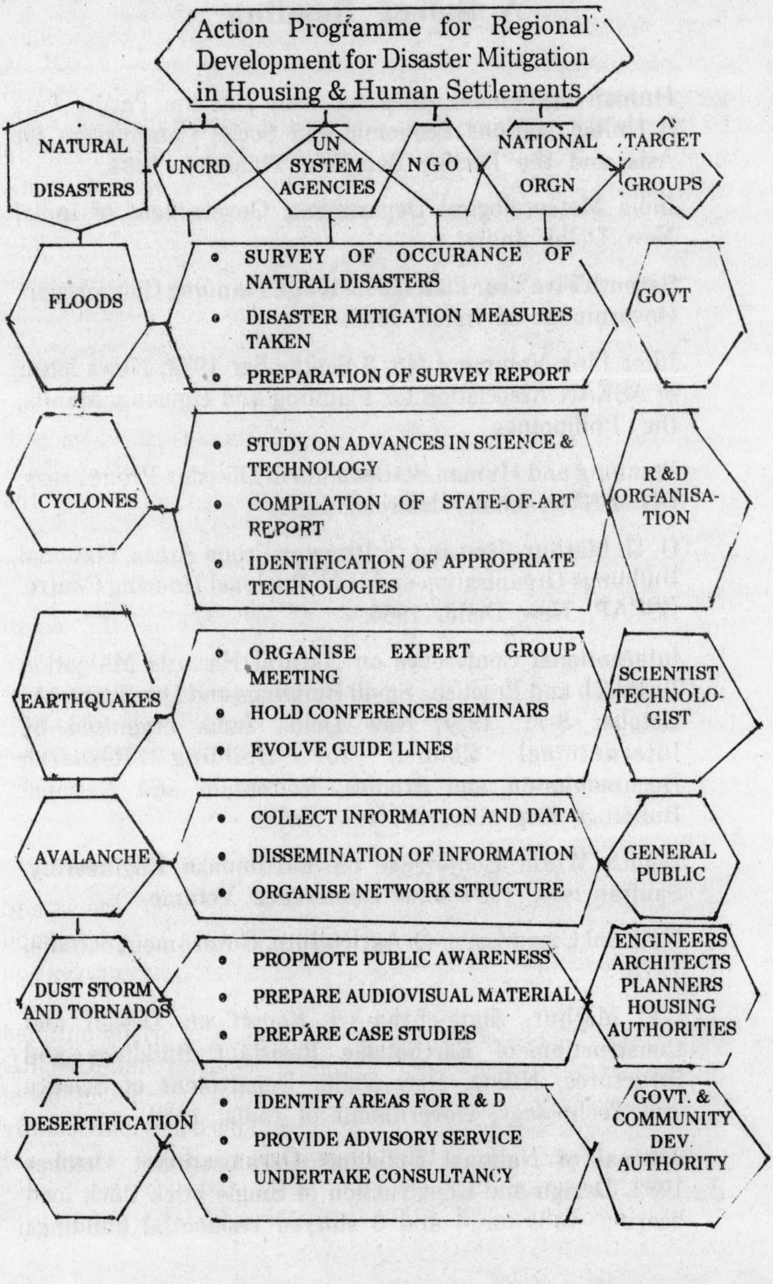
Action Programme for Regional Development for Disaster Mitigation in Housing & Human Settlements
NATURAL DISASTERS
UNCRD
UN SYSTEM AGENCIES
N G O
NATIONAL ORGN
TARGET GROUPS
FLOODS
• SURVEY OF OCCURANCE OF NATURAL DISASTERS
• DISASTER MITIGATION MEASURES TAKEN
• PREPARATION OF SURVEY REPORT
GOVT
CYCLONES
• STUDY ON ADVANCES IN SCIENCE & TECHNOLOGY
• COMPILATION OF STATE-OF-ART REPORT
• IDENTIFICATION OF APPROPRIATE TECHNOLOGIES
R &D ORGANISA-TION
EARTHQUAKES
• ORGANISE EXPERT GROUP MEETING
• HOLD CONFERENCES SEMINARS
• EVOLVE GUIDE LINES
SCIENTIST TECHNOLO-GIST
AVALANCHE
• COLLECT INFORMATION AND DATA
• DISSEMINATION OF INFORMATION
• ORGANISE NETWORK STRUCTURE
GENERAL PUBLIC
DUST STORM AND TORNADOS
• PROPMOTE PUBLIC AWARENESS
• PREPARE AUDIOVISUAL MATERIAL
• PREPARE CASE STUDIES
ENGINEERS ARCHITECTS PLANNERS HOUSING AUTHORITIES
DESERTIFICATION
• IDENTIFY AREAS FOR R & D
• PROVIDE ADVISORY SERVICE
• UNDERTAKE CONSULTANCY
GOVT. & COMMUNITY DEV. AUTHORITY

A Select Reading

Human Settlement Atlas for Asia and the Pacific Part I; United Nations Economic and Social Commission for Asia and the Pacific; Bangkok, Thialand, 1984.

India Meteorological Department, Government of India, New Delhi, India.

Seventh Five Year Plan (1985-1990), Planning Commission, Government of India, 1985.

Inter Link Volume 4 No. 3 September 1984; News letter of ASEAN Association for Planning and Housing, Manila, the Philippines.

Planning and Human Settlements in Disaster-Prone areas; UNCHS (Habitat), Nairobi, 1983.

G. C. Mathur, Housing in Disaster-Prone Areas, National Buildings Organisation and U.N. Regional Housing Centre. ESCAP, New Delhi, 1986.

International Conference on Natural Hazards Mitigation Research and Practice : Small Buildings and Development : October 8-11, 1984, New Delhi, India organised by International Council for Building Research Documentation and Studies, Rotterdam and National Buildings Organisation, New Delhi.

Eighth World Conference on Earthquake Engineering, Sanfrancisco, 1984 Post Conference Volume.

National Commission on Agriculture, Government of India, 1975.

G.C. Mathur, State-of-the-Art Report on Design and Construction of Earthquake Resistant Buildings and Structures, N.B.O. New Delhi. Department of Science and Technology, Government of India, 1986.

Journal of National Buildings Organisation : October 1983. Design and Construction of Single brick thick load bearing walls for 4 and 5 storyed residential buildings in earthquake zones.

Indo-U.S. Workshop on Earthquake Engineering, 1978, New Delhi.

Monograph on Earthquake Resistant Non-Engineered Construction, UNESCO.

Cyclone Damage and Rehabilitation, Invited talk by G.C. Mathur, Director N.B.O. at Asia Pacific Symposium on Wind Engineering, December 5-7,1985, University of Roorkee, Roorkee.

S.P. Mukherji, Preparedness including Flood Control Measures--A Guide for Relief Works : Department of Agriculture, Government of India.

Chandrasekaran, K.S., Floods--Problems and Solutions Paper presented at the International Conference on Flood Disaster, 3-5 December, 1981, New Delhi.

Symposium on Earthquake Disaster Mitigation, University of Roorkee, March 1981, Volume I, India.

Jai Krishna, Earthquake Disaster Paper presented at Annual General Meeting of the Indian Society of Earthquake Technology, March, 1982.

Position paper on Anti-Disaster Planning in Tamil Nadu by Directorate of Town and Country Planning, Government of Tamil nadu, India.

Technical Report on Cyclone Shelters by the Public Works Department, Tamil Nadu, India.

Cyclone and Building Behaviour, School of Planning and Architecture, New Delhi.

National Buildings Code of India, Revised Edition 1983, Indian Standard Institution, New Delhi.

2

Military Bridging Equipment and Boats for Disaster Management

*Y. P. Pathak**

and

*M. A. Sinare***

The natural calamities like river flood or tidal surge, cyclones and earthquakes have played havoc with lives of the people for ages. There is a colossal loss of human lives, cattles, crops, buildings, communication links and a hoard of other property when the large natural or manmade disaster strikes. The management of such large disasters is the responsibility of the entire nation and many a times international help is also sought to tide over the emergencies. The large scale relief and rescue operations have to be launched on warfooting to save the precious human lives and the property by mobilising the resources from all possible sources.

River floods with heavy rains and the large scale melting of snow, inundate the land around river banks, wash away the human habitat, snap the road links and damage the road and railway bridges. The flood waters surround and cut-off thé villages and housing pockets on river banks. Many a times people are marooned for days together and have to go without food and shelter, potable water, medicines and other essential supplies. The major rivers like Brahmaputra and Ganges have a perennial problem of flooding the large areas, washing away the big chunks of lands, changing the course and wrecking

* Deputy Director, Research and Development Establishment (Engineers), Defence Research and Development Organisation, Dighi, Pune.

** Scientist, Research and Development Establishment (Engineers), Defence Research and Development Organisation, Pune.

the large destruction along their way. There is hardly any year in which there is no news of devastating floods in Assam, West Bengal, Bihar and U.P.

India is blessed with over 4,000 kms of coast line which has been the source of livelihood for crores of people living along the coast. Fishing, shipping, harbouring, recreation and the consequent large scale industrial growth in coastal belt is a boon to the national economy. The same very blessing of proximity of sea turns into tears when catastrophic cyclones, hurricane winds, the mighty tidal surge batter the large coastline resulting in death of thousands of people, hundreds of thousands of cattles, destruction of houses and other property. The devastating cyclones and tidal surge that hit the Andhra Pradesh in mid-eighties, Bangla Desh, in 1970 and 1991 have left a very painful memory of mass destruction and misery.

Earthquake is another natural calamity which hits the large landmass without slightest warning. There is almost no limit to the scale of destruction of houses, roads, railways, bridges, dams, factories and the human lives. A few seconds of strike of this dancing devil razes to the ground the years of hard work put in to construct the human habitat and the means of livelihood. It traps the persons below the collapsed building debris, renders thousands of people homeless and leaves behind a challanging task of rescue and relief.

Mobilisation of Resources for Rescue and Relief Operations

Handling the natural calamities and major disasters requires large scale mobilisation of resources in the locality for relief and rescue operations, there is a necessity for preparing disaster control action plans for every state and all the districts in Indian Union, more particulary for the areas where the natural calamities are known to occur frequently. Action plans should methodically blend all the state and the central government agencies, local bodies and private sectors resources which could be pooled up at a short notice to conduct the operations. The drill for an early warning system, communication network and specific duties for each agency should be laid down taking into account the availability of resources with each of them.

Role of Armed Forces

Armed forces of the country have always played a major role in handling the natural calamities and have assisted the civil authorities in the hours of need. Precious lives and property worth crores have been saved by timely and expedicious help rendered by troops. Defence forces possess the necessary skills, discipline and the resources which could be deployed in the affected parts of the country within a short notice of few hours. Be it the battering received from cyclones and tidal surge in Bangla Desh, Andhra Pradesh or Kerala, the floods of mighty rivers like Brahmaputra and Ganges, earthquakes at Koyana or Rajasthan, the expertise and the resources of Army, Navy and Airforce have always come handy and were effectively used to save human lives and property. Use of helicopters and Airforce planes for air dropping of most essential supplies like food, medicines, drinking water and other items, is the quickest and the most effective way of saving human lives immediately after the disaster strikes. The timely help rendered by the troops also acts a big moral booster to civil population which otherwise is helpless.

DRDO Expertise

Defence Research and Development Organisation (DRDO) of Ministry of Defence is engaged in design and development of sophisticated equipments, arms, ammunition, missiles, aircrafts and a variety of other materials and processes required by the country's Defence forces. With its 47 major Research laboratories and establishments spread all over the country, it is in a unique position to undertake the design and development of equipment, materials, processes and systems required for disaster management. Many of the equipments like bridges, boats, shelters and tents developed by DRDO can directly be purchased and used, wherever required. Equipments developed by DRDO for use of Defence Forces against their specific requirements and specifications, are engineered to incorporate various redundancies to ensure high reliability. These measures and certain other requirements for deployment of equipments in varied operating environments result in high costs, which may not be warranted in civil usage. However, DRDO can develop and supply the equipments required by different agencies for disaster management which could be cost effective and simpler to use and maintain.

Military Bridging Equipment

The Army is equipped with portable light weight bridges, boats, portable shelters, earth moving and construction plants, trackway expedients and special purpose vehicles, which can be used in emergencies for rescue and relief operations. In a number of instances Army Engineers have speedily laid the portable bridges whenever the permanent road bridges were washed away or extensively damaged in floods, and restored the communication links for use by civilian population. The use of Army boats for rescue of persons stranded in flooded areas and delivering the essential supplies like food, clothing, medicines, potable water and other items is almost a permanent feature whenever the river flood or tidal surge inundate the adjoining areas and the land locomotion is impossible or difficult.

Military bridging equipment is held in different parts of the country by Army formations like Engineer Regiments, Brigades, Divisions and Engineer Store Depots. Local Army authorities like Station Commanders generally accept the specific requests made by the state government authorities such as district collector for rendering the help in rescue and relief operations in handling the natural calamities and disasters. Troops and equipment are deployed as per the requirement and the availability, and the operations are conducted in co-ordination with civil authorities. Troops generally man their own equipment. Mobility, flexibility and speed are the essential key elements in any task undertaken by the Army. A sense of urgency and devotion to duty is in-built in the training of Officers and Jawans of the Army. They will quickly survey the situation, assess the requirements of men, materials and equipment, deploy the available resources in optimum quantity at right places, plan and execute the task speedily. Army equipment and stores are normally not handed over to civil authorities for use.

This paper mainly describes and explains the utility of military bridging equipment and boats which are of interest from disaster management point of view. These have been extensively used in the past by Army for the rescue and relief operations. Some of these devices are now available for civil use and can be purchased and stocked by state government authoritoies for meeting the emergency requirements. Following types of equipment are described with the help of diagrams and photographs :

(a) Portable fixed bridges
(b) Portable floating bridges
(c) Mechanically launched bridges
(d) Boats for flood relief.

Portable military bridges have a vital role to play in quickly re-opening the communication lines whenever the permanent road bridges get damged because of floods, earthquakes or for other reasons. When one or two spans of road bridge fall, the portable bridges can be used to span these gaps (Fig.1).

Fig. 1 : Bailey bridge used for bridging broken span of road bridge

Broken span can be bridged in a short time of a day or two to carry the highest IRC load class traffic, i.e., 70R. When this is not feasible because of extensive damage to the bridge, a totally new temporary bridge can be constructed by the side of existing bridge. Bridge spans with piers are constructed using prefabricated bridge panels, pins and deck system. On a river with substantial flow of water floating bridges constructed on pontoons, can be used.

Portable Fixed Bridges

Bailey Bridge (BB)

This bridge in its different configuration was designed and produced in 1940 in UK and was extensively used by Allied Forces in the Second World War. It is fabricated in high strength steel, is of modular construction and is launched manually. Each component is designed in such a way that maximum six persons are required to carry the same during the construction. The bridge can be constructed across the river in a matter of hours and can be used to carry heaviest loads. This bridge is produced in India by

M/S Garden Reach Ship Builders and Engineers Ltd.
43/46, Garden Reach Road,
CALCUTTA - 700 024.

The different configuration of this bridge can be purchased and stocked by civil authorities, CPWD, state government and local bodies for use during emergencies. Washing away or damage to the existing bridge structures, particularly the low height bridges of vintage origin, is of very common occurrence. Bailey steel bridge ideally suits such situations for re-opening the road communication. Presently, the following four configurations are commonly used and are available :

Standard Baily bridge
Extra wide Baily bridge
Baily Pontoon bridge
Baily suspension bridge

Standard and Extra Wide Bailey Bridge

This bridge is of through type, the roadway being carried between two main girders. The roadway width of the standard Bailey is 3.27 m whereas for extra wide version it is 4.19 m. The main girder is formed from steel panels of welded construction - 3048 mm long × 1550 mm in height, each panel being pin jointed to its neighbour end to end. Fig. 2 shows the pictorial view of a bally panel.

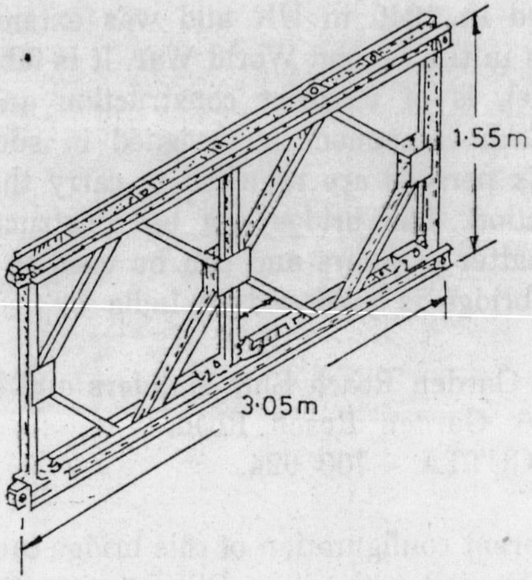

Fig. 2 : BB Panel

The load carrying capacity of the bridge girder can be increased by adding extra panels alongside and also on top of original panels. The different arrangements of panels are known as trusses and storeys, a girder made up of three panels alongside each other and none on top is known as triple truss, single story; while a girder made up of two panels alongside each other and one set of two on top is known as double truss, double storey.

The bridge is described according to the number of trusses and storeys which form its main girders. In all cases the number of trusses given first follwed by the number of storeys. *Single single* is the lightest combination possible and *triple triple* is the heaviest. *Single double* and *single triple* form unstable configuration and are never used. There are, therefore, seven possible combinations of girders, e.g., single single, double single, triple single, double double, triple double, double triple and triple triple. Some of the configurations are shown in Fig. 3.

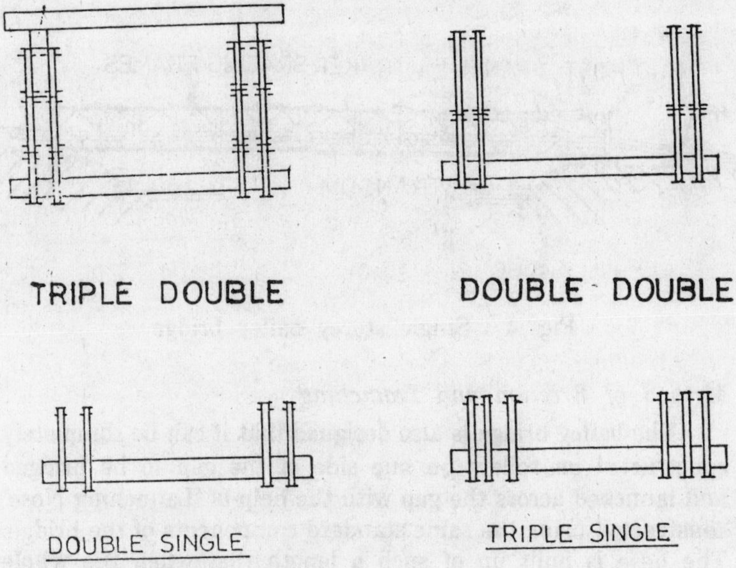

Fig. 3 : Bailey bridge configuration

With the exception of Double Triple and Triple Triple. the various constructions stated above can be reinforced by the addition of chord reinforcement to the top and bottom of each truss for increasing the load carrying capacity of the typical bridge. The girders are connected crosswise by transoms which rest on bottom chord of panels and carry the roadway superstructure. The girders are also connected by two diagonal braces, called sway braces, at each panel. Across the transoms, run the road bearers, which for ease of construction have been welded together in groups of three to four stringers and are 3048mm long, the same length as the panel bay. Running across the stringers are placed the wooden chesses which form the deck of the bridge. Ribands are provided to guide the traffic and to hold down the decking with the help of riband bolts. When required, 762mm wide footwalks foe padestrian traffic can be provided either on one side or both sides of the bridge. Ramps are provided at the either end for ease of access to the deck of the bridge. Side of single storey, double storeys and cross-section of the bridge are shown in Figs. 4, 5 and 6.

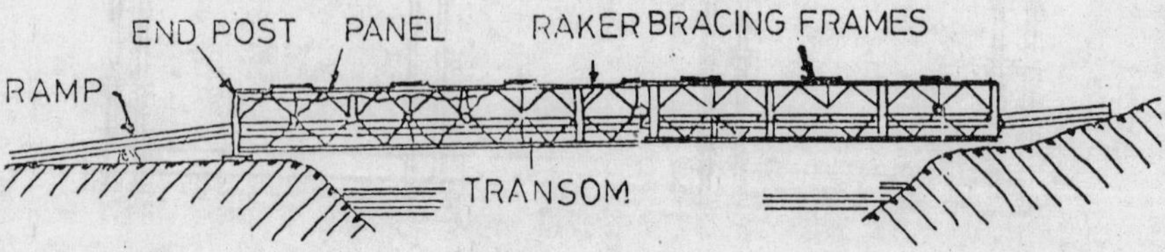

Fig. 4 : Single storey bailey bridge

Method of Erection and Launching

The bailey bridge is also designed that it can be completely constructed on rollers on one side of the gap to be bridged and launched across the gap with the help of 'Launching Nose' constructed using the same standard components of the bridge. The nose is built up of such a length that when the whole structure is rolled forward, the tip of nose lands on the rollers on the far bank before the point of balance is reached. Fig. 7 shows the launching of the bridge.

Bridge Erection Time

The components of the bridge have been so designed that a bridge can be constructed and launched by unskilled or semi-skilled labourer under the supervision of a trained engineer. No component is heavier than 300kgs and the heaviest component is carried by six men. An indication of the number of trained men and average time required for construction of the bridge, without the help of crane, is given below.

Type of bridge	Span in metres	Working party	Average Construction time	
			By Day	By Night
Single Single	15.2	45	2-3 Hrs	6 Hrs
Double Single	24.4	45	3-4 Hrs	8 Hrs
Triple Single	33.5	90	4-6 Hrs	8 Hrs

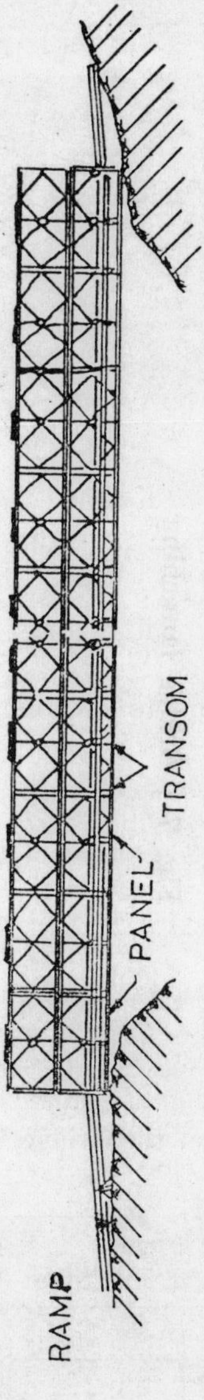

Fig. 5 : Double storey bailey bridge

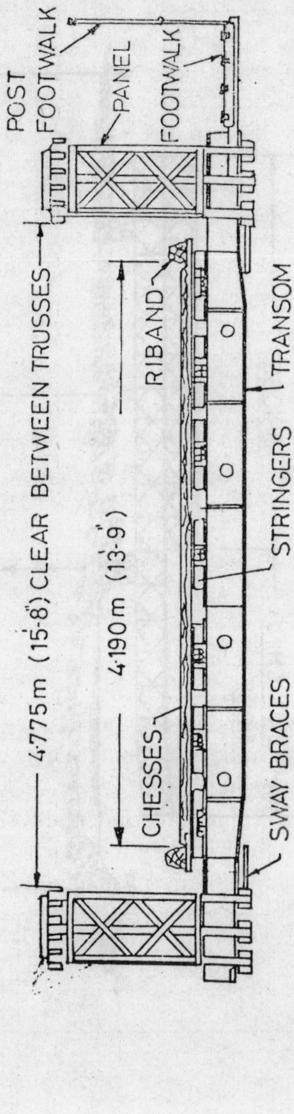

Fig. 6 : Typical cross section through extrawide portable steel bridge

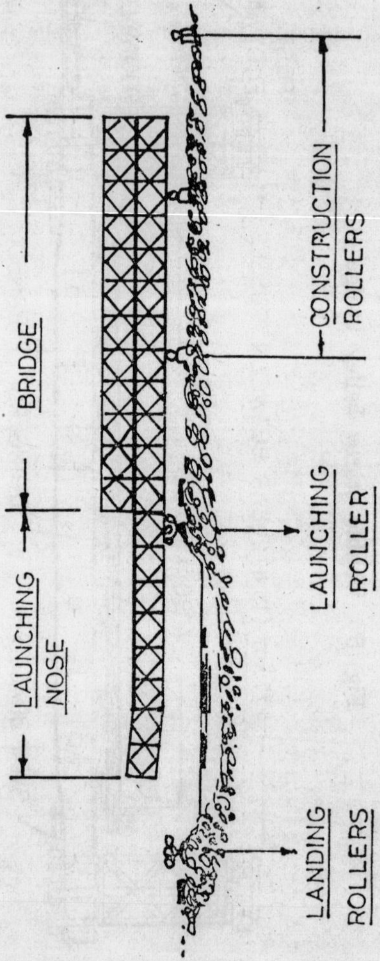

Fig. 7 : Bridge launching

Multispan Bailey Bridge

Bailey bridge can also be constructed in a number of continuous spans thereby covering much larger river width or gap. This is achieved by construction of crib-piers using Bailey Bridge (BB) main panels. Fig. 8. shows the multispan capability of the bridge.

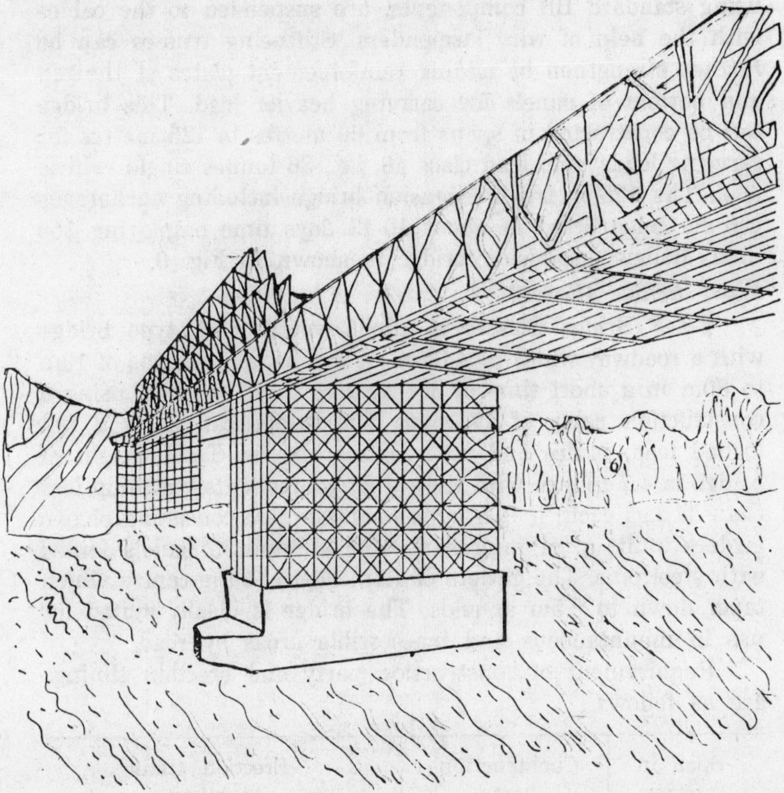

Fig. 8 : Multispan Bailey Bridge

Bailey Suspension Bridge

Whenever the river or the gap to be bridged is more than 60 metres wide and sufficient time is available for construction, Bailey Suspension bridge is very useful. It is constructed using standard Bailey Bridge set, Bailey conversion set and erection gear. Two towers are constructed at either bank of the river and suspension cables are supported on these towers. Suspension cables are anchored at either bank by constructing suitable anchorages. The roadway and the stiftening trusses, assembled using standard BB components, are suspended to the cables with the help of wire suspenders. Stiftneing trusses can be further strengthen by adding reinforcement plates at the top and bottom of panels for carrying heavier load. This bridge can be constructed in spans from 60 metres to 125 metres for carrying loads upto load class 40, i.e., 36 tonnes single vehicle load. The 125 metres suspension bridge including anchorages can be constructed in about 10-12 days time employing 150 men. Bailey suspension bridge is shown in Fig. 9.

Fixed Bridge Class-3

Fixed Bridge Class-3 is alight weight deck type bridge with a roadway width of 2.125m. It can be laid on gaps of 10m to 30m in a short time of 30 minutes to 40 minutes using a construction party of 17 men. The bridge can carry a full loaded jeep, mules and other similar traffic. Total weight of bridge is 4.7 tonnes with individual components weighing less than 41 kgs each. It is a light weight bridge consisting of two girders built up of interchangeable aluminium panels joined with steel pins. The girders of 1.1m depth at the centre which taper down to 0.5m at ends. The bridge is ideally suited for use in mountaneous and inaccessible areas by road.

Requirement of construction party and erection timings are as follows.

Span in metres	Construction party	Erection timing in minutes	
		By Day	By Night
10 M	17 Men	25	40
20 M	17 Men	35	50
30 M	17 Men	45	60

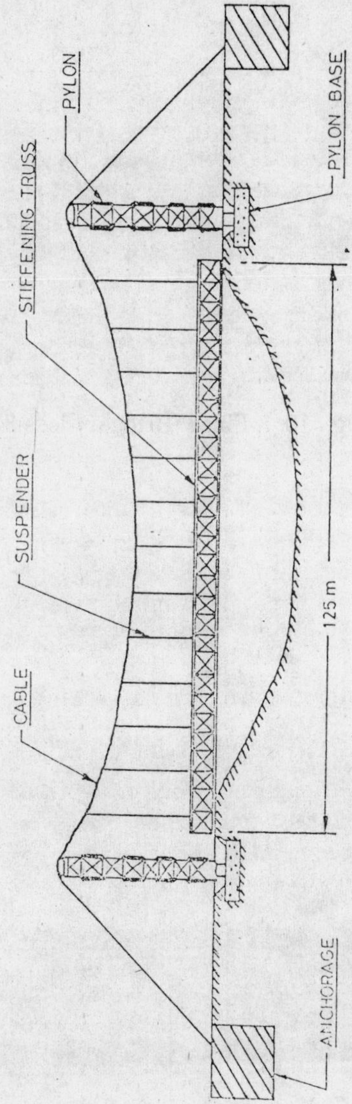

Fig. 9 : Bailey Suspension bridge

Figs. 10 and 11 shows the erected bridge and also carriage by males.

Fig. 10 : Fixed Bridge Class-3

Fig. 11 : Bridge Components Carriage by Mules

The bridge, in dismantled form can be carried by jeeps or mules for construction in inaccessible areas including mountaneous terrain. It has built-in capability of multispan construction using pier system. Therefore river gaps larger than 30m can also be bridged. Fixed Bridge Class-3 can be produced and supplied through DRDO to civil users like Central governments departments, state governments, public sector undertakings, local bodies and even private sector enterprises for use in emergency situations or otherwise.

Multispan Manually Launched Assault Bridge MLC -60 (MLAB)

This is manually launched bridge capable of bridging the dry as well as wet gaps ranging from 10 metres to 75 metres. It is designed for carrying vehicle loads upto class-60, i.e., 54.43 tonnes tracked loads. The bridge is launched and retrieved manully and is of modular construction, each module being of four to six men load. It is a two girder deck type bridge having capability of multispan construction and provides 4m wide roadway. Bridge components carried as palatised loads are delivered to the site of construction in vehicle and the bridge of requisite length and load class is constructed speedily across the river/gap/obstacle.

The two girder portable bridge is constructed using 1.8m length modules of top panels and bottom panels. Each panel weighs less than 200 kgs and can be handled by four men. The panels are of welded construction and have been designed and fabricated in high strength aluminium alloy having 400N/mm sq ultimate tensile strength. The bridge is basically a pin jointed structure and it can be launched from home bank, i.e., without having a foothold on the other bank of the river. It is constructed using following components in addition to launching aids.

Top Panel
Bottom Panel
Junction Panel
End Taper Panel
Bank Seat Beam
Deck
Ramp

Fig. 12 : MLAB Bridge Components

Launching Nose Heavy
Building Aids
Link Reinforcement Kit
Pier System
Anchorages

These components are assembled with the help of steel pins to form a bridge of requisite length and launched using launching nose heavy and building aids.

These components are shown in the photographs given below (Fig. 12).

Capability of the Bridge

This portable modular bridge can be used in a number of configurations for bridging the rivers or gaps ranging from 10m to 75m for various types of traffic. By using the basic components of the bridge, to suit the typical situation existing in the field as per the requirement of span and loading, a bridge can be designed and erected. Most common span configurations and loadings used by Army Engineers are described in succeeding paragraphs.

Single Storey MLAB Bridge

Single storey bridge can be constructed using only top panels bank seat beams, deck and ramps, for spans upto 50 metres.

Fig. 13 : Single Storey MLAB Bridge

Fig. 14 : 31m Double Storey MLAB Bridge

It can be launched in 20 to 40 minutes time. For 10 metres span its load carrying capacity is load class MLC-60, i.e., 54.43 tonnes which gradually reduces to load class MLC-16, i.e., 18.5 tonnes wheeled vehicle load at 50m span. Fig. 13 shows the erected bridge.

Double Storey MLAB Bridge

Double Storey MLAB Bridge can be constructed using top panels, bottom panels, junction panels, bank seat beam and taper panels, deck and ramps. This bridge can carry MLC-60 vehicle loads, i.e., 54.43 tonnes tracked loads at 31.1 metre span. It can be launched on gaps upto 49.4 metres. However, the load carrying capacity decreases as the span increases beyond 31.1 metres. Fig. 14 shows Double story bridge in launched condition.

Double Storey MLAB Bridge with Link Reinforcement Kit

This bridge is same as per the double bridge described above except that its load carrying capacity is increased by providing a link reinforcement kit below the bridge. It carries MLC-60 loads on 49.4 metre unsupported span. Fig. 15 shows the 49.4 metre bridge with link reinforcement kit.

Fig. 15 : 49.4m MLAB Bridge with Link Reinforcement Kit

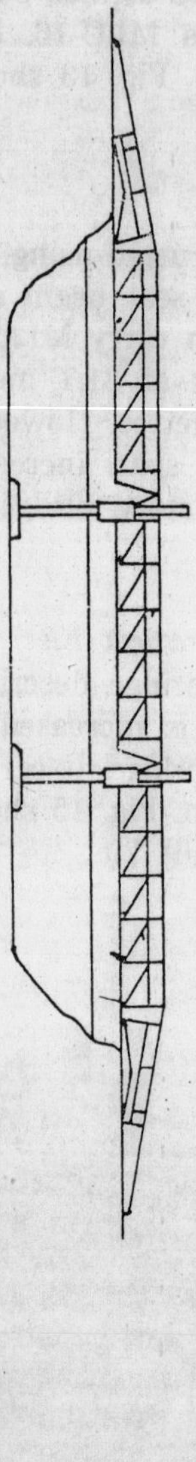

Fig. 16 : Double Storey Assault Bridge with Piers

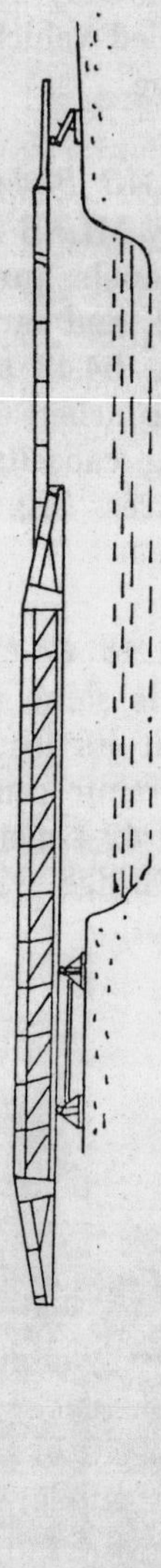

Fig. 17 : Launching of MLAB Bridge

Multispan MLAB Bridge with Pier System

Here again the construction of the bridge is same as that of double storey construction except that it rests on the piers at every 25 metre interval. It can be launched upto 75 metres span with two piers. Fig. 16 shows the MLAB Bridge on piers.

The launching of these bridges is done from one bank of the river using building aids and the launching nose heavy. Most of the construction is done manually except that a heavy vehicle is used for pushing the bridge on rollers till it lands on the far bank. Fig. 17 shows the bridge in launching mode.

This bridge system has been designed, developed and produced indigeneously by Research and Development Establishment (Engineers) Pune. It is a light weight equipment and very versatile in its applications and speedy in construction. Table below gives the typical timings of bridge launching/ construction.

Bridge Type	Span in metres	Load class	Time in hours	
			Day	Night
MLAB single storey	9.8	MLC-60	1/2	3/4
MLAB double storey	31.1	MLC-60	2	4
MLAB double storey with link reinforcement kit	49.4	MLC-60	4	6
MLAB double storey with two intermediate support piers	75	MLC-60	6	8

Multispan manually launched assault bridge (MLAB) which is of aluminium construction, can be produced and supplied by DRDO to civil users like central government departments, state governments, public sector undertakings, local bodies and even private sector enterprises for their use. Launching of the bridge is simple and unskilled labour, and the engineers with a few days training, can launch it across the rivers and gaps, though they may not be able to achieve the above timings which are achieved by trained jawans and engineers.

Portable Floating Bridges

Bailey Pantoon Bridge

Bailey Pantoon Bridge is similar to standard BB except that instead of cribs/piers the spans rest on the Pontoons or floats. This type of bridge is useful for rivers with plenty of flowing or stationary water and where construction of crib/ piers is not feasible. Ends of the bridge span rest on the pontoons for support. Depending upon the load class of the bridge, a number of pontoons have to be used. It is also called floating bridge because it floats on water with the help of pontoons. Pontoons are either manufactured using marine plywood or steel plates. Fig. 18 shows the erected pontoon bridge.

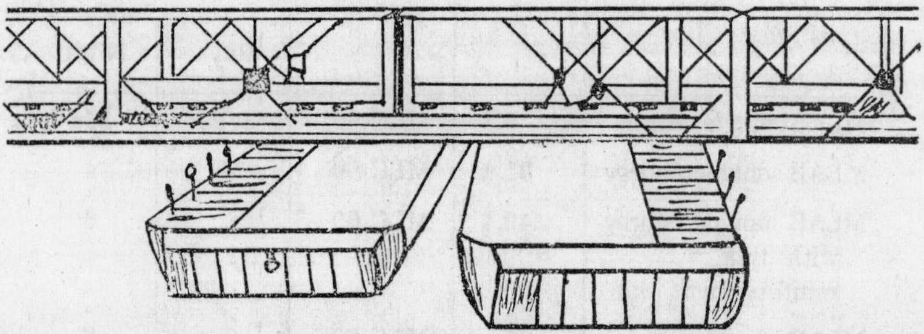

Fig. 18 : Bailey Floating Bridge on Pontoons

Heavy Assault Floating Bridge CL-50 (Kruppman)

It is a deck type floating bridge of German origin and is now produced indigeneously. The equipment can be assembled easily in different ways for various loads and spans of floating bridges. It is simple to construct. All parts are light, can be easily handled manually and carried in lorries. A bridge can be put across the river quickly. The 5.4m wide roadway is formed by using main girders which are supported on saddles fitted on the rubber float. Fig. 19 shows a rubber float which can be inflated as per requirement by air pumps.

The bridge consists of floating units joined together by joining members 'S' type. The construction of floating units differs for various load classes. At the ends, the ramps are connected to the floating units with joining members 'H' type and they can be raised and lowered mechanically with the

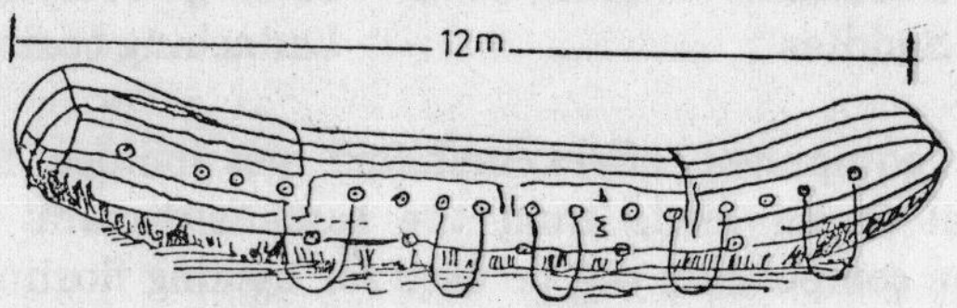

Fig. 19 : KM Bridge Float

help of ramps winches. Floating bridges upto 100 m length can be constructed using this equipment. The erected floating bridge is shown in Fig. 20.

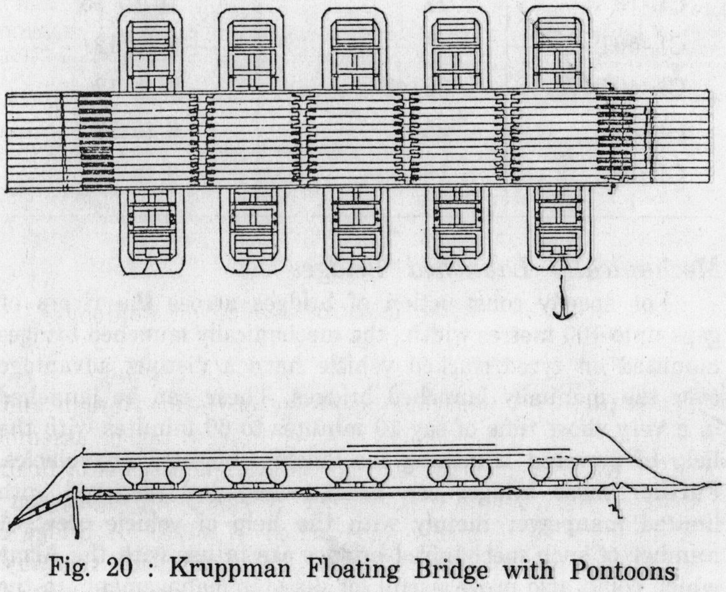

Fig. 20 : Kruppman Floating Bridge with Pontoons

The main components of the bridge are made of aluminium alloy and are floatable. The inflatable floats are made from nylone fabric coated with neoprene rubber. The equipment consists of the following main components:

Main girders	Anchors
Ramp girders	Winches
Cross girders	Erection tools
Pneumatic rubber floats	Joining components
Saddles	Launching boat with OBM

The equipment offers manifold possibilities for varied structural forms made from the same structural elements. The same components can be used for making floating bridges, ferries and short span bridges of different sizes for carrying various loads. The load carrying capacity and the erection time of the 100m floating bridge is as follows :

Load Class	Vehicle weight in tonnes	Erection time in hours
CL-70	72	10 to 15
CL-50T	45	8 to 12
CL-40T/W	36/42	8 to 12
CL-24	25	8 to 12
CL-18	18	8 to 12

Mechanically Launched Bridges

For speedy construction of bridges across the rivers or gaps upto 100 metres width., the mechanically launched bridges mounted on tyred/tracked vehicle have a distinct advantage over the manually launched bridges. These can be launched in a very short time of say 10 minutes to 60 minutes with the help of powered launching mechnisms mounted on vehicles. Further these bridges can be launched and retrieved with limited manpower mainly with the help of vehicle crew. A number of such mechanised bridges are in use with the Army which could also prove useful for disaster management in the areas where cross country movement and speedy construction is desired. Most of these bridges are mounted on tyred vehicles with very good cross country mobility.

Trestle-cum-Span Bridges

These are vehicle mounted mobile bridges of 10 to 13.5m individual span length with 4m wide roadway. The bridges are mechanically launched from the vehicle with the help of launching mechanism fitted onto the vehicle. Load carrying capacity of the bridge is 50 tonnes of vehicular load. Rivers or gaps with widths upto 100m can be bridged by laying this bridge in multiple spans with the help of integral portable pier system. Launching time varies from 10 minutes to 50 minutes depending on the length of the bridge or the day/night launching. Figs. 21 and 22 depict the launching of the bridge.

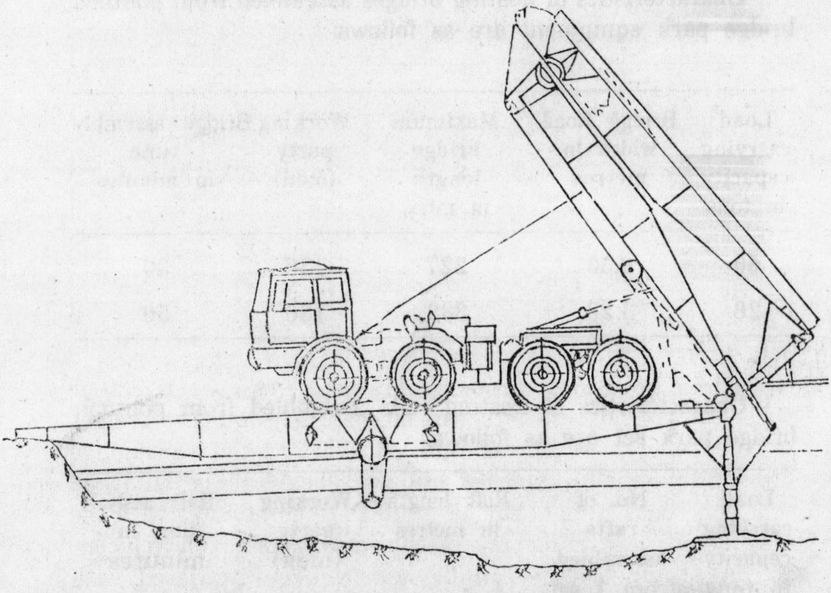

Fig. 21 : Multispan Bridge with Piers

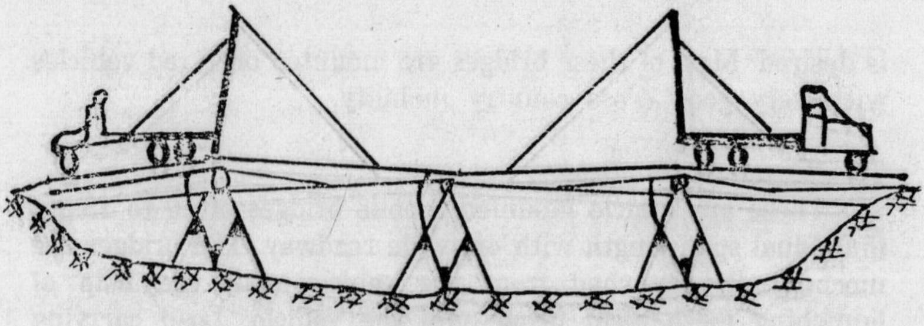

Fig. 22 : Fully Launched Bridge

Pontoon Bridge Park Equipment (PMP)

Pontoon bridge park equipment serves for organising of bridges and ferry crossings. The equipment is used for assembly of floating bridges of 20 to 60 tonnes in capacity and rafts are 40, 60 and 80 ton capacity assembled of pontoon sections and 110 and 150 ton capacity assembled of pontoon and end sections.

Characteristics of floating bridges assembled from pontoon bridge park equipment are as follows:

Load carrying capacity in tons	Bridge Road width in metres	Maximum bridge length in mtrs.	Working party (men)	Bridge assembly time in minutes
60	6.50	227	136	30
20	3.29	382	136	50

Characteristics of floating rafts assembled from pontoon bridge park set are as follows:

Load carrying capacity in tons	No. of rafts assembled from 1 set	Raft length in metres	Working party (men)	Raft assly. time in minutes
40	16	13.5	8	8
60	10	20.25	12	10

Load carrying capacity in tons	No. of rafts assembled from 1 set	Raft length in metres	Working party (men)	Raft assly. time in minutes
80	8	27.00	16	12
110	4/5	39.25	24	13-15
150	4	52.75	32	16-20

The equipment is fully mounted on vehicles having cross country performance. Fig. 23 shows the pontoon section mounted on truck.

Fig. 23 : PMP Bridge on the Vehicle

The bridge assembled from the equipment of the pontoon bridge park consists of floating pontoons. landing bays and approaches. The pontoons sections are used for assembly of floating portion of floating bridges and for assembly of rafts. The unfolded pontoon section is a ready bay of a 60 ton bridge of 6.25m in length. For assembly of 20 ton bridge, a pontoon section is deployed in two-half sections. The launching of the bridge on flooded river is shown in Fig. 24.

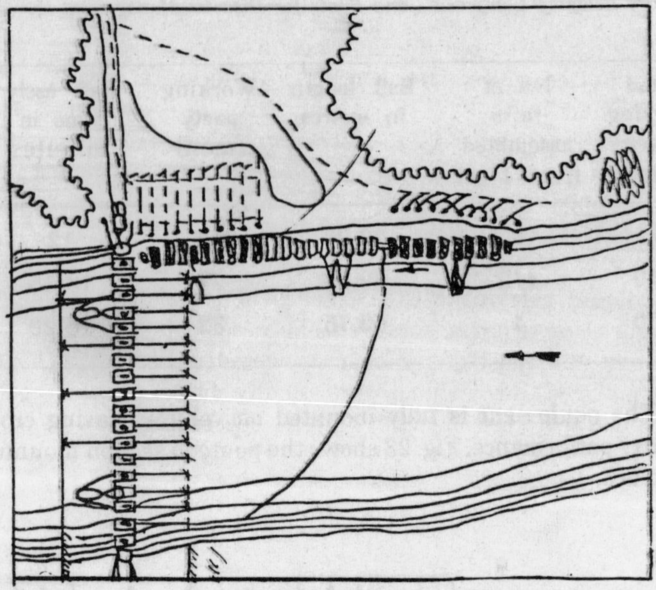

Fig. 24 : Launching of PMP Bridge

Boats for Flood Relief Operations

Boats used by the Army play a vital role in rescue and relief operations when the rivers get flooded and people staying in the low lying areas get marooned at many places. Military units are often requested by state government officials for sending Army boats for relief operations. Local Army Units generally accept such requests and despatch the available boats with operating crew. Sometimes, however, the flood affected area is far away from the nearest Army unit or the availability of boats is inadequate in number and the civilians find themselves at a disadvantage of not receiving the help in time. There is, therefore, a requirement of stocking some boats by state governments for flood relief operations. The flood relief boat which will be simple in design, low cost and easy for handling even by village folks, can be designed and engineered by DRDO.

This section, however, describes with illustrations, some of the boats presently available with the Army and which can be used for flood relief operations. It also includes a few boats which were developed for Defence use but have not been productionised so far. These could be offered for civil use in case they fit in the bill. The boats have been manufactured using different materials like wood, neoprene rubber coated fabrics, aluminium alloy sheets, fibre reinforced plastics (FRP) and steel plates depending upon the utility and considerations of light weight for easy handling and transportation. The designs of these boats have been worked out to suit the end use, desired load carrying capacity, speed of travel, handling and transportation requirements. Some of these boats can be paddled manually and most of them are powered either by outboard motors (OBM) or engines permanently fitted on the boats. Following boats are described in the succeeding paragraphs :

a. Pneumatic Assault boat
b. Boat Assault, Universal type
c. Assault Craft rigid bodied (Aluminium)
d. Assalut Craft rigid bodied (FRP)
e. Strom boat
f. Folding boat
g. Boat Bridge Erection
h. Boat personnel, 10 men
i. Motor Boat (Steel), 40 men

Pneumatic Assault Boat, Light Weight

Boat Assault Pneumatic, Light Weight, is made out of neoprene coated nylone fabric. It is capable of carrying 12 persons with luggage. It is propelled by 35/45 HP outboard motor and can also be paddled with oars provided with the boat. The boat has been developed by Research and Development Establishment (Engineers), Pune as shown in Fig. 25.

The buoyancy tubes are constructed out of high tenacity neoprene rubber coated fabric. The main buoyancy tubes have been divided into six air tight compartments with valves for inflation. In addition to these tubes, lower buoyancy tubes of small diameter have been provided for additional safety. The proofed fabric floor has been strengthened by FRP floor board.

Fig. 25 : Pneumatic Assault Boat

The accessories like foot pumps, paddles and bailers have been provided with the boat. It can be deflated after use, folded and carried in a valise by six men. The technical details of the boat are as follows :

(a) Overall dimensions in inflated condition	Length 5000 mm Width 1900 mm Hull dia 500 mm
(b) Dead weight	117 kg
(c) Speed in still water at 1200 kg load	3 knots - two men paddling 6 knots - Eight men paddling
(d) Load carrying capacity	At 300mm free board-1200 kg At 250mm free board-1500 kg At 200mm free board-2000 kg

Boat Assault, Universal Type

The boat is made of aluminium alloy sheets with rivetted construction and weighs 200 kgs. It is 5200mm long, 2100mm wide and 510mm deep with flat bottom and a trapezoidal hull.

The boat can be propelled manually by eight oars or paddles and can also be mechanically propelled by 34 KW OBM which can be fitted either at bow end or stren end. The loades boat is shown in Fig. 26.

Fig. 26 : Universal Assault Boat

Structural rigidity to this boat is given by providing corrugations to the bottom sheet, stifferners to the side sheets and the floor seat beams with buoyancy material. The boat is extrmely stable and the floor seat beams with the buoyancy material provide a reserve buoyancy of over 100 kgs and render the boat practically unsinkable. The boats are of nestable type, i.e., one boat can fit in other with only some addition of height. This way 10 to 12 boats can be carried at a time in a civil truck. This boat has been designed and engineered by Research and Development Establishment (Engineers), Pune and has been extensively used in flood relief and rescue operations. The characteristics of the boat are as follows :

(a) Load carrying capacity

(i) Carriage of persons	12-15 persons with some luggage
(ii) Cargo capacity at 310mm free board	1000 kgs

(b) Speed of travel

(i) Boat propelled by 34KW OBM

Unladen	15-20 knots
Laden with 1000 kgs weight	6-7 knots

(ii) Boat rowed annually by 6 to 10 men — 3-4 knots

Assault Craft Rigid Bodied, Aluminium

The boat is made out of aluminium alloy sheets with rivetted coonstruction and weighs only 92 kgs. It is 3250mm long, 1500mm wide and 510mm deep with a flat bottom and trapezoidal hull. The boat can be propelled manually with the help of paddles or oars and can also be mechanically propelled by 35HP OBM for attachment of which integral braackets have been provided at both ends, i.e., stern end and bow end. Two such boats can be joined together to form a single unit for carriage of larger and heavier loads. Single boat can carry 10 persons with some luggage. A loaded boat is shown in Fig. 27.

Fig. 27 : Assault Craft Aluminium

The boat has been designed and developed by Research and Development Establishment (Engineers), Pune and is presently in service with Army. Because of its low weight and excellent performance, it is ideally suited for flood relief and rescue operations. The boats are nestable type to minimise space for storage and also to economise on the transportation by trucks. Ten boats can be carried at a time in a civil truck. The performance details are as follows :

(a) Load carrying capacity-

- i) Ten persons with luggage
- ii) Pay load of 700 kgs at free board of 300mm
- iii) Pay load of 900 kgs at free board of 250mm

(b) Speed of travel

The boat is highly manoeverable. It is versatile boat capable of high speed as well as good cargo capacity.

i)	Boat propelled by OBM	
	Empty boat	15-16 knots
	Laden with 7-10 men with luggage	10-12 knots
ii)	Boat rowed manually	
	Fully loaded either with men or cargo	3-4 knots

Assault Craft Rigid Bodied, FRP

This boat is manufactured in fibre reinforced plastics and is an ultra light weight boat weighing only 70 kgs. It is 4600mm long, 2100mm wide in the centre and 700mm deep with slightly curved bottom and cup shaped sides. The boat can be propelled by two oares or seven paddles and can also be power driven by 35HP OBM. The boat loaded with persons is shown in Fig. 28.

The boat is of simple design and the performance details are as follows :

(a) Load carrying capacity

(i)	Persons with luggage	10-12 persons
(ii)	Cargo load at 250mm free board	800 kgs

(b) Speed of travel

(i) Manually propelled	3-4 knots
(ii) Powered with 35HP OBM	5-6 knots

Fig. 28 : Assault Craft FRP

This boat was designed and engineered by Research and Development Establishment (Engineers), Pune for use by the Army. However, it has not been productionised so far. The boat can be licensed out for production to civil users. It is a high performance boat and because of its ultra light weight, is ideally suitable and hence strongly recommended for use on relief and rescue operations.

Storm Boat

The storm boat is of wooden construction, 6m in length and 2m in width. It is powered by an outboard motor which gives it a speed of 20 knots empty and 6 knots fully loaded. The boat has seat tracks fitted along the sides, which serves either as seats or ramps for the wheels of the jeeps. Steel ramps are provided for loading or off-loading and can be used on banks upto 1m height. The Fig. 29 shows the boat.

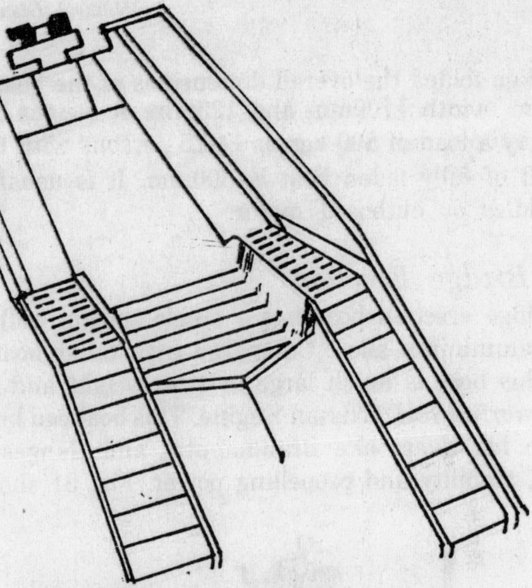

Fig. 29 : Storm Boat with Ramp

The boat can carry a load of 1.5 tonnes or 18--20 persons with luggage. It is powered by 35HP OBM and is very useful for ferrying the persons and stores. The boat is of vintage design but because of its simplicity utility and the ease of operation, it is still preferred and used by Army.

Folding Boat

It is a boat with collapsible canvas sides which was designed primarily to carry infantry across water obstacles in the war. The boat has the stiff marine plywood floor, canvas sides and gunwale. The canvas sides are held upright by side gunwale struts, and two stern pieces. When closed six webbing straps secure the gunwale to the bottom of the boat. The boat is shown in Fig. 30.

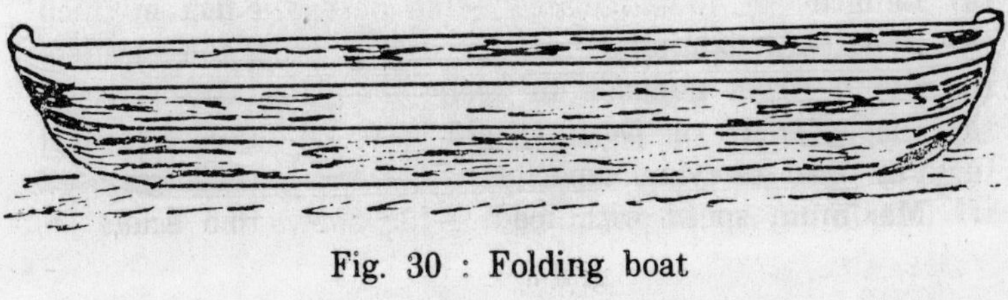

Fig. 30 : Folding boat

When folded the overall dimensions of the boat are, length 5000mm, width 1700mm and 125mm. It weighs 150 kgs and can carry a load of 800 kgs or 14-15 persons with luggage. The draught of fully laden boat is 500mm. It is usually propelled by paddles or outboard motor.

Boat Bridge Erection

Bridge erection boat has a single section hull fabricarted out of aluminium alloy. Compared with other boats described here, this boat is much large in size, weight and is propelled by a powerfull 76HP Nissan Engine. This boat can be confidently used in big rivers like Brahmaputra and Ganges because of its size, stability and propelling power. Fig. 31 show the boat.

Fig. 31 : Bridge Erection Boat

This boat was designed and engineered by Research and Development Establishment (Engineers), Pune mainly for use of Army engineers. It has been extensively used by troops for rescue and relief operations. The general features and technical data are tabulated below :

(a) Length	6.045 m
(b) Breadth maximum	2.454 m
(c) Depth (from gunwale to keel)	1.036 m
(d) Displacement or Dead weight	1900 kgs
(e) Pay load carrying capacity	1360 kgs
(f) Maximum speed with load	16.5 knots

Boat Personnel, 10 Men

It is a Twin Screw motor launch built for ferrying a full load of 2000 kg or 15 to 20 persons with cargo at a speed of 12 knots. The vessel is adequately strengthened to operate in fast flowing rivers having floating debris during rainy season. The hull of diesel driven motor boat is of full welded BILGE construction and is divided by two water tight bulk heads into three compartments. General view of launch is shown in Fig. 32

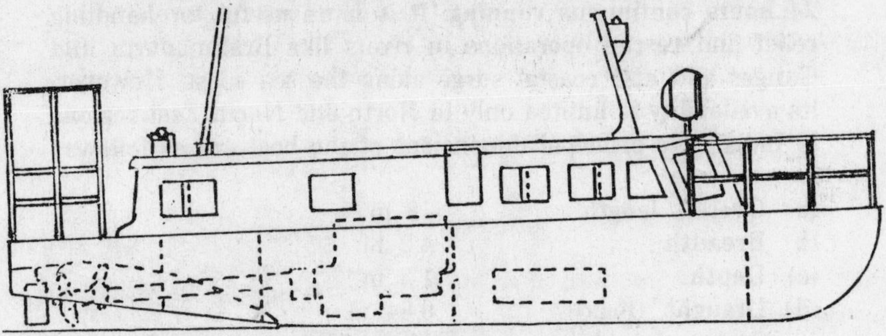

Fig. 32 : Motor Boat of 10 Men

Principal technical data of the boat are as follows :

(a)	Dimensions	Overall length	11.5m
		Bredth	2.75 m
		Depth	1.10 m
		Draft	0.60 m
(b)	Engines	Two nos. of diesel engines developing 78 BHP each	
(c)	Weight of the vessel	7800 kgs	
(d)	Speed	12 knots at 2000 kgs pay load	
(e)	Capacity	15-20 persons with cargo or 2000 kgs pay load	

The vessel is a very powerful and extremely stable speed boat designed for 15 hours of continuous running. It is more useful for large rivers like Ganges, Brahmaputra and also sea coast operations.

Motor Boat, Steel, 40 Men

The diesel engine driven twin screw motor launch is designed for transportation of personnel and cargo in the rivers of north and north-east. The vessel is adequately strengthened to operate in fast flowing rivers having floating debris and to withstand occassional groundings. It is built for carrying a pay-load of seven tonnes inclusive of 40 persons with luggage, nine crews and other accessaries at a speed of 10 knots. The vessel is a very powerful and extremely stable speed boat designed for 24 hours continuous running. It is more useful for handling relief and rescue operations in rivers like Brahmaputra and Ganges and also coastal surge along the sea coast. However, its availability is limited only in North and North East regions of India. The principal dimensions of the boat are as follows :

(a) Overall length	18 m
(b) Breadth	4.2 m
(c) Depth	1.3 m
(d) Draught (max)	0.84 m
(e) Service speed	10 knots
(f) Passenger capacity	50
(g) weight	30 tonnes

3

Housing in Areas Prone to Natural Disasters

*G. C. Mathur**

Natural disasters such as floods, cyclones, earthquakes cause large scale destructions to houses year after year. These create serious problems in thickly populated states like Uttar Pradesh, Assam, Bihar and West Bengal. The coastal districts of Andhra Pradesh, Tamil Nadu, etc., are susceptible to cyclones and storms. More than 55 per cent of India's land area particularly in the North Eastern region falls in the seismic zone of moderate Indo-Gangetic plains and Kutch and Kathiawad regions are earthquake prone. Other forms of natural disasters which some times occur in Northern India include avalanche in the snow-bound Himalayan regions and landslides in the North-Eastern Region.

Disaster Mitigation

The problem of disaster mitigation relief is of stupendous magnitude and involves coordination of a large number of agencies concerned with different aspects. In a vast country like India, with its widely varying geographical features, types of population, etc., housing in disaster prone areas has to take due account of the terrain availability of building materials, appropriate construction techniques, resources and skills available.

Development Group

The attention of the Planning Commission has been drawn to the housing and land use in disaster prone areas. It has been observed that there is a need for evolving guidelines for

---

* Former Director, National Buildings Organisation, New Delhi.

ensuring proper land use in disaster prone areas to minimise the damage and destrucion and for evolving design of low cost houses which are better resistant to the effects of natural calamities. The Working Group on Flood/Cyclone Management set up by the Planning Commission under the aegies of Ministry of Agriculture and the Rural Development in connection with the formulation of Seventh Five Year Plan had suggested to build suitable designs for structures in vulnerable areas particularly the coastal regions. In persuance of this recommendation, the Ministry of Urban Development (the then Ministry of Works and Housing) set up a Development Group (Task Force) on Housing in Disaster Prone Areas under the Chairmanship of the author, to go into various aspects of the problem and make suitable recommendations in the matter. The recommendations of the Development Group and the Strategy for the implementation suggested are as follows :

Recommendations

The subject of Disaster Mitigation with reference to housing involves numerous disciplines. The general approach to the problem of housing in disaster prone areas varies according to the type of the disaster, as each of them has its own special characteristics and varying parameters. As such the Group has given important recommendations applicable to all types of disasters and suggested areas for further action on long term basis. Nevertheles, a few recommendations for specific type of disasters have also been included, taking into account their uniqueness in finding suitable mitigation measures.

Technical Measures

(1) Many buildings and houses located in disaster prone areas are structurally inadequate to resist the destructive action of natural disasters. Efforts should be made to incorporate strengthening measures in important buildings, hospitals, community shelters, schools, cinema halls, office complexes and such type of buildings where a large number of people is exposed to risk. The old and temporary structures must

be given priority. The cost-benefit ratio in providing disaster resistant housing should be worked out for various types of disasters and local conditions so that cost effective solutions commensurating with needs are worked out.

(2) The level of reliability of a particular structure depends on the type and the quality and the disaster mitigation measures. In view of limited resources the cost-benefit ratio must be given due regard, incorporating such measures.

(3) (a) In flood prone areas, the building should be constructed as far as possible on soil of the best bearing capacity. It should be constructed on the highest ground available.

(b) Houses should be constructed over raised mounds. The mounds should be prepared with locally available soil and compacted thoroughly.

(c) The roof level should be sufficiently high above the 'design flood level' in order to provide protection in the case of emergency.

(d) The walls constructed with mud and soil blocks should be protected against the flood rendering water proofing treatment.

(4) All buildings in seismic zones should be designed and constructed for earthquake resistance as stipulated in the Building Codes. Proper architectural planning regarding shape and size of rooms and building as a whole, location and size of opening, etc., are found to contribute greatly to earthquake performance of the buldings. The provision of horizontal seismic bands on all walls integrating the action of individual rooms as well as the building as a whole is an essential feature of all masonary as well as mud houses for safety against collapse during earthquake.

(5) (a) Reinforced cement concrete flat roofs are suitable in cyclone prone areas because of their weight and rigidity. In other types of roof using light materials, sufficient slope should be provided.

(b) For cyclone resistance beams should be provided on all internal and external bearing walls. Vertical reinforcement in the walls and at corners and junctions should also be provided.

(c) Durable structures of RCC, brick, stone and

concrete block masonary are better suited in cyclone prone areas.

Siting and Control Measures

(1) Micro-zoning pattern should be evolved for disaster prone areas to provide guidelines for planning and siting of housing and human settlements.

(2) Guidelines for working out methodology of vulnerability analysis should be prepared for land use planning.

(3) Floods :

(a) Flood storage facilities in unoccupied flood plain areas should be developed for storing peak discharges of rivers during flood.

(b) To prevent inundation of flood plains, river banks should be constructed or the existing level of river banks should be raised.

(c) To relieve the flood pressure from the normal river channel, by-pass channels should be provided.

(d) The normal river channels should be improved to increase the conveyance of flood water by re-aligning or enlarging the cross-sectional area or increasing the bed slope.

(e) Well designed and maintained drainage system should be provided in towns for avoiding local flooding.

(f) Growing of regular plantation in the catchment area and on the banks of rivers as well as coastal area should be encouraged to retard run off.

(g) Plants and shrubs should be grown around the houses as they provide a measure of protection by breaking the force of gushing water.

(4) The importance of flood plain zoning should be recognised for orderly settlement free from undue hazards. Survey should be undertaken in flood prone areas to demarcate prohibited, restricted and warning zones and inhabitants should be made aware of these zones with proper demarcation.The concerned authorities should develop flood plain zoning maps which should be implemented in establishing human settlements.

(5) The Building Regulation should specify incorporation of strengthening measures in building and housing in order to enable them to withstand inundation from high velocity

water.

(6) Much attention should be given for drainage in forming new settlements and escape lanes should be incorporated in the layout for rapid flow out of water.

(7) There is a need for proper planning of human settlements taking into account the total effects of wind on the settlements particularly the infrastructure. Proper orientation and geometry of the structure are important for increasing the wind resisting capacity and should be given due regard. By proper siting of houses and other structures in a settlement, wind concentration can be avoided or minimised.

(8) Cyclone shelter belts should be created in the coastal areas by tree plantation. Temporary emergency shelters should be constructed in the coastal areas.

(9) The Municipal Bye-Laws and Building Regulations should incorporate mendatory provisions for strngthening of houses and buildings in disaster prone areas. Strict enforcement should be ensured. Building bye-laws should be examined in depth to identify shortcomings in the provisions for adequate and satisfactory strengthening arrangements taking into account the type and intensity of disaster experienced locally.

(10) Repair and reconstruction of buildings and houses affected by natural disasters are specialised subjects. The National Buildings Code of India should include a chapter devoted to this aspect. The National Buildings Code should also include chapters for rural buildings and houses which should incorporate measures of strengthening houses against natural disasters.

Research

(1) (a) There is a felt need for developing the methodology for precising prediction of formation, intensity and movement of tropical storms in the Indian subcontinent. Towards this end, facilities like aircraft reconaissance, special marine vessels and satellite observation should be augmented and improved.

(b) There is a felt need for collecting basic information pertaining to incidence of all types of structures. A Data Bank should be established to collect information from all sources.

(2) Surveys of different types of houses should be carried

out all over the country and mapping of housing zones and typology should be evolved. Data obtained will facilitate R and D work.

(3) Specific measures for disaster preparedness related to housing should be identified to mitigate their effects. Such measures include materials for repais and reconstruction, temporary shelters, etc.

(4) To study the structural response and optimise the design of a hazard prone structure, reasonable large scale disaster simulation and performance facilities need to be created. Large size shaking table, wind tunnel static and dynamic test floor, computer controlled loading and data aquisition system, instrumentation to obtain field data on hazard loads are some of the major facilities which should be established at the national level.

(5) As the facility of wind tunnel and large scale shaking table would be available at the Structural Engineering Research Centre in Ghaziabad, a close interaction between SERC and other agencies is essential to ensure that the design parameter of these facilities meets the requirement of disaster prone structures.

(6) (a) Research work should be undertaken to develop temporary houses and instant houses for sheltering disaster victims immediatly after the disaster as well as for temporary duration. The chief criteria are (a) Construction should be based on local building materials and appropriate technology (b) it should be light in construction; and (c) prefafab structure should be light, amenable for dismentalling and reusing.

(b) R and D work should be carried out to study the cost effectiveness of penultimatically supported tents used as a temporary shelters. The reseaech should aim at standardising design procedures, develop synthetic covering material and ancillary equipment required to maintain the shelters in operation.

(c) Mitigation of damages from natural disaster is possible through a good understanding of the structural behaviour of houses and buildings. Some of the priority areas of research are as follows :

(i) Structural design data pertaining to the terrain and to the intensity and frequency of the type of hazard being considered;
(ii) Study of structural damages caused in different kinds of hazards;
(iii) Characteristics of locally available materials and other common building materials to evaluate their suitability for disaster housing;
(iv) Hazard, resistant designs and strengthening measures;
(v) Development of design criteria; and
(vi) Appropriate construction techniques.

(d) In determining the degree of reliability of a structure, the combined effect of load and strengths which are themselves highly variable should be taken into account. The application of reliability theory to hazard resistant structure will give a clear indication of the relative influence of the parameter contributing to the risk.

(e) Appropriate materials and techniques should be developed for quick repair and rehabilitation of existing old and dilapidated buildings.

(f) Model studies should be conducted with different configurations of building to study their relationship with wind effects.

(g) Studies should be undertaken to improve the durability and performance of low cost buildings and houses in rural areas to withstand the effects of cyclone.

(h) Effecient jointing, bracing and anchoring details should be developed for structural members through research.

(i) Research work should be undertaken on structures built on silts to increase their flood resistance.

(7) (a) Data of rainfall, run off and sediment yield and other water shed characteristics should be collected over a period of time for all major rivers in order to obtain prediction models for estimating run off and sediment yield of ungauged water sheds.

(b) Flood frequency curve based on the data of frequency distribution, intensity of rainfall and water shed should be developed.

(8) (a) To utilise the enormous potential existing in the academic and research organisations, specific research needs to be organised. The research work should be coordianted by agencies such as NBO and DST.

(b) Research work should be undertaken on the aspect of strengthening existing structures to resist anticipated earthquake forces.

Strategy for Implementation

Considering the magnitude and complexity of the problem, it is imperative that a well planned strategy has to be adopted for evolving long-term and short-term measures towards the end. A good amount of research and development work as well as training extension and publicity are called for. Some of the specific measures recommended are given below :

(1) The short and long term steps for developing disaster resistant houses should be identified and implemented as per time bound programme.

(2) (a) The NBO should make a first hand study of the work carried out in other parts of the world regarding disaster housing with a view to utilising the knowledge and experience under Indian conditions.

(b) Suggestive type designs incorporating various strengthening measures should be worked out and distributed widely to the concerned departments.

(c) A permanent cell should be created in NBO to follow up and implement the recommendations. As this is a specialised job calling for multi-disciplinary approach and collaboration with a large number of departments all over the country, adequate staff should be provided to man the cell.

(d) The Regional Housing Development centres of the NBO should play an active role by carrying out extension work to promote wide scale adoption and research and technological developments pertaining to disaster housing.

(e) Demonstration houses and structures incorporating disaster resistant measures should be put up at various places prone to different types of disasters. The demonstration structures should incorporate locally available materials and should be used as tools to develop skills in disaster resistance construction.

(3) (a) Guidelines for house builders should be prepared suggesting ways and means of protecting houses against natural disaster by incorporating strengthening measures in Standards and Codes. The guidelines should be brought out in regional languages with good illustrations.

(b) Engineers, architectures and builders should be made aware of the latest technology available for strengthening structures in disaster prone areas, through seminars/symposia, lectures, distribution of publications, etc.

(c) Training Courses on Housing in Disaster Prone Areas, Disaster Mitigation and allied subjects should be organised for inservice personnel to impart knowledge on the latest technologies and innovations pertaining to construction and repaires of houses in disaster prone/affected areas.

(d) Training programmes for inservice personnel in planning design and construction of earthquake resistant buildings and houses should be organised. The training should also include the aspect of strengthening masonary buildings and mud houses.

(e) In flood prone areas, the importance of keeping the drains to avoid flooding should be brought home to the people.

(4) (a) Seminars, Workshops and Symposia should be organised with duel purpose of propagating technologies and strategies on disaster housing and to provide a forum for interaction of experts in field.

(b) Promotional work and publicity pertaining to disaster resistant construction in villages must commensuarate with needs and keep affordability in view. It should be easily comprehended by the villagers.

(c) Audio Visual Programmes using video films, movie films, slides, etc., should be prepared for propagating information and educating people at all levels.

(d) Books, instruction leaflets and manuals should

be prepared for the benefits of engineering personnels as well as laymen.

(e) Mass media like TV Radio and Press be utilised for countrywide publicity.

(5) (a) There is a great need to undertake promotional activities for transfer of technology related to construction in seismic areas. The NBO and Department of Earthquake Engineering should step up their activities. They should be adequately strengthened with the staff and requisite facilities.

(b) An Earthquake Engineering Research Centre should be established for taking up research on all aspects of seismic resistance construction and for propagational work.

(6) The ISI should take up formulation of Indian Standards and Codes of Practices on various aspects pertaining to planning, designing and construction of structures put up in the vulnerable areas.

(7) The curriculum of Engineering Colleges and Architectural Schools, etc., should include the subject of housing and building in disaster prone areas.

(8) A school on Housing in Disaster Prone areas should be set up to impart training to all professional people concerned with different aspects of natural disaster including house construction, restoration, retro fitting etc.

(9) The Last Decade of Century (1991-2000) should be designated as Decade for Natural Hazard Reduction to focus World attention on this important human problem. A strategy for finding satisfactory solution should be worked out by the end of the decade.

Technical Knowhow

To be able to build disaster resistant houses at low cost, technical advice and consultancy are required in order to adopt the appropriate building materials and construction techniques evolved through research. The author will be glad to provide necessary technical know-how and advice for planning, designing and construction of more durable houses at low cost in areas prone to natural disasters.

It is expected that during the International Decade for

Natural Disaster Reduction (1990-2000) announced by United Nations, high priority will be accorded by all concerned to construct more durable houses at low cost in areas prone to natural disasters.

Notes and References

The protection of low cost houses from heavy damage and destruction due to natural disaster depend upon various factors. The details of specific measures and construction techniques to be adopted could be obtained from technical literature on the subject particularly the following :

(a) Housing in disaster prone areas; Report of the Development Group, Government of India, National Buildings Organisation, New Delhi, 1987.

(b) Technical papers presented by G. C. Mathur at national and international conferences, symposia, workshops and training courses which are based on practical experience as per the selected titles given below :

(i) Durable Mud Houses in flood affected areas : International Conference on Flood Protection 1978, New Delhi, organised by Internal Commssion on Flood Control.

(ii) Cyclone Damage and Rehabilitation of Houses : Asia-Pacific Symposium on Wind Engineering, 1984 Roorkee organised by Asian Institute of Technology, Bangkok and University of Roorkee.

(iii) Appropriate Technology for Construction and Earthquake Resistant Mud Houses : International Conference 1883, New Delhi, organised by International Council for Building Research, Rotterdam and National Buildings Organisation, New Delhi.

(iv) Problems of Housing in Snow-bound Regions : National Conference 1978, New Delhi, organised by Snow and Avalanche Study Establishment, Manali.

(v) Social and Economic Contraints in Building Earthquake Resistant Houses : International Conference on Earthern Structures 1981,

Albuquerque, organised by University of New Maxico and Intertech, U.S.A.

(vi) Appropriate Technology for Construction of Houses in Desert Regions 1980, Jodhpur, organised by Indian Association of Desert Technologists.

(vii) Fire-safety in High-rise Buildings : Disaster Management Journal, 1982, Joint Action Committee, New Delhi.

(viii) Technological options for Shelter for Disaster Victims : Annual Conference 1987 organised by National Buildings Organisation, New Delhi for Regional Housing Development Centres.

(ix) Post-Disaster Shelter Management : Training Course organised by Social Institute and J.A.C. 1989, New Delhi.

(x) Mobilising Human Response to Disaster Preparedness, Mitigation and Management : 1989, New Delhi organised by Central Water Commission.

(xi) Planning and Managment for Prevention and Mitigation of Natural Disasters in Metropolitan Centres in India : International Seminar 1986, Tokyo organised by United Nations Centre for Regional Development, Nagoya and Government of Japan.

(xii) Sustainable Development and Natural Disasters Mitigations : Seminar 1989 organised by Friedrich Edbert Stiftung, Bonn Germany and J.A.C., New Delhi

(xiii) Shelter and Housing in Areas Prone to Natural Disasters : National Conference 1990, New Delhi organised by Disaster Management Institute, Bhopal and J.A.C., New Delhi.

4

Disaster Relief in India

*J. C. Pant**

Disaster relief comprises a wide spectrum of activities namely, pre-disaster assessment, emergency management, disaster relief, post-disaster rehabilitation and mitigation efforts. A disaster causes temporary disturbance to the societal equilibrium. Disaster relief is provided to tide over the situation during the crisis phase which enables the affected people to recover from the immediate impact of the disaster. This paper is devoted to the issues connected with disaster relief in the wake of natural calamities in India.

Evolution of Relief Policy

Disaster relief has been in vogue in India since olden times. One of the very first treatises on government, written more than two thousand years ago and commonly attributed to Kautilya, pronounces that when famine threatens, a good king should "institute the building of forts of water-works with the grant of food, or share (his) provisions (with them), or entrust the country (to another king)". The chief methods of famine relief adopted by Indian rulers included free distribution of raw foodgrains, opening of free kitchens, opening of public grain stores to the people, remission of revenue, payment of advances, remission of other taxes, construction of public works, canals and embankments, sinking of wells, encouragement to migration and increase in pay of soldiers. However, available evidence is too scanty to judge the real efficiency of relief efforts prior to 19th century.In the earlier periods and upto India's Independence (1947), famine relief policy held good for all other types of natural disasters also.

---

* Additional Secretary, Department of Agriculture and Cooperation, Ministry of Agriculture, New Delhi.

Under the rule of East India Company, as famines were frequent and severe, sometimes extremely severe, as with the calamitous famine of 1770 in Bengal, relief efforts were, moreover, at best half-hearted and in any case lacking in effectiveness. The observation of the Famine Commission in 1880 clearly brings out the status of relief efforts which prevailed at that time :

> "........the earlier despatches of the Bengal Government, while breathing a tone of sincere compassion for the sufferings occassioned by famine, are busied rather with its fiscal results, as affecting the responsibility of the Company towards its share holders, than with schemes, which would have seemed wholly visionary, for counteracting the ineviatable loss of life." (Famine Commission Report, 1880, pp 31).

The Famine Commission regarded the greater"market integration" permitted by the railways as one of the sure ways of rushing foodgrains to the famine struck areas. The Commission did feel uncomfortable about the occasional facilitation of exports of food stocks from famine stricken areas. But on the long run advantages of the railways, they had no doubt, and the Famine Commission of 1898 stated that "one of the most remarkable features in the recent famine was the uniform level of prices all over the country which is attributable to the over extending system of railways and which, greatly diminished the intensity of distress."

The famine prevention during the period 1858-1880 showed one inverse correlation between the determination of relief efforts and the intensity of distress. The impact of relief efforts on alleviating the intensity of distress was discernable during the period. These efforts were, however, evaluated as excessively costly.

This period of error and trial came to an end after the Famine Commission 1880, keenly aware of the vital importance of "prompt and decided action" in matters of famine relief, recommended the promulgation of *famine codes* as follows which would contain authoritative guidelines for the anticipation, recognition and relief of famines :

"The duties involved in relief measures are complicated and multifarious, their successful performance necessitates the utilisation of large stores of accumulated experience and a carefully considered and prepared plan; they cannot be safely left to individual energy and resources, or be dealt with on a system improvised only when the emergency has risen. Prompt and decided action in carrying out these measures is of primary importance, and by considering well beforehand the principles that should guide them, much of that hesitation and uncertainty of purpose, which have been found to be so detrimental in the past, will be avoided in the future. We recommend, therefore, that the Governemnt of India should, as soon as possible, issue a set of rules embodying the main principles that should govern the administration of famine relief, and that these rules should be authoritative in all parts of British India". (Famine Commission Report 1880, pp. 37-38).

The promulgation of the Famine Codes has undoubtedly represented an essential step towards the successful prevention of famines in India. However, the Famine Codes were not able to provide necessary guidelines in other kinds of natural disasters.

An examination of the incidence of famines in India before and after the Famine Codes strongly suggested a contrast between the earlier period marked by frequent famines even on account of local crop failures and the latter period when a few large-scale famines occurred. The period from 1860-1880 witnessed frequent famines. From 1880 to 1896, by contrast local crop failures were generally prevented from developing into famines. In 1896-97 and again in 1899-1900, famine struck with renewed force. During the 20th century, the incidence of famines was less even before Independence except the Bengal famine of 1943. The above trend became a testimony to the fact that whereas the Famine Codes were somewhat effective in tackling the situations created by the local crop failure, they were ineffective to prevent large-scale famines.

The main reasons why large-scale famines kept occurring even after formulation of famine codes in the pre-independence era were as follows :

(i) existence of famine codes did automatically ensure their applications;

(ii) famine had an excessively punitive character in relation to selection of relief works, wage rates;

(iii) non-interference with private trade resulted in unprecedented price rise and no concious attempts were made to prevent food exports from famine stricken areas; and

(iv) no serious attempts were made to prevent epidemics in the case of serious famine situations.

The above factors point to shortcomings in the relief system in the pre-independence era.

After independence, a need was felt to revise the Code to provide for the social and economic goals of a welfare state, as embodied in the Constitution and the successive Five Year Plans. Different state governments have since carried out and introduced many changes in their relief manuals.

Bihar famine episode accelerated the process of transition and thus modernisation of relief efforts was given definite shape. In the memories of Suresh Singh, who was a District Collector in Palamau (one of the worst drought affected districts in Bihar in 1967) has succinctly brought out the transition:

> "We start our operations within the framework of the Bihar famine code and Bihar had the advantage of having an updated code. The famine code was originally based on three assumptions: the Indian famine was a famine of work, not a famine of food; famine relief was *ad hoc* in nature; a large financial commitment to famine relief could be more fatal than famine itself and so a set of stringent rules had been framed restricting the scope of the relief. Famine relief was a negative concept; it was preventive rather than protective. All this very well fitted the colonial frame, but these assumptions were incompatible with the norms of democratic society and militated against the compulsion of a developing economy. After the Bengal Famine (1943) and particularly after independence most of the assumptions were

> modified, for instance, the State assumed the responsibilities for the public distribution of foodgrains as the Bengal famine was found to be not only a famine of work but also a famine of food. The concept of stringent famine relief was also watered down because the state undertook comprehensive measures of welfare. But the transition to a new system was not complete in the early 1960s.

In the crucible of experiences in 1966-67, the process of transition was accelerated. We started with the famine code and improved upon it. We introduced changes in the structure and function of famine relief; famine relief was thus modernised."

The Famine Relief Codes of the erstwhile provinces were replaced in the fifties and sixties by the Scarcity Relief Manuals of various states which describe 'scarcity' as a marked deterioration of the agricultural season due to the failure of rains or floods or damage to crops from insects resulting in severe unemployment and consequent distress among agricultural labour and small cultivators. The Scarcity Relief Manuals also make provision for dealing with all natural calamities including drought. In assessing the state of a season for the purpose of determining whether scarcity is to be declared or not, factors such as the *annewari* of crops in the current and in the previous two years, the availability and prices of foodgrains and fodder, the state of employment and trends in wages, unusual movements of labour from rural areas, the state of crime and other factors indicating signs of distress such as malnutrition among children are taken into consideration.

Scarcity manuals lay down measures to provide reasonable purchasing power to the affected people as well as ensure availability of goods and services. The more recent drought manuals also lay down measures not only towards alleviating distress of the affected population but also to bring out alternative arrangements in maintaining crop production through contingency planning and better water management and developmental efforts by creating assets through employment generation works to the extent necessary.

Every major disaster contributed in bringing about qualitative improvements in disaster management efforts. Drought of 1965-66 contributed to building up of a reliable Public Distribution System (PDS) to take care of the food emergencies. The privations suffered during this drought and also spurred the country into embarking on certain fundamental changes in the agricultural strategy which ultimately ushered in the Green Revolution making the country self-sufficient in foodgrains production. The drought of 1972 focussed on the need for evolving massive employment generation programmes for enhancing the purchasing power of the people rather than running free kitchens, while the drought of 1979 underlined the need for creating durable and productive assets for enabling the people of the affected area to withstand future droughts with greater resilience.

The Government of India (GOI) issued guidelines in 1980 for preparing relief manuals in the light of changes in approaches towards drought management. The State Government of Andhra Pradesh brought out a Drought Handbook and the Government of Gujarat and Maharashtra prepared Draft Relief Manuals. The other state governments are in the process of drafting or updating their relief manuals in the light of guidelines issued by the GOI.

The drought of 1987 focussed not only on the need for providing access to food to the affected people but also on maintaining their quality of life. It is no more a question of saving life from the threat of widespread starvation during such a natural calamity. The central theme of relief today is to meet the food and nutritional needs of all sections of the people keeping in view their normal energy requirements, supply of drinking water, providing adequate health care and fodder for the cattle also.

The severe floods on various occasions and the cyclone of 1977 in Andhra Pradesh, brought qualitative changes in policy measures to undertake counter measures against the impact of natural disasters.

The disaster management policy presently under implementation seeks to provide relief and arouse the energies of social groups and non-governmental organisations in a total effort to ensure that damage to the affected population in facing a natural calamities is minimised to the extent possible. The objective is not only that no one should die of starvation but more importantly to prevent physical deterioration and destitution of the people and to enable them to resume normal pursuit of life at the earliest. It also aims to encouraging community effort by sharing a common concern and to fashion or shape events and social infrastructure so that the recurrence of scarcities and other calamities is minimised. The relief measures are, no longer to be conceived in isolation but are expected to be integrated with the development ethos and programmes under implementation under various Five Year Plans in order to minimise their recurrences.

Prior to 1878, no special financial provision was made to meet the obligations imposed by periodic recurrence of famines. They were treated as extraordinary calamities and the expenditure entailed was also regarded as extraordinary. During 1878, an annual sum of Rs. 1.5 crores was earmarked by Government of India for famine insurance. It was to be utilised for distribution of relief when famines occurred, but when there was no famine, the amount was utilized for protective works like railways and irrigation. After the financial decentralization under the Mont-Ford Reforms of 1919, the famine relief became a liability upon the provincial governments. Each provincial government was required to maintain with the Government of India a Famine Insurance Fund by contributing a fixed sum of money every year. Bombay was required to provide about R. 63 lakhs annually. Out of the annual contributions, funds would be spent on construction of protective irrigation works and on relief measures, when necessary. The balance to the credit of the fund was regarded as invested with the Central government.

In 1928-29, the Famine Insurance Fund was changed into the Famine Relief Fund and it was decided that all annual assignments made to this fund from revenue as well as its balance should be spent only on the relics of famine. On introduction of provincial autonomy in 1937, famine relief was left entirely to the provincial governments, as the Government of India Act of 1935 did not provide for a separate famine relief fund. The fund was therefore discontinued and the balances due to the provinces were returned to them. Thereafter, it devolved upon the provincial governments to devise proper arrangements for avoiding and alleviating the distress caused by famines.

The Indian Famine Commission 1880 had expressed an opinion that the then government made efficient arrangements for delivering the famine-stricken. They also felt that there was no reason for appealing to the public to aid the government by contribution, but that charitable assistance should be welcomed and encouraged for certain purposes. The Government of India laid down its policy regarding private charity in 1897. The government fully accepted general responsibility for saving the lives of the people in tracts in which famine prevailed. It was felt that private charity, while working side by side with it, should not interfere with or overlap the operations which were organised for this purpose by the government. The Indian Charitable Fund was created in 1897 to channelise funds from public for relief purposes.

For collection and administration of private subscriptions, a Central Committee called the Indian Committee was appointed. The Central Committee allotted funds to the provincial committees, which in turn, formed local committees for administration of the funds for relief, in the provinces.

The fund of 1897 was subsequently replaced by the Indian People's Famine Trust. The Indian People's Famine Trust was constituted by the Government of India on the basis as a donation of Rs. 15 lakhs given by the Maharaja of Jaipur for the purpose of charitable relief in seasons of general distress. The IPFT was renamed as Indian People's Natural Calamities Trust in 1986. Out of this fund Rs. 142 lakhs were given to next of kin of deceased in the cyclone of May, 1990 which struck Andhra Pradesh and partially affected Tamil Nadu, Pondicherry and Orissa.

After Independence it has been a well accepted practice that the primary responsibility for providing relief measures to people affected by natural calamities is that of the state government concerned. The Central government supplements the efforts of the state governments by providing additional resources in accordance with recommendations of the Finance Commissions from time of time.

The Central-State share of relief expenditure was governed by recommendations of Finance Commissions from time to time. The policy reviews in relation to financing relief expenditure underwent change after periods of fair trials. The policy of following years will be of interest to the readers :

Year	*Pattern of Financing*
1953	The Central government gave 50 per cent of the expenditure of gratuitous relief as grant and 50 per cent of expenditure on pest relief works as a loan besides concessional supply of foodgrains.
1955	In February, 1955, the assistance policy was revised. The state government could then expect grants to cover half the total expenditure of gratuitous relief upto Rs. two crores and 3/4 of the expenditure above that limit. Not only did the central policy of 1955 thus covered the different components of relief expenditure but it was also envisaged that the assurance for a State Plan outlay could be kept intact.
	The Second Finance Commission, for the first time, recommended the *margin money* for each state for relief expenditure.
1961-62	The states were required to inform the Centre when they felt that the expenditure of relief will be in excess of Rs. one crore. The Central government, thereafter, constituted a team of officers for an on-the-spot assessment of the situation. The central assistance was normally limited to half the expenditure of the relief items including works undertaken as a preferable alternative to gratuitous relief, when new assets were either not created or were of value less then the expenditure. In a calamity of very considerable magnitude, the Central government would consider additional *adhoc* grants.
1966	The additional expenditure over and above the Annual Plan provisions as assessed by the central teams was to be shared by the Centre. The shareable

Year	*Pattern of Financing*
	items included relief works' expenditure. The central assistance was limited to 75 per cent of actual expenditure in excess of margin money. two-third of which were given as grant and one-third by way of loan. The balance of 25 per cent of the expenditure was to be borne by the state.
1974-75	Assistance given to the states for relief expenditure is to be adjusted within the ceilings of central assistance for the State Plan.
1979	The Seventh Finance Commission recommended that if the ceiling of expenditure for drought relief is upto five per cent of the state's annual plan outlay, the Central government should give Advance Plan Assistance to the state. If the ceiling of expenditure exceeds five per cent of the annual plan, half of excess expenditure will be treated as loan. In the case of floods, 75 per cent of the ceiling of expenditure would be non-plans grant from the Centre and remaining 25 per cent would be met by the states.
1985	The Eighth Finance Commission recommended the same pattern of financing relief expenditure, with the modification that fire was also included as one of the natural calamities eligible for Central assistance and provision was made for sharing of 50 per cent of margin money by the Centre.
1990	A Calamity Relief Fund (CRF) has been constituted for each state with an allocated amount 75 per cent of which shall be provided by the Central government as a non-plan grant in four quarterly instalment and the remaining 25 per cent shall be met by the state government concerned from their own resources. A state level committee headed by the Chief Secretary of the state shall decide on all matters connected with the financing of the relief expenditure. The progress of the relief

Year *Pattern of Financing*

expenditure will be monitored by the Central government in the Department of Agriculture and Cooperation.

Following the constitution of the Calamity Relief Fund, it is now the responsibility of the state government to meet the entire expenditure on management of the natural calamities unless a particular calamity is a calamity of 'rare severity' which requires handling at the national level. The Ninth Finance Commission has recommended state-wise allocations after taking into account the average of the ceiling of expenditure approved for various natural calamities by the Central government for each state during the last 10 years ending 1988-89.

Funds from the Chief Minister's Relief Fund and the Prime Minister's Relief Fund are released for providing assistance to the affected people from time to time.

The extent of central assistance approved for states for natural calamities relief from the First Five Year Plan to Seventh Five Year Plan as well as average annual assistance sanctioned in various plan periods are given below :

Sl.no.	Period	Total amount sanctioned (ceilings of expenditure)	Average annual assistance (ceilings of expenditure)
1.	I Five year Plan (1951-52 to 1955-56)	28.18	5.64
2.	II Five Year Plan (1956-57 to 1960-61)	38.55	7.71
3.	III Five Year Plan (1961-62 to 1965-66)	32.55	6.41

Sl.no.	Period	Total amount sanctioned (ceilings of expenditure)	Average annual assistance (ceilings of expenditure)
4.	Annual Plan (1966-67)	58.36	58.36
5.	Annual Plan (1967-68)	99.97	99.97
6.	Annual Plan (1968-69)	105.54	105.54
7.	IV Five Year Plan (1969-70 to 1973-74)	1197.97	239.59
8.	V Five Year Plan (1974-75 to 1978-79)	651.40	130.28
9.	Annual Plan (1979-80)	341.43	341.43
10.	VI Five Year Plan (1980-81 to 1984-85)	2791.97	558.39
11.	VII Five Year Plan (1985-86 to 1989-90)	5129.91	1025.00

It may be seen that the central assistance to the states for financing relief expenditure was less than 10 crores per annum in the first three plans. The annual expenditure increased steadily during the three annual plan periods. The ceiling of expenditure approved declined during the 5th Plan to only Rs. 130 crores per annum. From the Annual Plan 1979-80 and thereafter the ceiling of expenditure increased steadily and attained a peak during the later half of Seventh Plan period.

It may be seen that there was a drop in the annual average central assistance sanctioned during the Fifth Plan period as compared to previous years and also there was a sharp rise in the subsequent years. During the Fifth Plan period recommendations of the Fifth Finance Commission were applicable. The Sixth Finance Commission for the first time recongnising the rising trend of expenditure of relief recommended that a reasonable marginal may be provided in the forecast of state expenditure to cover relief expenditure and that in the case of drought and floods the central assistance should be in the form of advance plan assistance within the overall ceiling of Central government assistance in the plan period.

The increasing trend of relief expenditure in the recent years may not solely reflect the increasing incidence of natural calamities. The kind of financial arrangements that are made to manage natural disasters have a bearing on the role of relief operations. Financial arangements are in a way a reflection of the government's perception of the magnitude of the relief to be provided to the affected people. The role of relief administration keeps changing with time depending on the changes in the socio-economic statue of a state. What is considered adequate relief effort at one time may be regarded to be sharply inadequate in another time frame. This changing perception generates a demand for change in financial arrangements. The role of relief administration *vis-a-vis* financial arrangements is therefore interactive and mobile. The increasing expenditure in recent times generally reflects the rising level of expectations of the affected population and the responsibilities of the administration in tune with the expectations of the people.

Upto late sixties India struggled hard to provide relief to the affected people from its own resources. During the severe drought period of 1965-67, India had to import around 13 million tonnes of foodgrains to distribute them to the drought affected areas. This made a severe dent in the balance of payment position which had serious consequences on the development programmes of the country. Out of total expenditure of Rs. 722 crores incurred during the period 1965-67 on drought relief, 28 per cent was borne by the Central government, 27 per cent by the state government and 43.8 per cent by the international aid agencies and other donor countries. Contrary to this, from the early 1970 India attained self-sufficiency in foodgrains and was able to meet the relief expenditure from its own resources. The major droughts of 1972-73, 1979-80 and 1987-88 were entirely financed by the Central and state governments. During the drought of 1987, it was decided as a national policy that no external assistance should be sought for financing the drought and the situation should be managed with our own efforts and resources. Severe cyclones in November, 1977 and May, 1990, sever floods from time to time were managed without seeking any assistance from external agency.

Relief and Management

Natural disaster management approach has significantly moved from crisis management to risk management in the late 1970s and thereafter integrated disaster preparedness approach through reliable early warning arrangements, carefully planned emergency response and better community preparedness. This approach has led to notable success in providing timely relief to affected people.

A comparison of major cyclone disasters in 1977 and May, 1990 clearly brings out the role of disaster preparedness strategy in minimising the impact of disasters. The cyclone of 1990 had similar destructive potentials like 1977 cyclone in regard to wind speed of 240-250 kms per hour, tidal waves of four metres height and accompanying heavy rainfall of 50 cms in 48 hours. In some respects, the cyclone of 1990 was more severe than 1977 as the tidal wave moved into 20-25 kms inland compared to 10-12 kms in 1977. The population affected due to 1990 cyclone was over 7.7 million people as compared to 3.4 million people affected due to cyclone of 1977. In 1977 the loss of life was about 10,000 whereas the loss of life due to May 1990 cyclone was restricted to 910. While 2.3 lakh cattle perished in 1977, the loss due to 1990 cyclone was about 27,000. The coordination mechanism at different administrative levels was activated so effectively and the meteorological forecasts were so accurate and timely that as many as 6.5 lakh people were evacuated from vulnerable areas well in time. The ability to warn in local dialect and to communicate accurately the probable threat to life and property with sufficient lead time for action was the basis for the successful management of 1990 cyclone disaster.

In the wake of unprecedented floods in August, 1986 in Godavari basin the Central Water Commission issued frequent forecasts and warnings. On the basis of the forecast, the Andhra Pradesh government authorities were able to move people living within 10 kms of the flood banks to places of safety and over one million people were evacuated from the vulnerable areas. Through a systematic disaster management approach thousands of people were saved from being washed away by floods.

With the ushering in of the quality change in disaster management approach it has been possible to restrict the relief expenditure of unproductive components of the relief activities such as gratuitous relief, etc., to the minimum and to gradually increase the resources for building productive and durable assets to enable the affected people to withstand disaster better in the future. During 1966-67 drought over 2.3 million were provided gratuitous relief. Over million people were fed on free kitchens. In contrast to this, less than five lakh persons received gratuitous relief and generally no free kitchens were arranged during 1987-88 drought. Similarly in the case of floods in Assam while relief assistance was given to the affected people for about a month during October, 1968 the same was provided for about a week during severe floods in 1988. Recovery from the ill-effects of calamities is a crucial test of the disaster management strategy. An early recovery of the affected people from the impact of disaster would reflect on the disaster management strategies adopted and would indicate that the development status of the affected people had improved. While it took several months for the people to recover from the ill-effects of drought of 1966-67, recovery was far quicker in 1987-88 drought. In fact one of the important features of the 1987 drought was the ability of the people and the economy to recover quickly from the impact of the drought as soon as the monsoon of 1988 commenced. The agricultural operations began in the country with the onset of monsoon in 1988 and the large number of irrigation works constructed as part of the employment generation programme during the drought period became functional as sources of irrigation in the ensuing season. The household assets like cattle which had been preserved through the calamitous drought could be employed in the agricultural operations immediately on the commencement of South-West Monsoon 1988.

The impact of natural disasters not only damages the life

support systems but also forces the nation to divert precious resources meant for development purposes to undertake immediate relief and rehabilitation programmes. The recurrent disasters act as obstacle to economic development. For instance, the country had to abandon the five year plan after 1965-67 drought, it is estimated that out of Rs. 722 crores which were incurred on relief expenditure, Rs. 142 crores utilized for productive schemes. However, an analysis of the sectoral share of expenditure for drought management for 1980-81 to 1987-88 reveals the following trend :

Sector	Share (%)
Employment generation	55
Drinking water schemes	25
Cattle conservation	10
Agriculture input subsidy	5
Supplementary nutrition	2
Gratuitous relief	2
Others	1
	100

From the above, it may be seen that in the new strategy of disaster management around 90 per cent of the relief expenditure is utilized for creating productive and permanent assets to safeguards farmer's assets.

Vulnerability reduction through development programmes has progressively strengthened the fighting capacity of the population living in the disaster prone areas to cope with their ill-effects. The higher the development status of a society the lesser will be their dependence on the government support through relief programmes. An analysis of peak level labour strength and population affected in selected drought years is given below :

S.No.	Drought year	Population affected (lakh)	Peak level labour strength (lakh)	Labour strength to affected population(%)
1	2	3	4	5
1.	1965-66	476.00	32.04	6.70
2.	1972-73	2000.00	92.00	4.60
3.	1979-80	2204.83	62.00	2.81
4.	1987-88	2854.19	60.42	2.11

Number employed against affected population has been declining over the years. It has been noticed through a survey conducted by National Council of Applied Economic Research that there is an increase of share of non-farm income over the farm income over the years. Between 1970-71 to 1981-82, the survey revealed that the share of non-farm income in rural households increased from about 23 per cent in 1970-71 to 33 per cent in 1981-82. This inference from the survey reveals that as a result of increase of the share of non-farm income in the total income of rural households the vulnerability of the rural population to natural disasters like droughts has reduced considerably. This has also reduced the dependence of the affected population on the government over the years.

In a populous country like ours, people will have to live perforce in disaster prone areas. Ways and means will have to be found to protect their life and property and ensure that their socio-economic activities are not adversely affected permanently. Our strategy while making efforts to further strengthen our disaster preparedness aspects, should focus on incorporating disaster mitigation measures with overall development plans to minimise the impact of disasters.

While the objective of disaster preparedness strategy is to protect lives and property from an immediate threats, the new strategy of disaster mitigation is to lessen the impact of disasters in the long run also. The disaster mitigation programmes if implemented well, may effectively contribute to reduce the physical, social and economic vulnerability of the disaster prone areas.

Construction of disaster resistant buildings, appropriate planning of transportation network, industrial establishments, drinking water facilities in the disaster prone areas, proper land use methods may reduce their physical vulnerability. Crop diversification, appropriate cropping strategies, mechanism to spread losses through insurance and other financial instruments may reduce the farmers economic vulnerability. Appropriate community preparedness programmes through well designed public awareness campaigns, increasing the capacity of local institutions like Panchayat, local community and voluntary organisations to cope with disasters may reduce social vulnerability of the disaster prone areas. Communities have evolved their own coping mechanisms over the years against the onslaught of disasters, and our effort should be to strengthen these mechanisms. The management of major disasters reveals that better disaster preparedness can reduce deaths and injuries to the local population but they do very little to prevent property damage and the devastating economic impact associated with such disasters. Losses due to natural disasters and the associated relief expenditure result in depletion of resources which could otherwise be used for socio-economic development. For instance, while it was possible to save human lives, flood-damages reported from 1985-86 to 1988-89 were Rs. 15,500 crores and relief expenditure for the same period was Rs. 1800 crores. While eight lakh houses were damaged due to 1977 cyclone, 16 lakh houses were damaged due to 1990 cyclone. This underlines the importance of undertaking disaster mitigation programmes as part of development activities.

The United Nations General Assembly has proclaimed 1990's as International Decade for Natural Disaster Reduction (I.D.N.D.R.) The U.N. General Assembly has enjoined on all governments to adopt specific policy measures at the national level to achieve disaster mitigation and to participate in concerted international effort for reduction of the impact of natural disasters. In this context, even though we have been successful to a large extent in tackling disasters, the International Decade provides us an opportunity to impart a sense of urgency to improve our strategies and also to ensure an integrated approach to achieve the overall objective of mitigating the impact of natural disasters in the years to come.

5

Coastal Erosion and Protection

*J. S. Mani**

Periodic arrival of hurricane along either a barrier island or a coastal region and long term wearing away of rocky cliffs result in coastal erosion. Coastal erosion is a complex interaction of physical processes and the coastal region. The physical processes such as the water motions of the waves, tides, storm surges and near-shore currents combine and interact with coastal regions which in turn have considerable inherent variability in their features.

Before embarking on the aspects related to coastal erosion, above agents which play a vital role in coastal erosion need brief introduction.

Waves--their Generation, Propagation and Decay

The waves one sees every day on the ocean, and those primarily responsible for coastal erosion, are generated by winds blowing over the surface of water. Though there are other types of waves, the wind generated waves are important as energy transfer agents. The water body first obtains the energy from wind, transfers it across the expanse of the ocean and then delivers it to the coastal zone, where it becomes the primary cause of erosion or causes variety of near shore currents and sand transport patterns. This transfer of the energy results in generation of ripples on the water surface at the initial stages of wind blow which later grows into a full-fledged wave, with the prolonged wind blow over the water surface. Water surface profile that results from the interaction of wind and water body (at the end of generation area) is termed as "wave".

* Assistant Professor, Ocean Engineering Centre, Indian Institute of Technology, Madras.

Fig. 1 shows the wave profile with terminologies usually adopted to describe the wave.

The waves as they advance from deep water ($h/L>0.5$) to shallow waters change their characteristics, i.e., the celerity (c), wave height (H) and wave length (L) change, but wave period (T) remains constant. The decrease in water depth towards shore causes the change in celerity and direction of wave approach such that the waves are more or less aligned parallel to the shoreline. This phenomenon is known as wave refraction. Refraction of waves cause either an increase or decrease in wave height depending on the nature of water depths prevailing in the near shore region. If there is an increase in wave height, the increase cannot be continuous and at certain water depth the waves have to collapse which is termed as "wave breaking". It is estimated that the waves break according to eqn. 1.

$$H/h = 0.78 \qquad \ldots\ldots\ldots\ldots \quad (1)$$

Thus depending on the height of the wave, the waves may break at appropriate depths and waves reformed have a chance to break again at the shore line. Most of the incoming waves break at the shore line (because of flat beach slopes) which is the primary cause of coastal erosion. Fig. 2. shows the near shore region, the beach profiles and the terminologies used to describe them.

Large size waves breaking in comparatively deeper water and smaller waves in shallow waters (according to eqn. 1.), generate a zone in the near shore known as breaker zone. The width of the breaker zone depends on the wave size, range and the beach slope. After the waves breaking occurs some broken waves transform into either bores or small waves. These regenerated waves either rush-up along the beach face or break again in appropriate water depths.

The nature of the beach profile, and hence the pattern of near shore waves depends on the grain size of the beach sediments and on the energy level of the waves. Normally coarser the sediment grain size, steeper would be the overall beach slope. The morphology of the beach profile also depends on the wave energy level, high wave conditions tending to shift sand offshore, eroding sand from the beach berm and

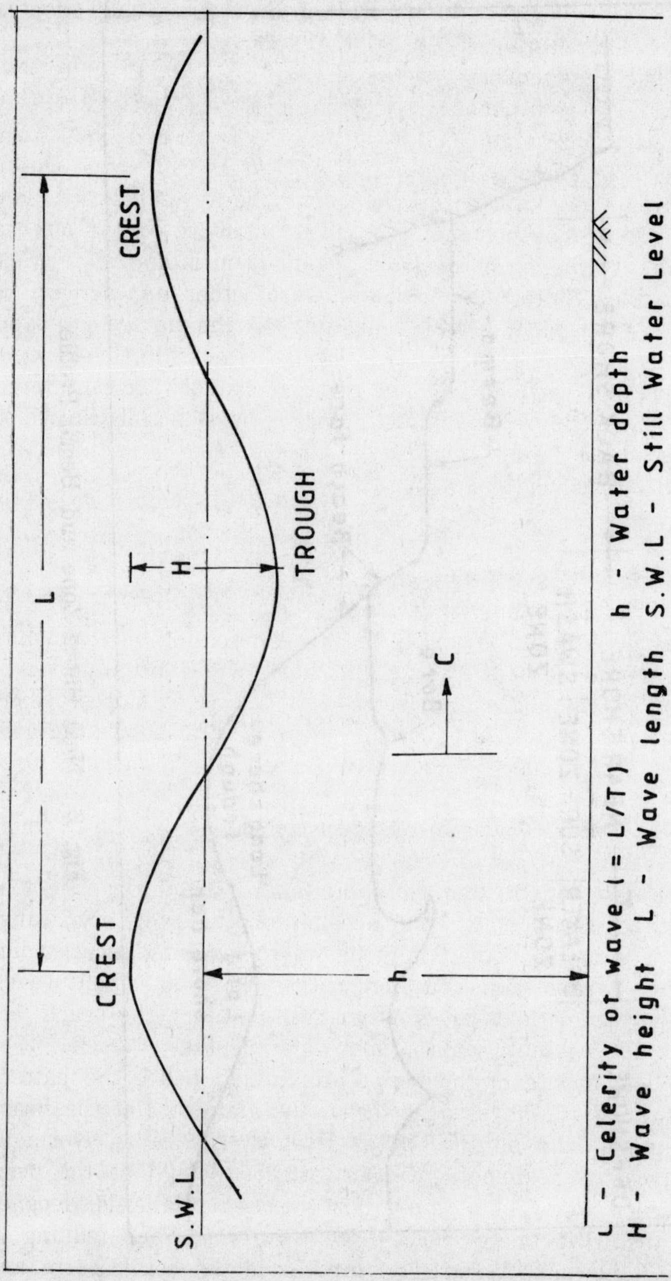

Fig. 1 : Definition sketch for a Wave Profile

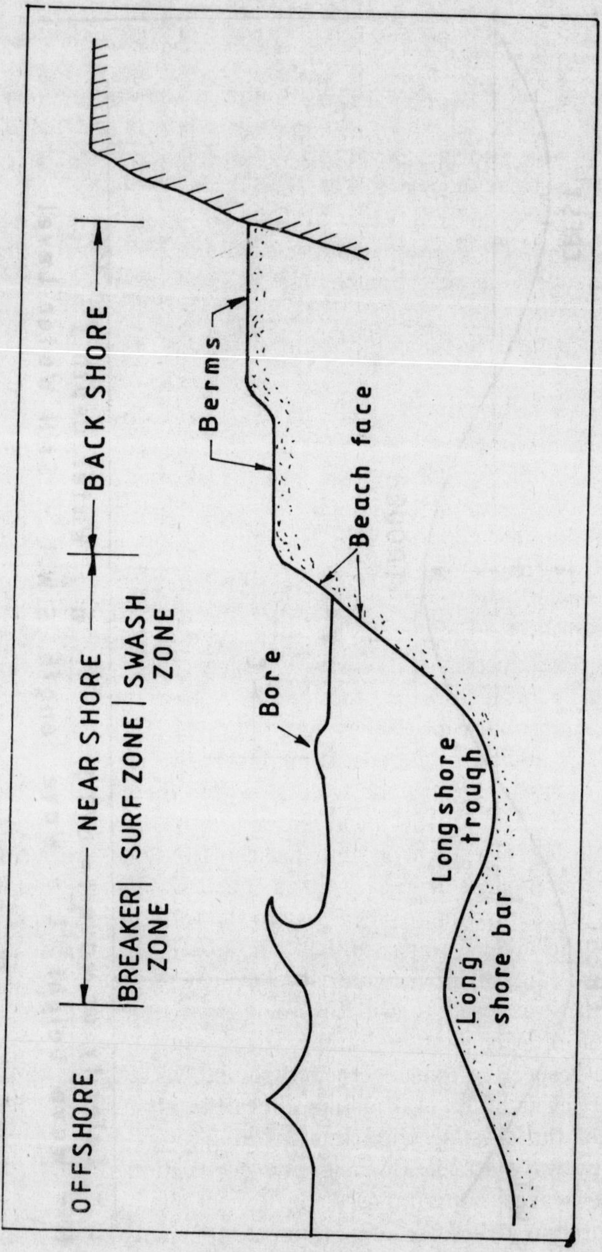

Fig. 2 : Near Shore Zone and Beach Profile

depositing in offshore area to form bars in the region of breaker zone. A return of low waves reverses the process. Along most coastlines there is a seasonality to the wave energy levels, wave heights tending to be larger during winter storms and smaller during summer producing a seasonal change in the beach profiles as shown in Fig. 3.

Due to this seasonally two profiles are often termed, *viz.*, the summer of swell profile and the winter of storm profile. It is interesting to note the change in position of shore line during summer and winter seasons. This aspect is quite important from the coastal erosion point of view.

The Tides--Storm Surges

A factor which is important in the severity of coastal erosion is the change in a water level in the sea due to tides. The severity of coastal erosion is felt strongly when there is a shift in the surf zone towards land due to increase in water level (tides) coinciding with occurrence of storm.

The most significant water-level change caused by the meteorological factors such as strong winds and abrupt atmospheric reduction is the storm surge. The rise in water level may be rather abrupt, induced by strong onshore winds and low atmospheric pressures accompanying a hurricane or typhoon. In addition to generating large surface waves, the winds of hurricanes can push water towards the coast, holding it there as a set up of the mean water level. The exceptionally low pressures of the storm system also contribute by "humping" up the water level. A drop of 3 mb in the atmospheric pressure produces and approximate 35 cm rise in the water level. Another factor is the heavy rains, which commonly accompany the hurricanes, cause rise in water level which means more land areas getting exposed to the severe wave action resulting in erosion of interior land adjoining the coast.

With respect to coastal erosion, the storm surge may rise the water levels by several meters above the highest high tides normal for the coastal zone, thus covering areas generally not affected by wave attack. Considerable destruction results from the large waves superimposed on exceptionally high levels since shoreline structures are brought under surf zone. Storm surges are also important in producing barrier island wash overs and breaching.

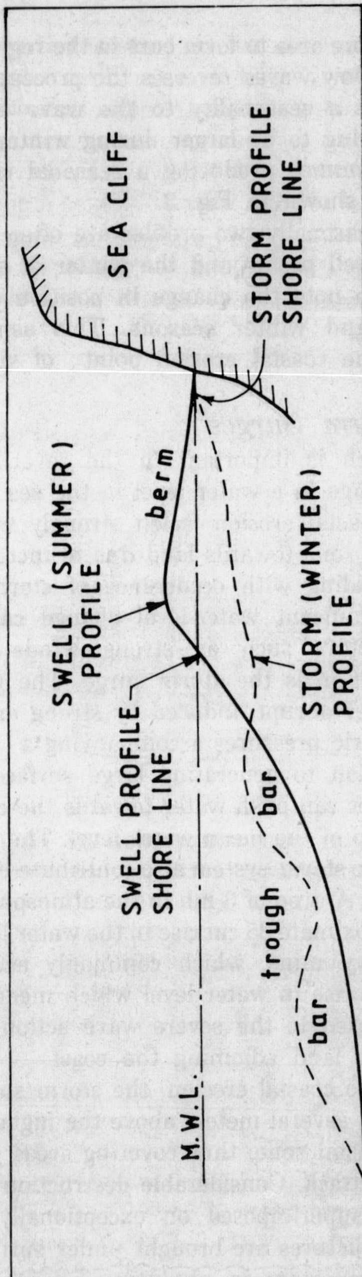

Fig. 3 : Changes in the Beach Profile brought about by High Energy Storm *vs.* Low Energy Swell

Nearshore Currents

Waves reaching a beach generate a variety of nearshore currents, the patterns of which depend (in large part) on the angle of wave breaking. One extreme is that when the waves are parallel to the shore, the dominant nearshore current that results is usually as seaward flowing rip current (Fig. 4a). Other extreme is when the waves break at a significant angle (roughly $5^\circ < \alpha_b < 10^\circ$). This produces as longshore current that is continuous along the shore line (Fig. 4b). In general both the above cases combine to produce a flow pattern as shown in Fig. 4c.

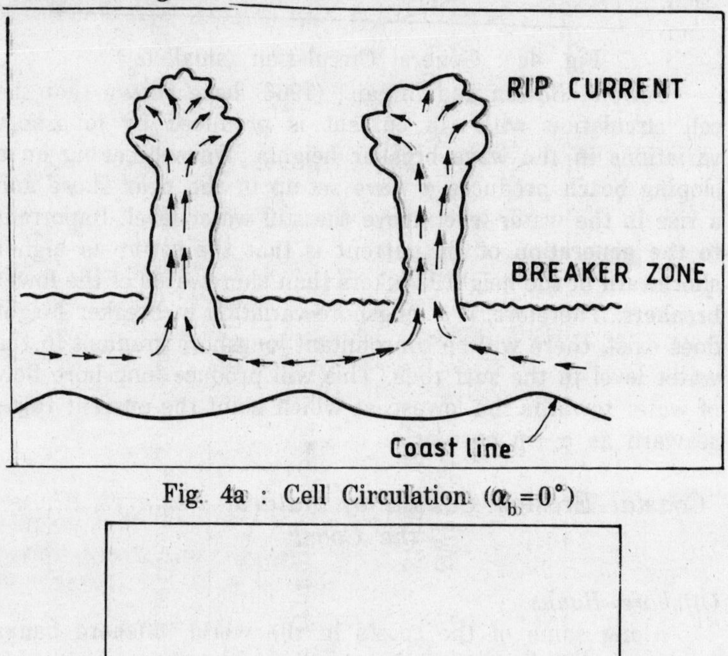

Fig. 4a : Cell Circulation ($\alpha_b = 0^\circ$)

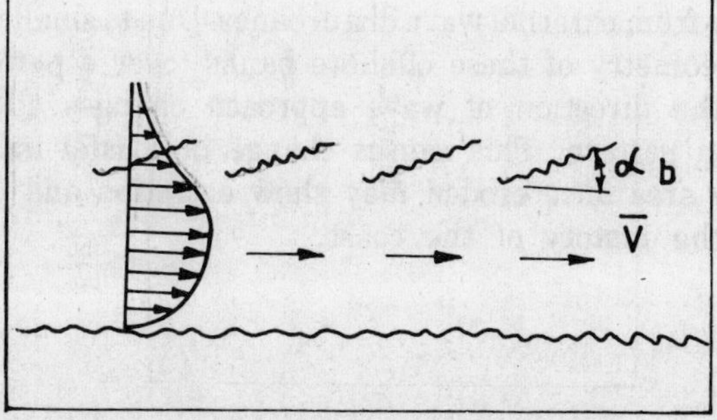

Fig. 4b : Oblique wave approach

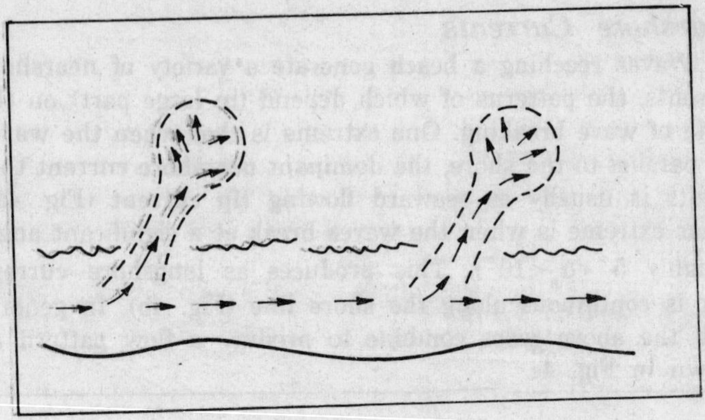

Fig. 4c : General Circulation (small α_b)

Bowen', Bowen and Inman', (1966) have shown that the cell circulation with rip current is produced by longshore variations in the wave breaker heights. Wave breaking on a sloping beach produces a wave set-up in the near shore and a rise in the water level above the still water level. Important to the generation of rip current is that the set-up is higher shoreward of the height breakers than shorewards of the lower breakers. Therefore, if a longshore variation in breaker height does exist, there will be concomitant longshore gradient in the water level in the surf zone. This will produce longshore flow of water towards the lowest, at which point the current turns seaward as a rip current.

Coastal Erosion Caused by Natural Features Along the Coast

Offshore Banks

Along some of the coasts in the world, offshore banks have provided shelter to the coastline as well as small scale harbours from external wave disturbance. Due to small variations in the geometry of these offshore banks (over a period of 200 years), the direction of wave approach changes altering the refraction pattern. This causes change in coastal morphology. Thus an area once eroded may show accretion and *vice versa* during the history of the coast.

Offshore Bars

The offshore bars can be either of the type shown in Fig. 3 or the other common form of bar submerged for all parts of the tide, formed at the entrance to a river of coastal inlet (Fig. 5). This type of bar is caused by the decreasing capacity of the seaward ebb current with or without a river discharge, to maintain its bed load or suspended load which will generally be much greater than that of the sea. A river bar is most likely to be formed where there is an adequate supply of sand, a fairly flat area offshore and a confined areas of discharge to the sea. The latter feature will tend to create a seaward jet current of the ebb, gradually expanding and diffusing as shown in Fig. 5. The tendency of the flow (both during flood and ebb) is to adjust its path according to the alignment of the offshore bar. The change in flow path, sometimes causes an increase in flow velocity which results in removal of banks of the river. The areas prone for erosion are shown in Fig 5.

Sand Spit

A spit is generally formed at any point where a projecting head land is associated with a strong littoral drift and a offshore shoal. Under these circumstances, there will be a sudden change in the longhsore component of expenditure of wave energy resulting in deposition of sand or shingle at the point. This accretion generally accumulates in the shape of finger and extends several kilometers from the point of commencement. The shore line in the updrift direction shows traces of erosion due to the existence of spit. Further advancement of the spit causes increase in the degree of erosion along the updrift shore line (Fig. 6).

Tombolo

Tombolo is the name given to a isthmus of mobile material that may develop from a coastline to form an attachment of an offshore island. The development of a tombolo can be explained as follows. The partial shelter of an offshore island leads to a cusp-shaped accretion on the adjacent coast of the mainland. This cusp-shaped feature develops or grows till a link between the mainland and the offshore island is made. Fig. 7 shows the stage-wise development of the tombolo formation. Depending on the direction of wave attack, the coast-line adjoining the

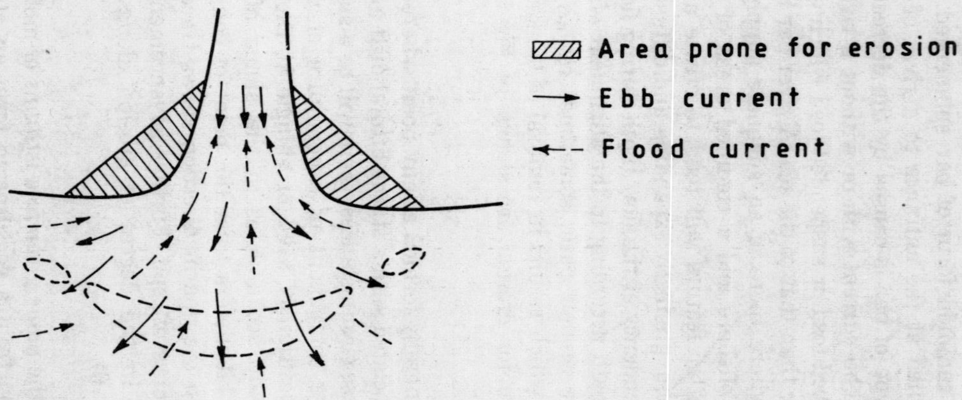

Fig. 5 : Offshore bar at an entrance to a river

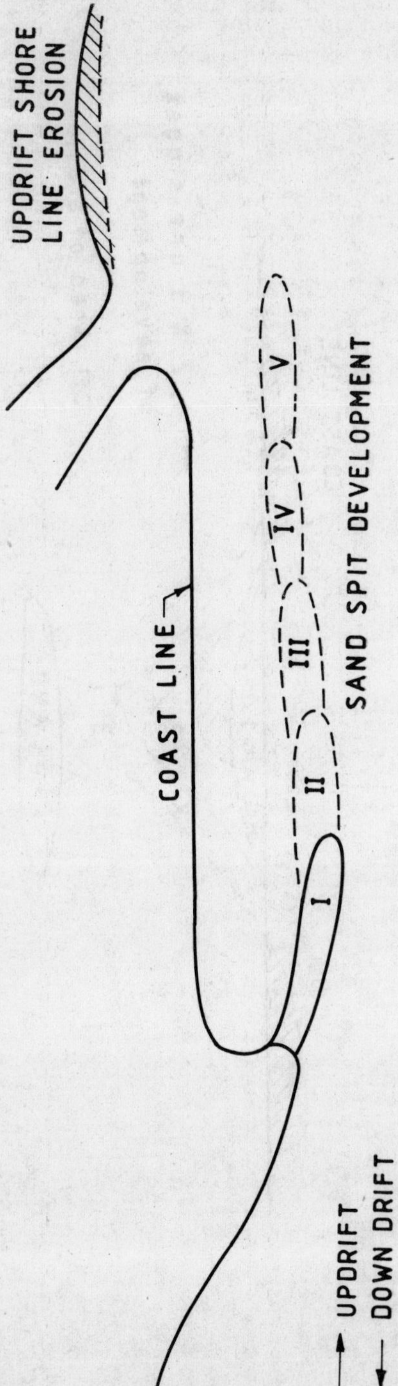

Fig. 6 : Sand Pit Development

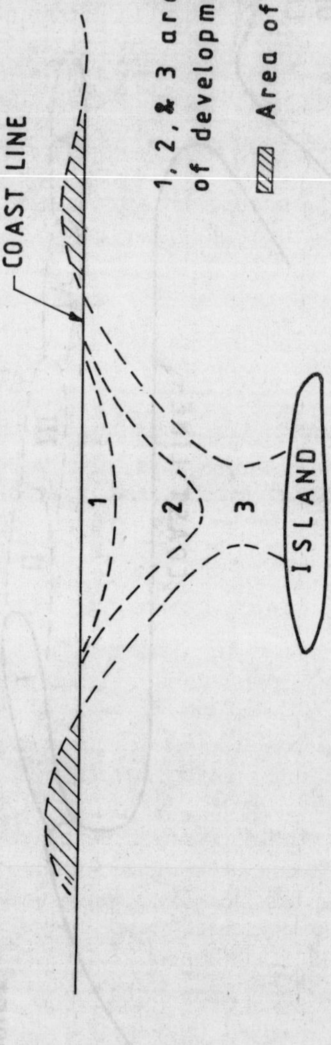

Fig. 7 : Formation of Tombolo

tombolo shows the sign of erosion which is because of the fact the tombolo, when fully developed, acts as a littoral barrier.

Bays

A bay usually owes its existence to the presence of relatively durable rock constituting the headlands. The form and composition of the foreshore and the offshore zone will depend to a greater extent on the degree and relative direction of exposure to wave attack. The variation in beach composition and profiles in the bays depends on the direction of wave attack. Usually, the change in wave direction causes movement of sediment within the bay from one side to the other (Fig. 8). Thus there is an apparent erosion along certain regions with in the bay while the other region showing accretion. Change in wave direction reverses the phenomenon. The net sediment movement causing this change remains the same.

Coastal Erosion Caused by Man-Made Structures

Ever since mankind had occupied the coastal belt for his livelihood, he has been threatened by the sea due to various human errors. Attempts have been made by the mankind to make modifications along the coastal region to suit his requirement. The kind of activities that the human being carried out along the coast can be classified in two groups, *viz.*,

(i) Providing artificial harbours in open sea/acquiring additional land

(ii) Protecting the access to artificial inner harbours by providing jetties of stabilization of coastal inlets.

Acquiring Additional Land

World wide, both the developed and the developing countries involve in constructing harbours along their coastal region to provide shelter to the ships from external wave disturbance. The dimensions of the harbour area provided by each country has grown in length and breadth and the trend now-a-days is to provide large size harbour basins to accommodate deep draft vessels. Provision of such harbour involves construction of shore connected breakwaters to form an enclosure of water

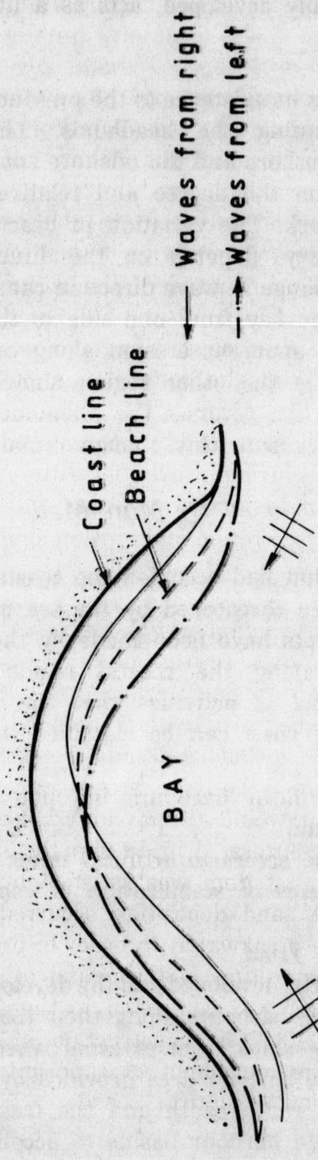

Fig. 8 : Beach Line Change in a Bay

body free from wave disturbance. In the case of littoral drift prone coastal regions, construction of harbours should be carried out with sufficient care A few examples on the construction of harbours in littoral drift prone coastal region are given below. These examples indicate the long term effect of construction of harbours on the coastal morphology, *viz.*, the accretion and erosion patterns in the vicinity of the harbour site.

Madras Harbour : The advancement in the construction of harbour since 1876 caused accumulation of sand on the southern side of the harbour. This resulted in the shift in shore line towards sea at a rate of 10 metres per year. The effect of obstructing the littoral drift caused erosion on the northern side of the harbour. With the construction of the fisheries harbour in the north, the magnitude of erosion due to storm waves is so high that at some of the locations severe damages have occurred especially to highways, etc. Attempts are being made to contain the furious action of waves on the coast line. Fig. 9 shows the area of accretion and erosion along the Madras coast.

Coastal Erosion and Accretion along Santa Barbara Coast

A comparable example to the Madras harbour is the breakwater constructed at Santa Barbara, California, U.S. Construction of a detached breakwater, intended for providing a shelter zone adjacent to a headland, caused enormous problem to the coastal engineers. When the breakwater was installed it was expected that it would (i) provide shelter on the lee side and (ii) allow the littoral drift to slip through the area. As was expected, the first item was satisfied but the second did not materialize. A sand deposition occurred propagating from land towards the breakwater. In order to prevent further growth of the sand deposition and shoaling of shelter zone, the detached breakwater was connected to the shore line on its updrift side (Fig. 10). The construction of the link, no doubt, had stopped the movement of sand into the shelter zone but caused erosion of updrift coast.

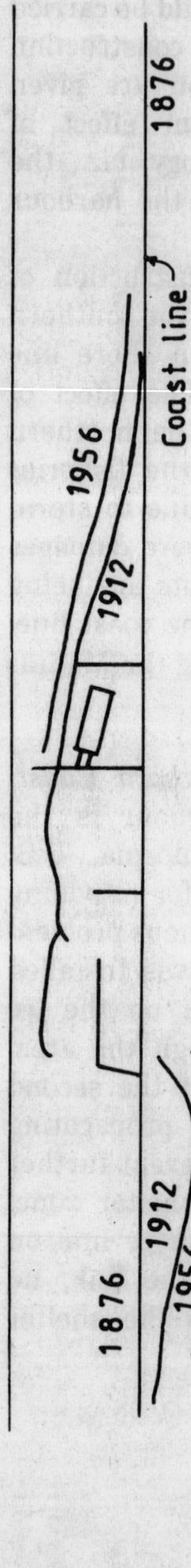

Fig. 9 : Accretion and Erosion Pattern along Madras Coast

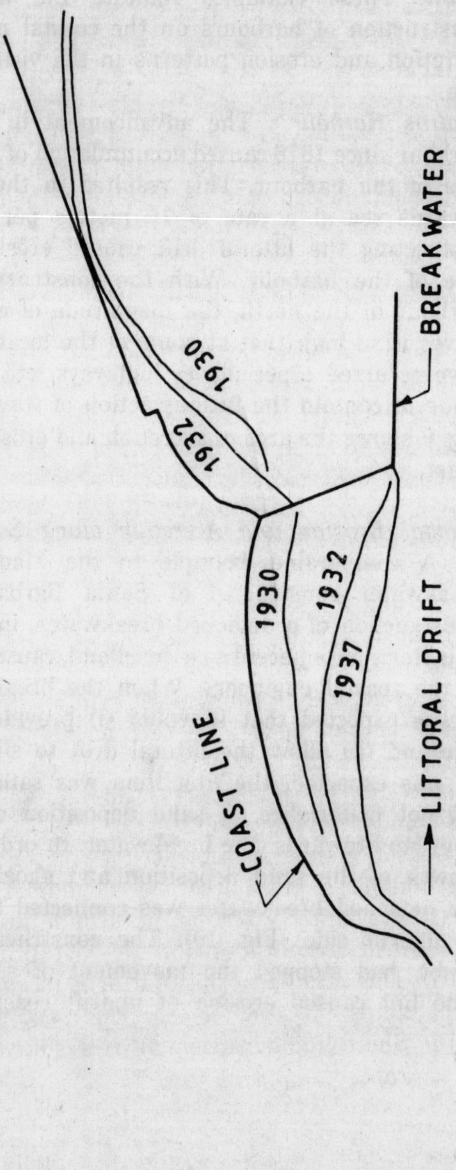

Fig. 10 : Deposition and Erosion Pattern at Santa Barbara, California

Protecting the Access to Artificial Inner Harbours by providing Jetties for Stabilisation of Coastal Inlets

Jetties have been constructed at many inlets on the east coast of U.S. For example jetties were built to stabilize the inlet, south of Ocean city, a sea side resort. These blocked the south littoral drift. However due to loss of supply of sand, the barrier Assateague Island to the south eroded and the shoreline retreated about 450m in 20 years following jetty construction. In 25 years time, the south beach had eroded to the point where it actually separated from the inner end of the south jetty, leaving a gap of almost 240m of open water. In the 26th year of construction of the jetty a sever storm opened a breach over a kilometer wide, 2.5 kms south of the jetties. Subsequent dredging and fill have partially restored the beach but such problems cannot be avoided.

Along the west cost of India, an artificial inner harbour has been built at Mangalore with its entrance protected by a 500m long jetties. The construction of these jetties had caused accretion and erosion of the coastline along the updrift and down drift sides of the coast respectively.

Coastal Protection

A natural beach of sand of shingle is an economic means of absorbing the energy of breaking waves and thus protecting an erodible coastline. It is also necessary to consider how the regime may be affected by maritime works interfering with the natural processes of littoral drift. After allowing for such factors, the engineers have to consider the sufficiency of the natural beach material for continuous protection, making provision for possible short term and long term variations (Wood and Fleming, 1969).

The Coastal engineer, before suggesting on the type of coastal protection for a given location, should know the following :

(i) Prevailing direction of littoral drift, up drift down drift magnitudes and the net drift.

(ii) The variation of littoral drift (regionwise) for a given zone.

(iii) Shore line advancement-recessment process and their rate.

(iv) The trend of shore line changes based on observations over a few years or so.
(v) The likely changes that the shoreline would exhibit after executing the protection work.

Types of Coastal Protections

Following are the types of coastal protection works that are usually carried out either to protect the existing beaches or to build up the beach lost due to erosion.

(i) Restoration of beaches
  (a) Groyne system
  (b) Artificial beach nourishment
  (c) Sediment by-passing
  (d) Offshore breakwaters
(ii) Protection of the beaches
  (a) Seawall
  (b) Bulk head
  (c) Revealment

Restoration of Beaches

Groyne System

One of the methods adopted for restoration of beaches in the littoral drift zone is to construct a series of structures called groynes along the affected part of the coastal region. These groynes, protruding into the sea for a short distance, are arranged at regular intervals along the coast. The spacing between the groynes, their geometry, and configuration depends on the extent to which the coast line is to be rebuilt or acquired. There are several types of groynes each suiting a certain requirements, *viz.*,

(i) Long and short gorynes
(ii) High and low groynes
(iii) Timber, steel, rubble groynes
(iv) Straight, and z-shaped groynes
(v) Fixed or adjustable type

A groyne system comprises a series of groynes placed with certain spacing, starting from the down drift side to up drift side. Usually at the end, a terminal groyne is placed. A groyne system is shown in Fig. 11.

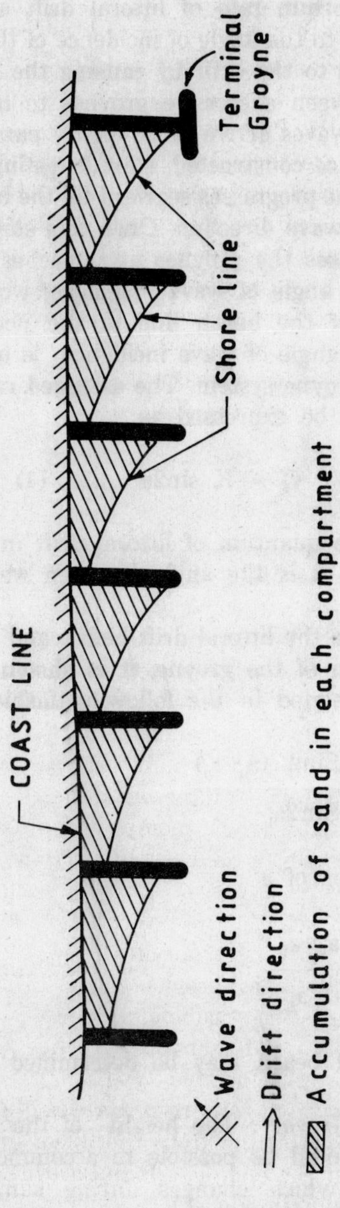

Fig. 11 : Groyne System

Role of Wave Approach Angle in the Layout of Groynes.

The equilibrium rate of littoral drift along a particular shore is related to the angle of incidence of the waves. Groynes act as arresters to the drift by causing the orientation of the beach line between successive groynes to be altered so that the prevailing waves arrive more nearly parallel to the beach. The groynes once constructed, start arresting the littoral drift and the shoreline progresses seaward till the beach line becomes parallel to the wave direction. Once this stage is reached, the material by-passes the groynes and reaches the updrift side. Any change in angle of wave incidence, would cause change in alignment of the beach line in the pocket between the groynes. Thus, angle of wave incidence is quite important in the design of groyne system. The assumed rate of littoral drift in an area can be expressed as

$$Q = K \sin 2a \quad \text{.........} \quad (1)$$

Where Q is the quantum of littoral drift in m^3/annum, K is a constant and a is the angle between wave crest and the shoreline.

If Q_0 and Q_9 are the littoral drift before and immediately after the introduction of the groyne, it is shown that the a_o and a_g can be correlated in the following fashion, *viz.*

$$\frac{Q_9}{Q_0} = \frac{\sin 2\,(a_0 - a_9)}{\sin 2a_0} \quad \text{..........} (2)$$

For small angles of a

$$\frac{Q_9}{Q_0} \simeq \frac{a_0 - a_9}{a_0} \quad \text{..........} (3)$$

and the line of beach may be determined approximately.

Height of the Groyne : The height of the groyne should be such that it should be possible to accommodate any type of beach profile (which changes during summer and winter seasons). The stability must take account of the extreme conditions of the beach entailing the simultaneous effects of

(1) the beach having a storm profile;
(2) the beach crest being inclined at the maximum angle to the gerneral line of foreshore; and
(3) local scour.

Length and Spacing of the Groyne : (a) The length of the groyne is related to the desired effectiveness of the groyne system. If the ratio of Qg/Qo is small then the length of the groyne should be extended further to see to that Qg/Qp > 1. As far as spacing between the groynes is concerned it is suggested to have a spacing of two to three times the groyne legth, measured from berm crest to seaward end as a general rule. Beach line variations due to change in direction of littoral drift is shown in Fig. 12.

Artificial Beach Nourishment

"Artificial beach nourishment" is a method by which the beach lost to the sea is regained by artificially supplying suitable beach material to the eroded beach from zones where coastal accretion occurs. In order to carry out artificial nourishment three major questions must be answered, *viz.,*

(i) What kind of artificial nourishment method should be selected?
(ii) What grain size and what amount of sand should be supplied to the beach? and
(iii) Where will the material to be used come from?

Therefore field investigation should be done first to resolve the above problms and ensure that the construction work would be successful. Fundamental data related to beach change and to coastal sediment phenomena at spectified localities should be collected. For example, the predominat littoral drift direction, the rate of littoral drift, the size of the berm as well as the long shore bar and and the foreshore slope of stabilized beach profile be known in as much detail as possible.
Artificial nourishment methods can be classified under

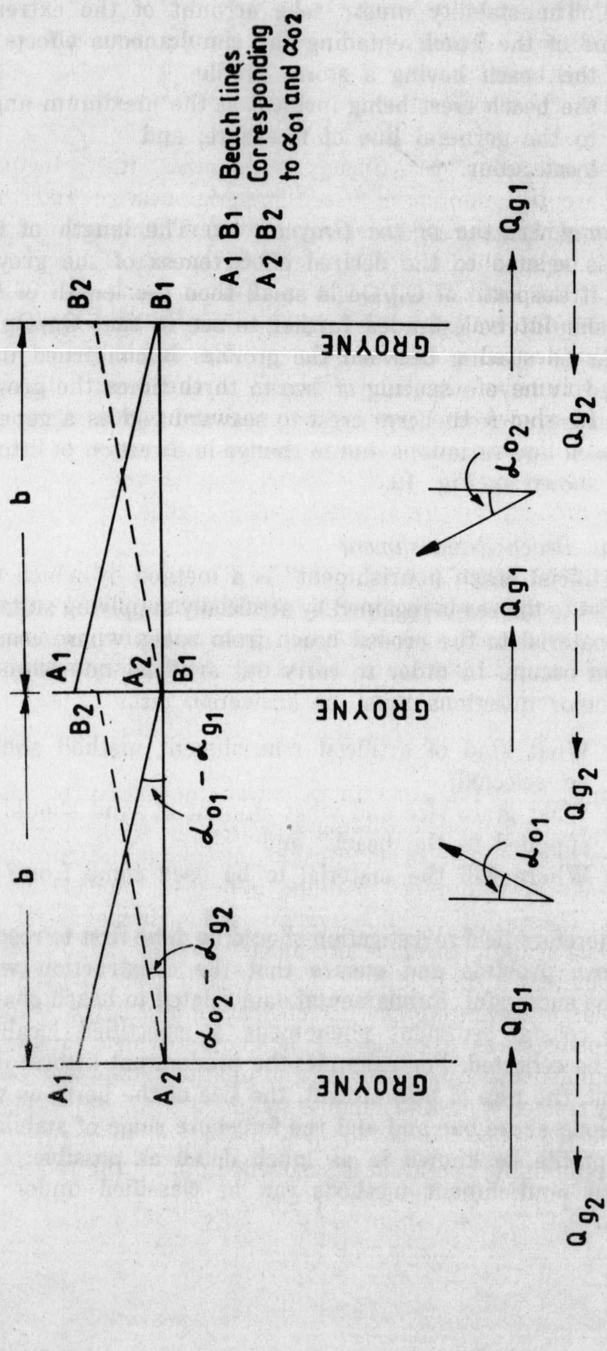

Fig. 12 : Variation of Beach on Groyne Shore

(i) Continuouns nourishment
(ii) Offshore deposits
(iii) Stock pile
(iv) Direct displacement

In the execution of artificial nourishment, the principal concerns are the amount of beach material desired and the place from where the material can be taken. The amount of material to be supplied is closely related to the rate of longshore sediment transport. The longshore transport rate and the nourishment interval plus the sand volume which is needed to form the desired stabilized beach profile should determine the total volume of the sand supplied to the coast.

Fig. 13 shows the process of continuous nourishment. The material is borrowed from the offeshore area with the help of dredger and the material is transported through pipes from the dredger to the affected coastal regions.[5]

Sediment Bypassing

Fig. 14. shows the sediment bypassing methods adopted in coastal zone. It is a conventional practice to provide either land-based pumping station or a dredger for continuous supply of sediment to the eroded coastal region. Depending on the coastline configuration, either the land-based pumping station or the dredger can be employed.

In the case of tidal outlets with training structures such as jetties, the impounded sediments on the updrift side is by-passed with the help of land-based pumping station. The sediment slurry is pumped through a floating pipe to cross the inlet. These floating pipe system is detachable so as to facilitate navigation through the inlet.

In some cases the width of the navigable water way may be quite large preventing the use of floating pipe lines. Under these cirucmstances a dredger is employed which dreadges the impounded material either on the updrift side or adjacent to the low crested wier, and supplies sediment through pipelines to the affected coastal zone. To allow navigation through such inlets, the pumping operation is suspended during the required period.

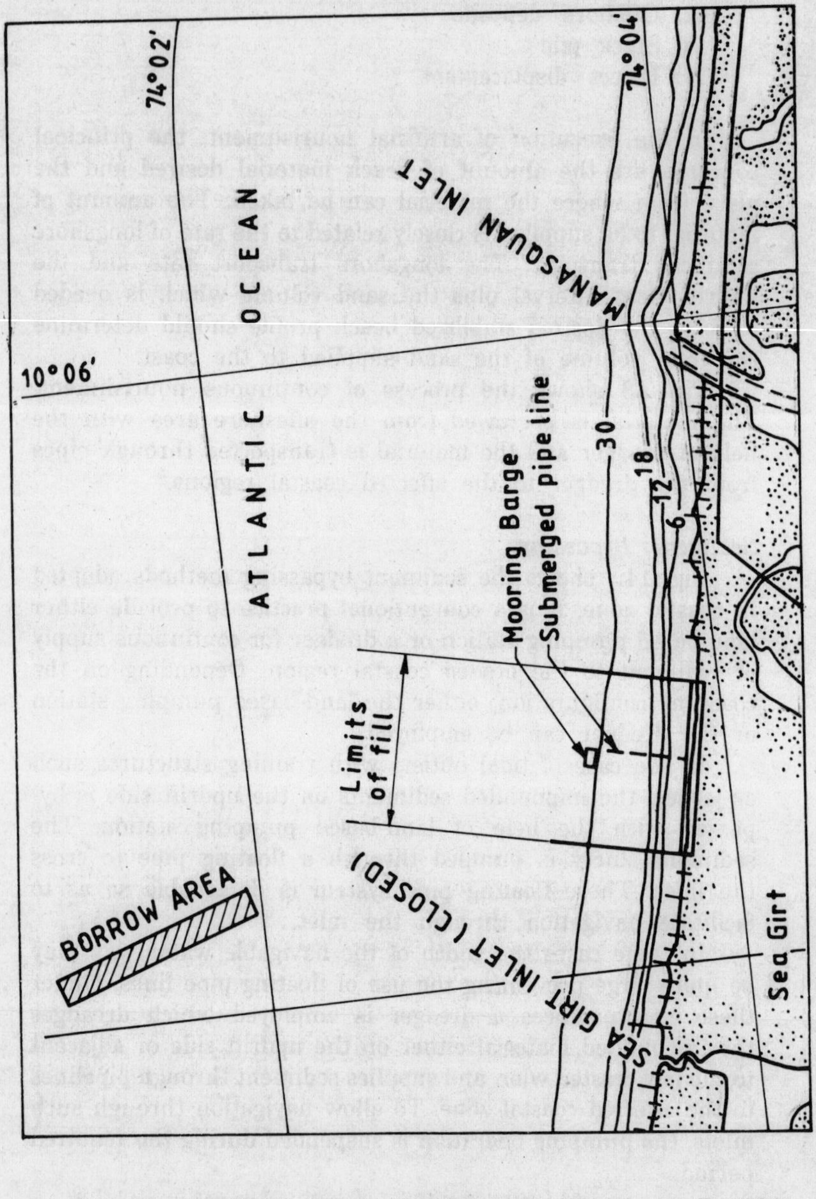

Fig. 13 : Artificial Beach Nourishment *(Contd. on P 120A)*

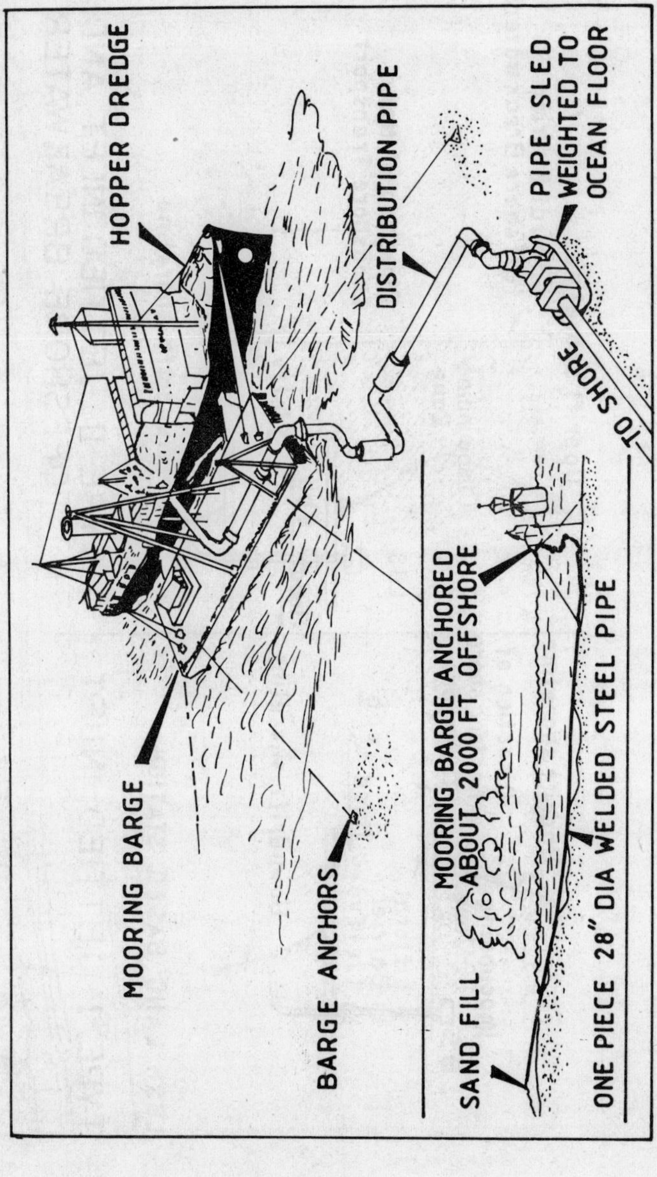

Fig. 13 : Artificial Beach Nourishment

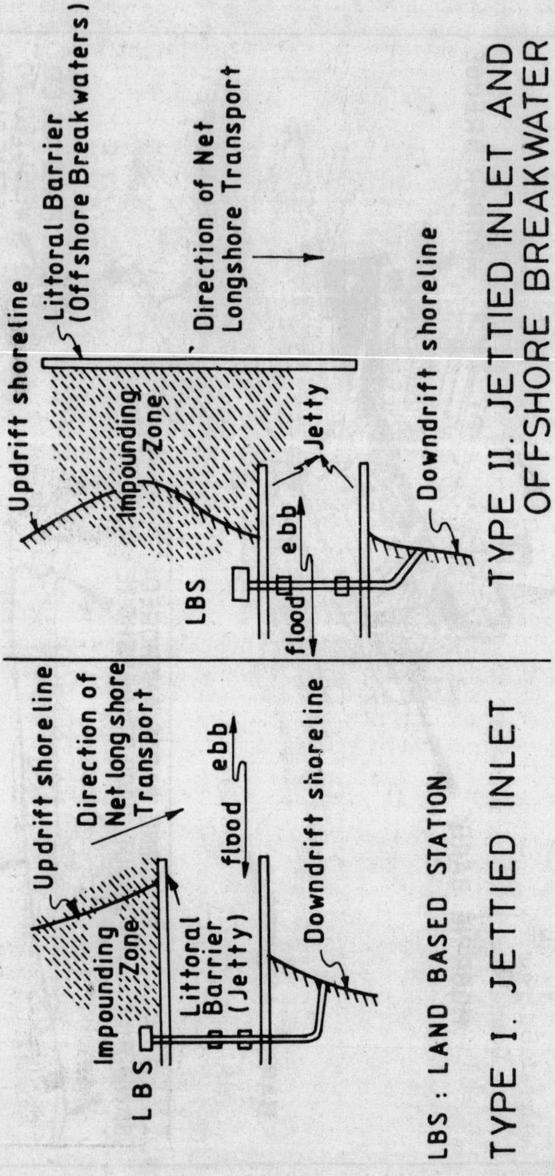

Fig. 14 : Sand by Passing *(Contd. on P 121A)*

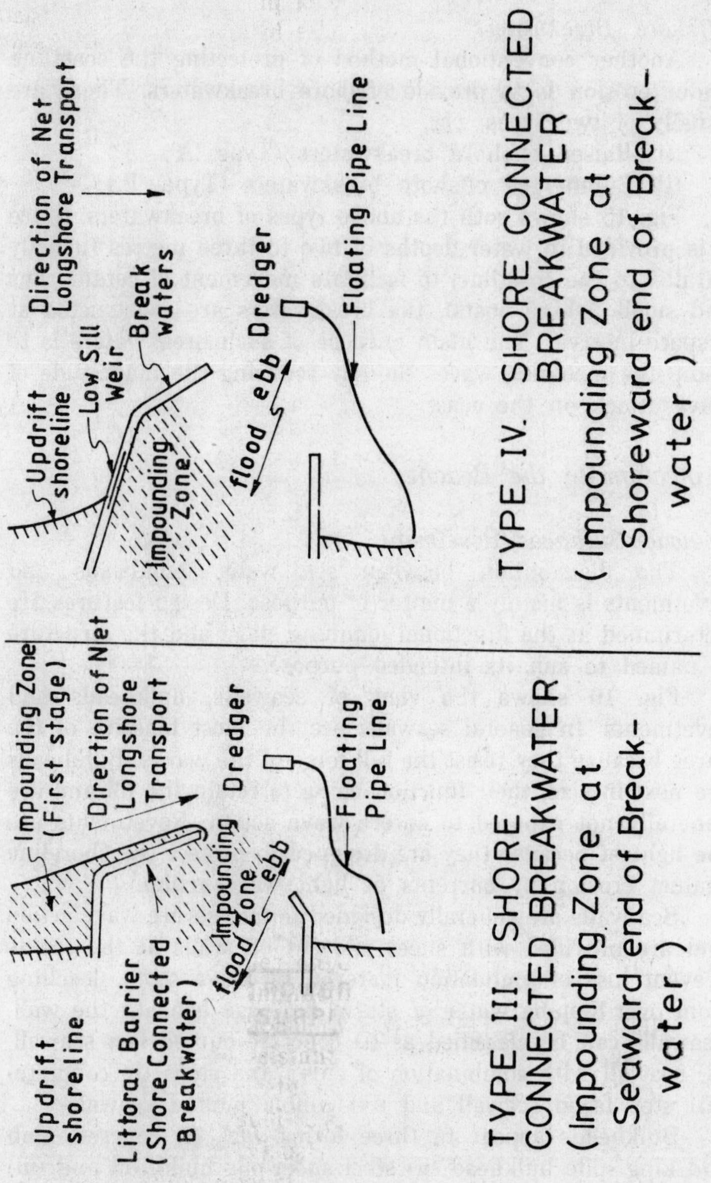

Fig. 14 : Sand by Passing

Offshore Breakwaters

Another conventional method of protecting the coastline under erosion is to provide offshore breakwaters. There are usually of two types, *viz.*,

(i) Raised offshore breakwaters (Type 'A')

(ii) Submerged offshore breakwaters (Type 'B')

Fig. 15 shows both the above types of breakwaters. Since it is provided in water depths of two to three metres (usually parallel to the coastline, to facilitate movement of catamarans and small fishing boats), the breakwaters are constructed at a space interval. The main purpose of such breakwaters is to damp the incoming waves thereby reducing the magnitude of wave attack on the coast.

Protection to the Beaches

Seawall/Bulkhead/Revetment

The distribution between sea walls, bulkheads and revetments is mainly a matter of purpose. Design features are determined at the functional planning stage and the structure is named to suit its intended purpose.

Fig. 16 shows the view of seawalls, bulkheads and revetments. In general seawalls are the most massive of the three because they resist the full force of the waves. Bulkheads are next in size, their function being to retain the fill and are generally not exposed to severe wave action. Revetments are the lightest because they are designed to protect the shoreline against erosion by currents or light wave action.

Sea walls are generally designed to face severe wave action and are provided with sheet pile cut off walls at the toe to prevent loss of foundation material by wave scout, leaching from over-topping water or storm drainage beneath the wall. Seawalls can be classified as (i) concrete curved face-seawall, (ii) seawall with combination of curve and steps (in concrete) (iii) step faced seawall and (iv) rouble mound seawall.

Bulkheads appear in three forms, *viz.*, (i) concrete slab and king -pile bulkhead (ii) steel sheet-pile bulkhead and (iii) timber sheet-pile bulkhead.

Revetments are of two types, *viz.*, (i) concrete revetment and (ii) rip rap revetment.

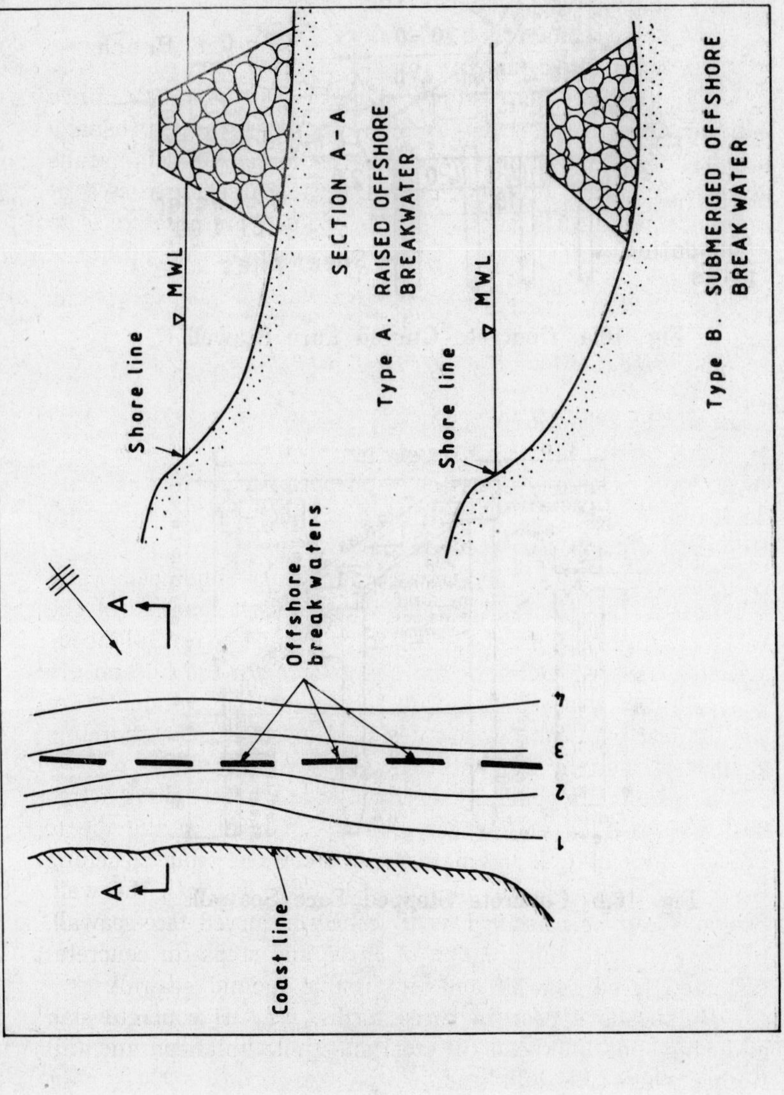

Fig. 15. Offshore Breakwaters

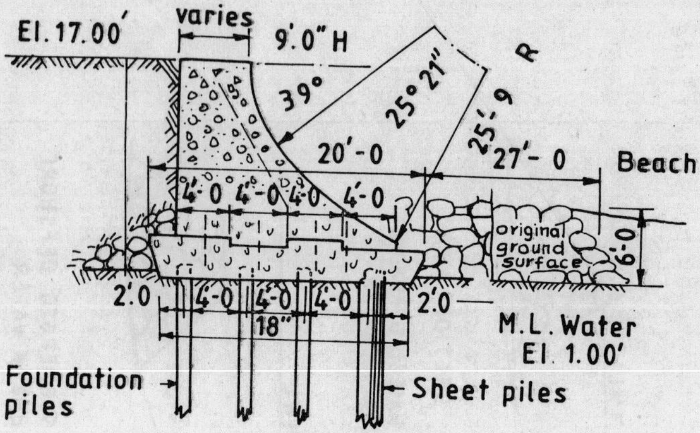

Fig. 16.a. Concrete Curved Face Seawell

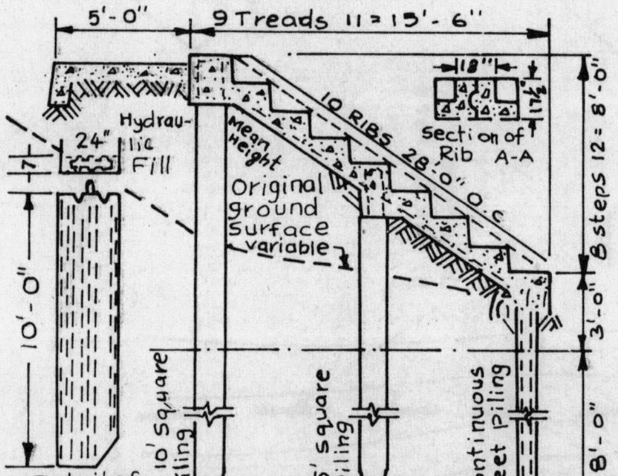

Fig. 16.b. Concrete Stepped Face Seawell

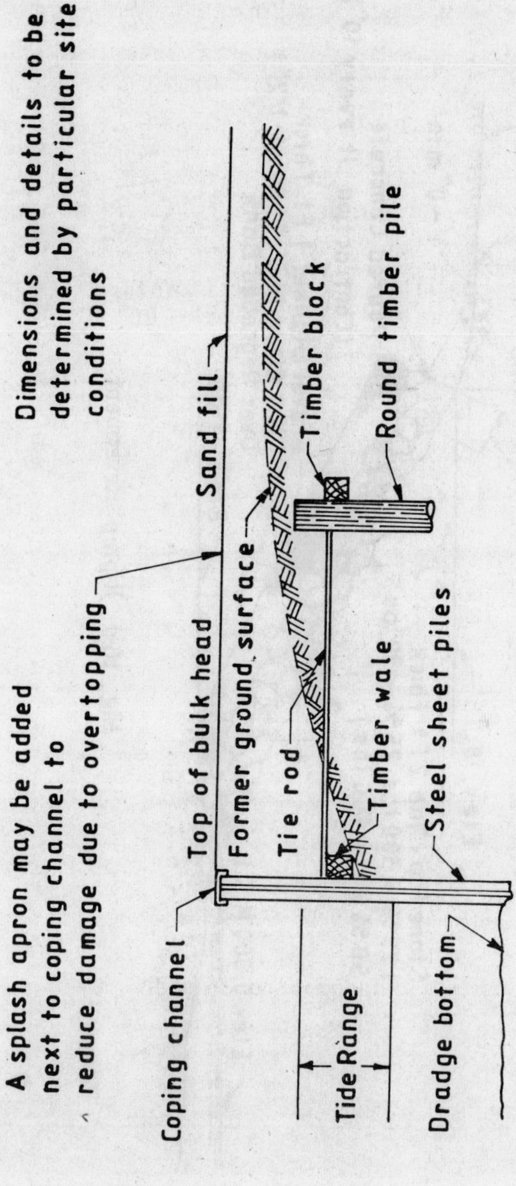

Fig. 16.c. Steel Sheet - Pile Bulkhead

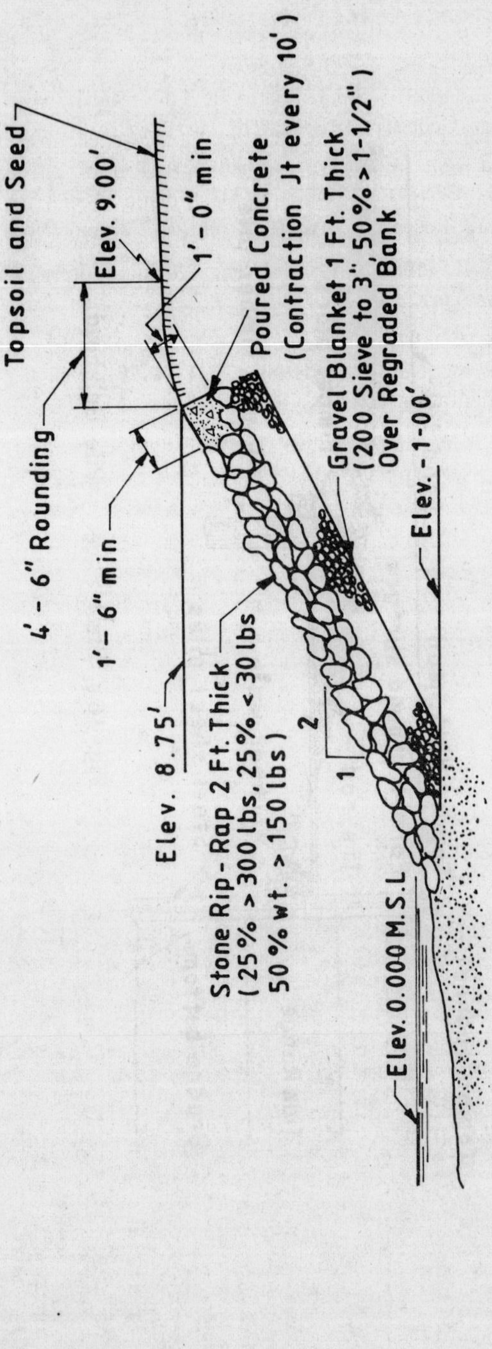

Fig. 16.d. Riprap Revetment

References

1. Bown, A.J. (1969) : Rip currents. 1, Theoretical Investigations, Journal of Geophysics Research 74,5467.
2. Bown, A.J. and Inman, D.L. (1966) : Budget of Littoral Sands in the Vicinity of Point Arguello, California U.S. Army Coastal Engineering Research Centre, Technical, Memo No. Tm-19
3. Horikawa, K. (1987) : Coastal Engineering, John Wiley and sons, New York.
4. King, C.A.M. (1972) : Beaches and Coasts, Second edition, St. Martin's Press, New York. Homar, P.D. (1976) : Beach Processes and Sedimentation, Prentice-Hall, Englewood Cliffs, New Jersey.
5. Sorensen, R.M. (1978) : Base Coastal Engineering : John Wiley and Sons, New York. Wood, A.M.M., and Fleming, C.A. (1969) : Coastal Hydraulics, MacMillan Press Ltd. London.

6

Tropical Cyclones and Their Warning System

*G. S. Mandal**

From a vantage point in space the tropical cyclones look to be quite innocent, small flat spirals, drifting on the sea, gentle eddies in the endless flow of the planet's atmosphere. But when they meet the shipping lanes, islands and the coasts of continents, they prove to be extremely fatal.

The tropical cyclones are the off-spring of ocean and atmosphere, powered by the heat from the sea, driven by the easterly trades and temperate westerlies, the high planetary winds and their own fierce energy. In their cloudy arms and their tranquil core, winds blow with lethal velocity, and the ocean develops devastation surge, inundating vast coast line.

Though there is no common terminology, but everywhere tropical cyclones are classified according to the wind speed in their circulation. They bear different names in different oceans and hemisphere. The intense tropical cyclones with wind speed 64 Nautical Miles per hour (knots or kts) or more in the circulation known as "Severe Cyclonic Storm with a Core of Hurricane Winds" over the north Indian Ocean (the Bay of Bengal and the Arabian Sea), "Hurricanes" in the Atlantic and eastern Pacific and 'Typhoons" in the northwest Pacific.

Compared to the great extra-tropical cyclones, tropical cyclones are moderate in size and their worst winds do not approach tornado velocities. Still, their broad spiral base may dominate weather over thousands of square kilometers and from the earth's surface to the top of the tropical tropopause. The associated winds often exceeding 200 kmph, rainfall

* Deputy Director General of Meteorology, Chief of the Director General of Meteorology, Mausam Bhavan, New Delhi.

exceeding 50 to 100 cms in 24 hours and, worst of all, very high storm tides (storm surge combined with astronomical tides) often exceeding 20 feet bring worst human disasters over the coastal areas where they strike. Today, records are available for the wind speed of 317 kmph gusting to 360 kmph, rainfall of 117 cm in 24 hours and storm surge of 41 feet in association with tropical cyclones. The lowest pressure of 870 mb ever recorded on the earth was in association with a tropical cyclone (Typhoon "TIP") in the Pacific formed in 1979. The life period of tropical cyclones is measured in days and weeks and not in minutes or hours. Combined with duration, size and violence the tropical cyclone makes the most destructive atmospheric disturbance. On positive, though less dramatic side, tropical cyclones provide essential rainfall over much of the land they cross.

Special Nature of the Problem in the Region

Over the warm water (sea surface temperature greater than 26°C or 27°C) in the tropical ocean, a little away from the equator within the belt of 30°N and 30°S the occurrence of tropical cyclone is almost a world-wide phenomena. However, their characteristics like frequency, intensity and coastal impact vary from region to region. Compared to elsewhere in the world, the tropical cyclones in the North Indian Ocean are less frequent (in fact the frequency of tropical cyclones in the North Indian Oceans is the least in the world) mostly moderate in intensity, short lived and smaller in size, but they are the deadliest.

Table1 below provides the list of human loss associated with some of the noteworthy tropical cyclones in the past two and a half centuries in various parts of the globe.

Table1

Human Loss Associated with Some Tropical Cyclones 1737-1923

Year	Country	Deaths
1737	(Hoogly, West Bengal), India	300,000

Year	Country	Deaths
1881	China	300,000
1923	Japan	250,000
1876	(Backergunj), Bangladesh	200,000-250,000
1970	Bangladesh	200,000
1897	Bangladesh	175,000
1822	Barisal 1 Backergunj), Bangladesh	50,000
1864	(Contai, West Bengal), India	50,000
1833	(Sagar Island), India	30,000
1864	(Masulipatnam), India	30,000
1831	(Balasore), India	22,000
1788	Antilles	22,000
1779	(Masulipatnam), India	20,000
1787	(Coringa, Andhra Pradesh), India	20,000
1789	(Coringa, Andhra Pradesh), India	20,000
1839	(Coringa, Andhra Pradesh), India	20,000
1965	Bangladesh	19,229
1942	(Contai, West Bengal), India	15,000
1963	Bangladesh	11,520
1961	Bangladesh	11,468
1971	(Paradip, Orissa), India	10,000
1977	(Chirala, Andhra Pradesh), India	10,000
1963	Cuba Haiti	7,196
1900	Taxas	6,000
1960	Bangladesh	5,490
1885	(False Point, Orissa), India	5,000
1960	Japan	5,000
1923	India	5,000

Data show that 19 out of 22 cases of large loss of life (10,000 or more deaths) occurred over the Indian sub-continent due to the tropical cyclone originating in the Bay of Bengal.

A favourable combination of meteorological forcings generated by tropical cyclones with some non-meterological factors of the region like very this astronomical tide, shallow Bay, low flat terrain and funnelling coastal configuration generates devastating storm tides by the tropical cyclones over the coastal areas of the North Bay of Bengal by the storms of even moderate intensities. In the past, the world's highest storm tide of 41 ft was reported from this area in the case of Backerganj cyclone of 31 October 1876. High density of population along the coast of North Bay of Bengal and socio-eccnomic conditions of the people living in these areas are the other factors, to some extent, responsible for such heavy loss of life and damages to properties. The above facts indicate the special nature of the problem in this region and the importance of cyclone warning system and long and short term mitigation measures against tropical cyclone disaster.

Because of very adverse impact of tropical cyclones on human activities, interest of mankind was drawn towards this problems from quite some time. In fact, many nations established the meteorological services towards the end of last century and in the beginning of this century for organising cyclone warning services for the mariners and coastal populations. India Meteorological Department (IMD) is one among them established towards the end of the century, although cyclone warnings in India in some form started even earlier than the formal establishment of IMD. It is due to this interest even the name "cyclone" meaning "coils of snake" in Greek was also coined in India towards the middle of last century by Henry Peddington, the then President of the Marine Court in Calcutta. With the revelation of spiralling nature of winds and rainbands of tropical cyclones by modern observing tools like satellites, radars and aircrafts show how appropriate is the name given to these weather systems at that time.

The prevention of tropical cyclone formation is not within the realm of possibility. However, the loss of human lives and destruction of properties can be minimised by taking prescribed short and long term mitigation measures. While cyclone warning system is the most important constituent of the short term mitigation measures against the cyclone disasters, the risk assessment of tropical cyclone falls under long term mitigation measures.

Fortunately, these days good advance warning systems against tropical cyclones have been developed and loss of human lives can be minimised by taking proper actions on the warnings. Adequate tropical cyclone data and their analysis for risk assessment required for long term disaster mitigation measures are also available.

Classification

Tropical cyclones are intense low pressure areas. These are large revolving vortices in the atmosphere extending horizontally from 500 to 1000 kms and vertically from surface to about 12 to 14 kms with fierce winds spiralling anti-clockwise inward towards calm centre in the lower levels in the northern hemisphere. Above 8-9 kms the wind directions are opposite to those of the lower levels. They move generally 300 to 500 kms per day over the ocean. While doing to they pick up energy from the warm water of the ocean and some of them grow into devastating intensity.

The classifications of cyclonic disturbances (low pressure areas) are made by the strength of the associated winds. The classifications used in India are given in Table 2.

Table 2
Classification of Cyclonic Disturbances

Disturbance	Wind speed in knots
1. Low	Less then 17 kts
2. Depression	17-27 kts (32-50 kmph)
3. Deep depression	28-33 kts (51-62 kmph)
4. Cyclonic storm	34-47 kts (63-88 kmph)
5. Severe cyclonic storm with a core of Hurricane winds	48-63 kts (89-118 kmph)

Climatology

Tropical cyclones form over all the tropical oceans except

over the south Atlantic and south Pacific, east of 140°W. Tropical cyclones are most commonly observed in the northern hemisphere from May to November and in southern hemisphere from December to June. The frequencies of tropical cyclones, however, vary from ocean to ocean. The annual average frequency ranges from 5.6 (the least) in the north Indian Ocean to about 30 (the highest) in the northwest Pacific. About 70 per cent of the tropical disturbances which later develop into tropical storms form in the northern hemisphere. There are approximately 80 tropical cyclones with maximum sustained winds of 20-25 ms^{-1} form over the globe per year. About half to two-third .of these disturbance weaken the intensity of every cyclonic storms with a core of hurricane winds (wind speed 64 kts or more). Fig. 1 shows the annual frequency of tropical cyclones with surface wind speed of 20-25 ms^{-1} over the globe.

The long term average of tropical cyclones in the north Indian Ocean (the Bay of Bengal and the Arabian Sea) is 5.6. This is about six per cent of the global total. The frequency of tropical cyclones is the north Indian Ocean is the least in the world. On an average, 2-3 out of six tropical cyclones intensify to severe cyclones. The frequency of tropical cyclone is more in the Bay of Bengal than in the Arabian Sea. The ratio is 4.1. The monthly distribution of tropical cyclones from 1891 to 1989 for the Bay of Bengal and the Arabian Sea is shown in Fig. 2. Quite different from other oceans tropical cyclone frequency in north Indian ocean is by-modal in character having primary peak in November and secondary peak in May. There are two distinct seasons of tropical cyclones in the North Indian Ocean. One is from May to June and the other is from mid-September of mid-December. May, June, October and November are known for sever tropical cyclones. Although the cyclonic storms have occurred in the monsoon season, the real severe ones are rare. Cyclones during the monsoon season are generally marked by rainfall which often leads to floods in different parts of the country.

The annual average of severe cyclonic storm with a core of hurricane winds in the north Indian Ocean is very small (about 2.5 per year; considering data for the last 25 years). Year to year variation of tropical cyclones in our area, however,

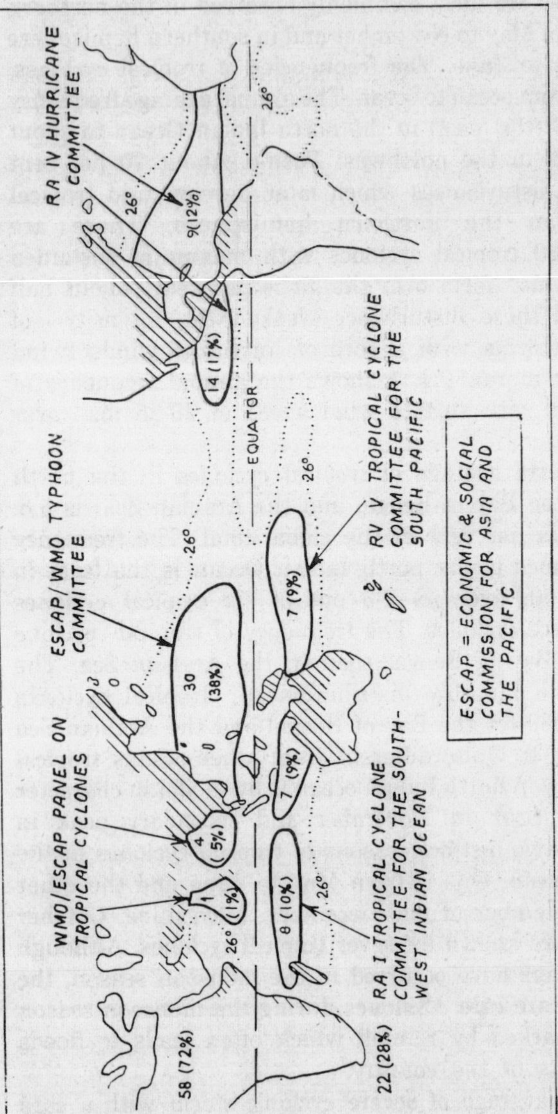

THE GLOBAL OCCURRENCE OF TROPICAL CYCLONES OVER THE GLOBE (AFTER W.M. GRAY 1975). THE NAMES OF TROPICAL CYCLONE BODIES AND THE TROPICAL CYCLONES BASINS COVERED BY THEIR PROGRAMMES ARE ALSO INDICATED.

The area enclosed by the dotted lines is the area where sea surface temp. is greater than 26°C.

Fig. 1

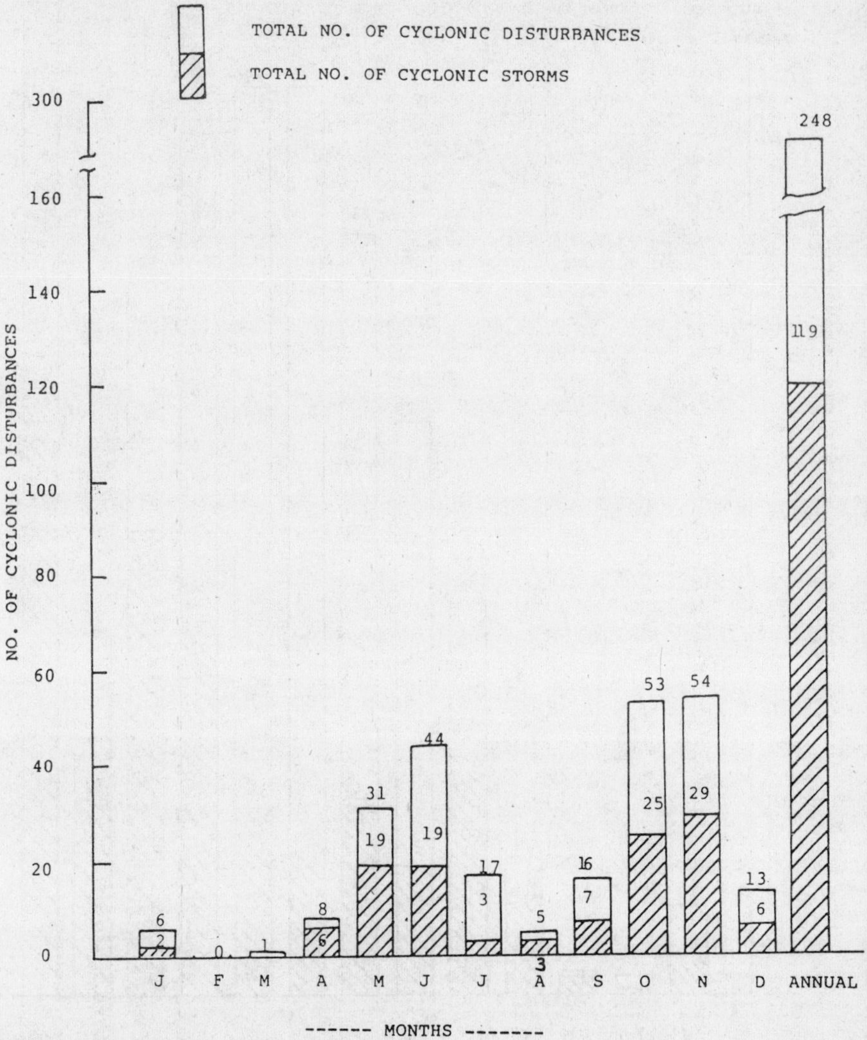

MONTHLY DISTRIBUTION OF CYCLONIC DISTURBANCES AND CYCLONIC STORMS FOR THE PERIOD 1891 - 1989 (ARABIAN SEA).

Fig. 2 contd....

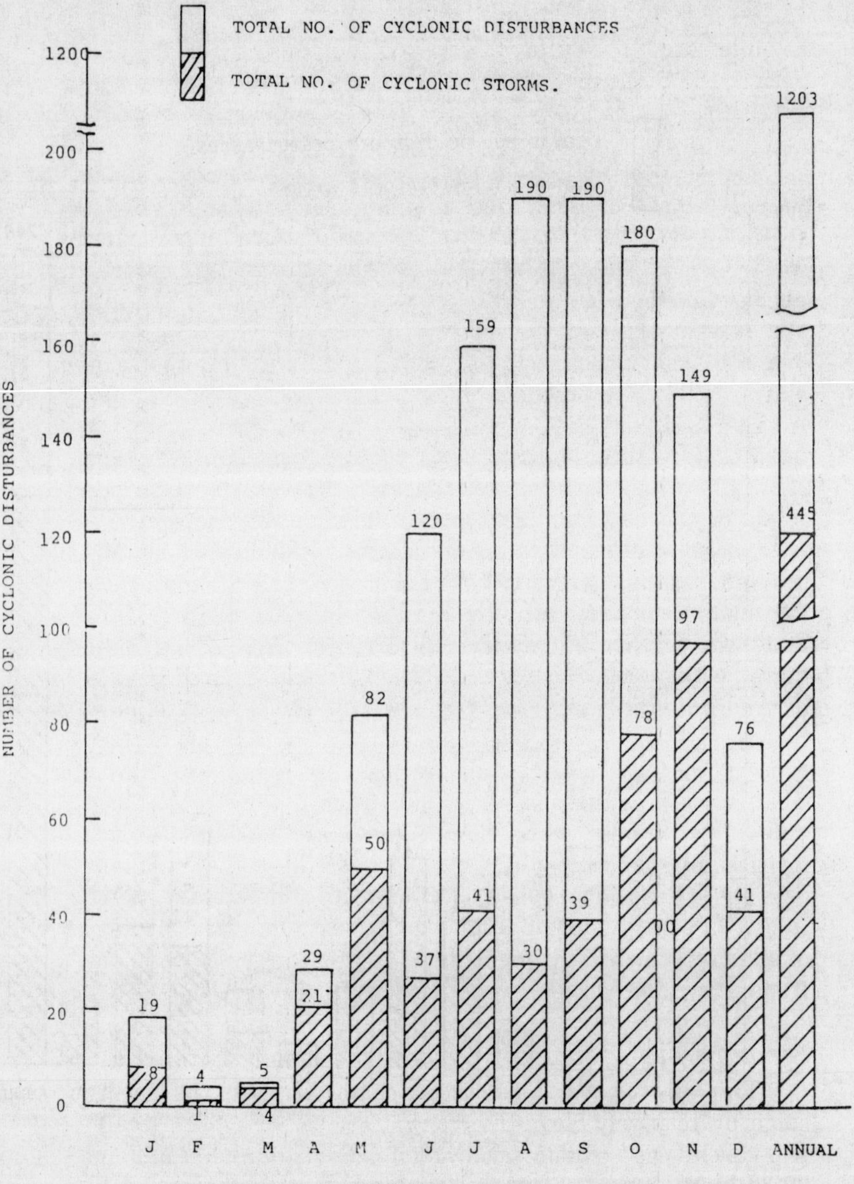

MONTHLY DISTRIBUTION OF CYCLONIC DISTURBANCES AND CYCLONIC STORMS FOR THE PERIOD 1891-1989. (BAY OF BENGAL).

Fig. 2

is quite large. It has been observed that during the 99 year period, the frequency of tropical cyclones has varied from one in 1949 to 10 on four occasions. The variations are random and there is no trend or periodicity.

Cyclones which move west, northwest or even north strike the east coast of India. Some of the Arabian Sea cyclones strike west coast of India mainly Gujarat and north Maharashtra coast. Out of these storms that develop in the Bay, over 58 per cent of them approach or cross the east coast in October and November. Only 25 per cent of the storms that develop over the Arabian Sea approach west coast. In the pre-monsoon season, the corresponding figures are 25 per cent over the Arabian Sea and 30 per cent over the Bay of Bengal. The important feature is that along the vast stretch of Indian coast, there are a few preferred zones which are more vulnerable (both in the east and west coast) to tropical cyclones.

In Table 3 the number of tropical cyclones that crossed different coastal districts of India are shown. This table provides information on tropical cyclone risk to coastal districts. The table shows that 24-Parganas districts of West Bengal are more vulnerable to cyclones followed by the Nellore district of Andhra Pradesh in the east coast of India. Interestingly, no storm struck West Godavari and Kanya Kumari district even in the east coast during the past 99 years. Along the west coast the Junagarh district in Gujarat state is the most vulnerable. Similarly, the risk of very sever cyclones to each district can be computed.

The average life period of tropical cyclones in the north Indian Ocean is about 2.5 days as against the world average of six days which means, compared to other oceanic areas, the tropical cyclones in the north Indian Ocean are short lived.

Structure of Tropical Cyclone

Tropical cyclone has a structure characterised in the mature stage by relatively cloud-free central region with nearly calm win called "eye" (winds usually well below 20 kmph), of about 20-30 km radius. The eye is characterised by low pressure at sea level, high temperature aloft and very little cloudiness. Pressure in the centre is the lowest and the temperature the highest in comparison to the surroundings. Eye radius can be 40 to 50 kms in large mature storms. The eye, like spiral rain

WEST COAST		EAST COAST	
STATION COASTAL DISTRICTS	NUMBER OF CYCLONIC STORMS DURING 1891-1989	STATION COASTAL DISTRICTS	NUMBER OF CYCLONIC STORMS DURING 1891-1989
KERALA		**WEST BENGAL**	
TRIVANDRUM	1	24 PARGANAS	23
QUILON	0	MIDNAPORE	12
ALLEPPEY	0	**ORISSA**	
ERNAKULAM	1	BALSORE	19
TRICHUR	0	CUTTACK	17
MALAPURAM	1	PURI	10
CALICUT	2	GANJAM	7
KARNATAKA		**ANDHRA PRADESH**	
CANNANORE	1	SRIKAKULAM	14
S. KANARA	2	VIZAG	8
N. KANARA	0	E. GODAVARI	8
GOA		W. GODAVARI	0
GOA	0	KRISHNA	14
MAHARASHTRA		GUNTUR	3
RATNAGIRI	2	NELLORE (Including PRAKASAM)	21
COLABA	3	**TAMILNADU**	
THANA	1	CHINGLEPUT	15
BULSAR	1	S. ARCOT (Including PONDICHERRY)	5
GUJARAT		TANJUVAR (Including PUDUKOTTAI)	13
SURAT	0	RAMNATHPURAM	3
BAROACH	1	TIRUNELVELI	2
KAIRA	0	KANYAKUMARI	0
AHMEDABAD	0		
BHAVNAGAR	2		
AMRELI	0		
JUNAGAD	10		
JAMNAGAR	3		
KUTCH	3		

Table 3 : Frequencies of cyclones crossing coast in the various districts of east and west coast of India during 1891-1989.

bands described below is unique to the tropical cyclones. Not other atmospheric phenomenon has similar structure. The eye is surrounded by an eyewall, an approximately 15-20 kms wide annulus of intense convection, torrential rainfall and deep thick cloudiness (marked by a large number of cumulonimbi) and at a distance of about 25-50 kms from the centre. The zone of maximum winds coincidence with the eyewall and therefore, this is the most dangerous zone of tropical cyclone. Outside the eyewall are convective rain-bands that appear like pinwheels or logarithmic spirals in some satellite and radar photographs. Because of the special nature of cloudiness associated with tropical cyclones they are easily detectable in radar and satellite photographs. The radar and satellite photographs of a tropical cyclone in its mature stage are shown in Fig. 3 (a) and 3 (b).

The hurricane force winds (120 kmph or more) begin at the eyewall and extend outward 75-100 kms. The winds usually decrease outward and at a distance of about 150 to 200 kms from the centre, the wind speeds are normally of the order of 70 to 80 kmph. In the low level the winds spiral inward and in anti-clockwise manner in northern hemisphere while in the upper troposphere, the wind directions are just opposite to that of lower level winds, i.e., wind flow is in clockwise manner in northern hemisphere and air mass goes out from the centre. In another way the tropical cyclone is a giant rotating machine of atmospheric air mass of about 1,000 kms in diameter and 12-14 kms in height where air mass moves inward in the bottom and outward in the top maintaining the upward flow of moist air very much essential for the survival of the atmosphere's giant rotating machine the 'Tropical Cyclone". Because of the nature of wind flow when a tropical cyclone strikes coast, in one sector the winds are from ocean to land (on-shore wind) and in other sector in the opposite side the winds are from land to ocean (off-shore wind). Along the coast the winds in the right forward sector are, therefore, from ocean to land and in the left forward sector from land to ocean. Because of this nature of the flow storm surge is generated in the right forward sector with its maxima coinciding with the zone of maximum wind. Therefore, about 150-200 kms stretch from the centre in the right forward sector is known for extreme devastations.

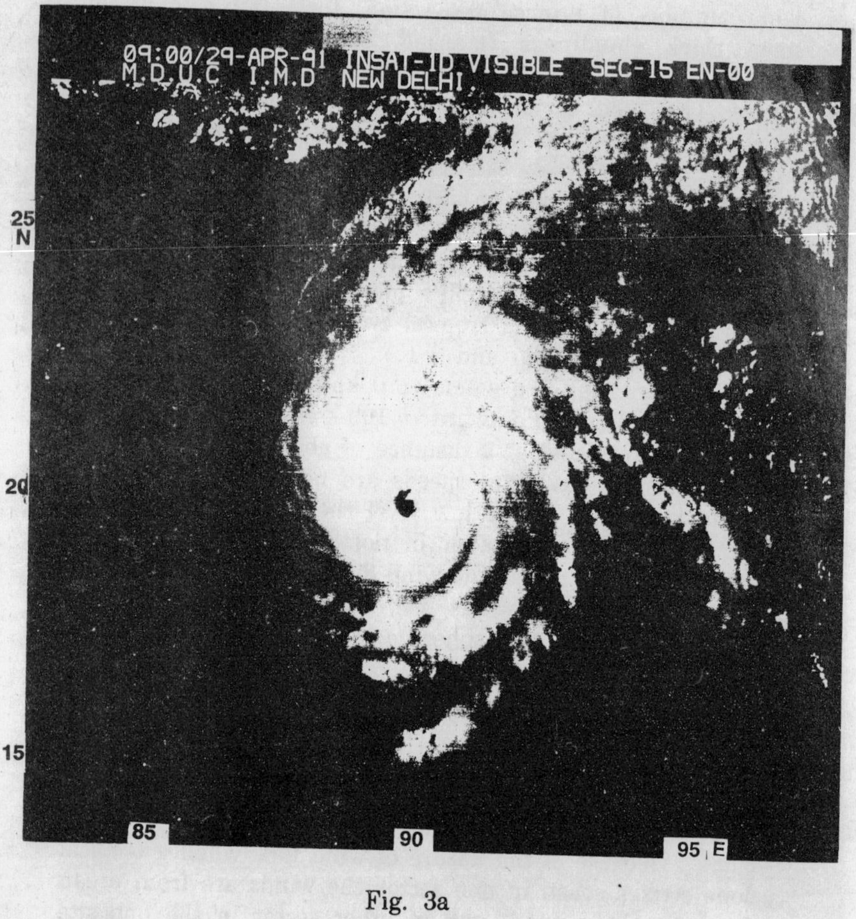
09:00/29-APR-91 INSAT-1D VISIBLE SEC-15 EN-00
M.D.U.C I.M.D NEW DELHI
25 N
20
15
85
90
95 E

Fig. 3a

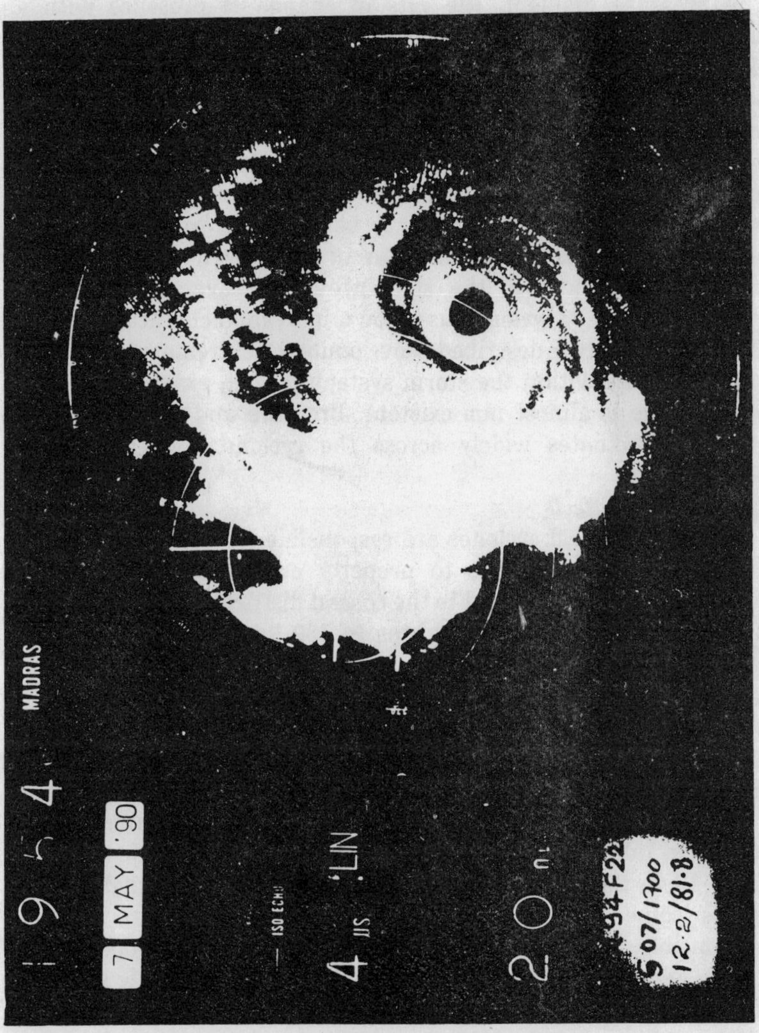

Fig. 3b

Like all winds, hurricane winds in tropical cyclone are produced by difference in atmospheric pressure of density. The pressure gradient, the rate of change of pressure with distance produced in tropical cyclone is the most severe in the atmosphere, excepting only the pressure change across the narrow funnel of a tornado. The record lowest pressure estimated in the tropical cyclone in the north Indian Ocean so far, is 911 millibar but still much higher than world record of lowest pressure of 870 millibar. The millibar is the unit of pressure which equals to 1/1000 of bar. A bar is equal to pressure of one million dynes per square cm in the metric system.

Discused above is the structure of an average tropical cyclone. But every cyclone has its own individual characteristics. The average picture described above omits the extreme variability and instability within the storm system. In fact, exact analogue of a cyclone is almost non-existent. Pressure and temperature gradient fluctuates widely across the cyclone.

Destructive Effects

Severe tropical cyclones are responsible for large casualties and considerable damage to property and agricultural crop. The destruction is confined to the coastal districts; the maximum destruction being within 100 kms to 150 kms from the centre of the cyclone and to the right of the storm track where wind is from ocean to land. The principal dangers from cyclones are: (1) fierce winds, (2) torrential rain and associated flooding, (3) high storm tides (combined effect of storm surge and astronomical tides) leading to coastal inundation.

Most of the casualties are caused by coastal inundation by storm tides. the maximum penetration of storm tide varies from 10 to 20 kms inland from the coast. Heavy rainfall and floods come next in order of devastation. They are often responsible for large loss of lives and damage to properties. Death and destruction purely due to winds are relatively small. The collapse of buildings, falling of tress, flying of debris, electrocution, aircraft accidents and disease from contaminated food and water in the post-cyclone period also contribute to loss of lives and destruction of properties. Some of these destructive features are discussed below in some details.

Winds

The wind structure in general (in the case of tropical cyclone) has already been discussed. The highest sustained winds ever recorded in the case of tropical cyclone in the globe is 317 kmph. Maximum gusts exceeded 360 kmph. In north Indian ocean, however, tropical cyclones are of moderate intensity and in most cases wind speeds are less than 185 kmph. Only in 10 per cent cases the winds exceeded 185 kmph in the past. It is difficult to record the wind speed beyond certain limit as wind recording instruments normally breakdown. The highest wind speed, therefore, can only be estimated with the help of indirect methods like estimation of wind speed with the help of satellite photograph of clouds. However, this is possible for the tropical cyclones formed after the satellite era (i.e., after sixties). The estimated highest wind speed associated with tropical cyclones in this region in the past is about 145 knots (270 kmph) in the case of Andhra Pradesh cyclone of 1977 which is so far the severest storm on record in the north Indian Ocean. The wind distribution around the storm is not the same even at same distance from the centre. There is certain amount of asymmetry in the wind distribution around the centre of a cyclone. The strongest winds are often observed to the right of the cyclone's track.

It is known that pressure increases at the rate of square of wind velocity. Therefore, for the tenfold increase in wind the pressure increase against and object is 100-fold. For some structures added force is sufficient to cause failure. Cyclone winds may also produce an inverse effect, as and when atmospheric pressure outside a closed structure is reduced enough to cause normal pressure inside to flow outward explosively. Tall structures like radio towers fretted by gusting hurricane-force winds, may be made to oscillate until structural failure occurs. Although hurricane wind itself is less destructive out of the cyclone's battery of destructive elements, wind driven barrages of debris can be quite dangerous.

Rainfall

Floods generated by the cyclone rainfall are more destructive than winds. Impact is more in the mountainous areas. The rainfall is the heaviest around wall cloud zones. Rainfall of the order of 20 to 30 cms per day is very common. Associated with tropical cyclone, 24 hours rainfall over 100 cms was reported from other regions. In extreme cases observed rainfall associated with tropical cyclone was as low as trace and as high as 250 cms. Outside the eyewall, the precipitation rate falls off roughly linearly with distance from the centre of tropical cyclone.

In India, during monsoon season in normal monsoon year, most of the rivers and revulets get filled up and fields and soil do not have any more holding capacity. Therefore, towards the end of monsoon season or in the beginning of October if a cyclonic storm crosses Indian coast, then it can cause very severe flood as at that time there is no space to accommodate heavy rainfall from tropical cyclones in the natural streams or soil. Flood in India is very less in association with the pre-monsoon cyclones when the rivers and revulets are dry and the lands are parched.

Storm Surge

Tropical cyclone's worst killer comes from the ocean, the storm surge. Over the deep oceans wave generated by hurricane-force winds may reach height of 50 feet of more. Below the storm centre, the ocean surface is drawn upward by a foot or so above normal due to the reduced atmospheric pressure. As the storm crosses the continental shelf and moves coastward mean water level increases. This abnormal rise in sea level caused by cyclone is known as storm surge. The surge is generated due to interaction of air, seas and land. The cyclone provides the driving forces in the form of very high horizontal atmospheric pressure gradient and very strong surface winds. As a result, the sea level rises and continues to rise as the cyclone moves over shallower water, and reaches a maximum on the coast near the point of landfall. Sea water inundates vast stretches of coastal areas and washes away all that comes in its way. Behind the storm centre, off-shore hurricane-force winds may cause a decrease in mean water level, setting up strong currents.

There is another kind of sea level rise, *viz*, astronomical tide, which is well known. The rise due to the tide may be as high as 4.5m above the mean sea level in some parts of Indian coasts. The advancing storm is superimposed on normal astronomical tides, and in turn, wind waves are superimposed on surge. This build up of water can cause severe flooding in the coastal areas. The worst devastation takes place when and where peak surge occurs at the time of high tides. Storm tides (surge-tide combination) can bring catastrophe over the flat coast like Bangladesh coast and northeast coast of India. When the surge water is forced up in a narrow channel, like river bed the surge may appear as a wall of water. The funnel shape of the coast like coasts adjoining the north Bay of Bengal adds further dangerous dimension to the storm tides.

The wave and current action associated with the surge also cause extensive damage. Currents set up along the coast by the gradient in storm surge height, and wind combine with the waves to weaken coastal structures. Waves and current severely erode beaches and highways, and in confined harbours, damage to shipping may be extreme. In estuarian region intrusions of salt water endanger the public health. However, greatest loss of life associated with cyclone is caused by flooding due to the storm surge.

Historical records indicate that significant storm surge affected almost all parts of the Indian east coast and the coast of Bangladesh although the most intense and the most frequent occurrences have been in the north Bay of Bengal causing terrible destruction of life and property. According to available records perhaps the highest sea level elevation in the world due to combined effect of storm surge and astronomical high tide occurred in 1876 near Bakerganj (Bangladesh). It was estimated that sea level rose by about 40 feet above the mean sea level on that occasion.

Storm surge and tide data are very important for frequency analysis of surge heights along different sections of the vulnerable coastline required for designing harbour installations, coastal planning and coastal engineering works. Available data on these elements in the north Indian Ocean are not adequate for frequency analysis as either the observing stations are far apart or these are not at all available on some sections of coastline. However, there are some good survey reports of past tropical cyclones where records of the highest water marks as revealed on buildings tress and embankments are available. Based on such data, efforts of preparing their catalogue are continuing in the National Meteorological Services and by individuals in the region.

Fortunately, these days it is possible to forecast storm surge heights with reasonable accuracy and tide estimates are available in tide tables. Theoretically, utilizing the past data it is also possible to calculate maximum probable storm surge in a particular place. The computational results of probable maximum storm surge over the east coast of India are shown in Fig. 4.

Energy

Unlike extra-tropical cyclones of middle latitudes, which derive their energy from large scale temperature contrast and vertical wind shear (variation of wind per km along the vertical), the primary source of energy for the genesis and maintenance of tropical cyclone is the diabatic heating--especially, latent heat release in clouds, surface sensible heat and radiation. Out of these processes the latent heat release in clouds is the primary source of energy driving the cyclone's circulation. The main energy, therefore, comes from the warm water of the ocean. Sensible heat extracted from the sea surface temperature is the main source of its energy. Within the life period of tropical cyclones transaction of energy within its circulation is immense. As discussed below, cyclone can be considered as an inefficient heat engine of the atmosphere. The conversion from thermal to mechanical energy is quite low, only about three per cent. Nevertheless, the heat energy released by the condensation of water vapour in a cyclone in a day often is the equivalent of that released by fusion of 40020 megaton hydrogen bombs. In a popular way it may be stated that the energy released in a day by a tropical cyclone if converted to electricity, it would be sufficient to meet all the electricity requirements of USA for about six months.

The Theory

Tropical cyclone is an intense low pressure area where pressure is very much below normal. There are a few known theories to explain the formation of tropical cyclones. One among them, based on physics is the Conditional Instability of the Second Kind; well known in meteorology by its acronym

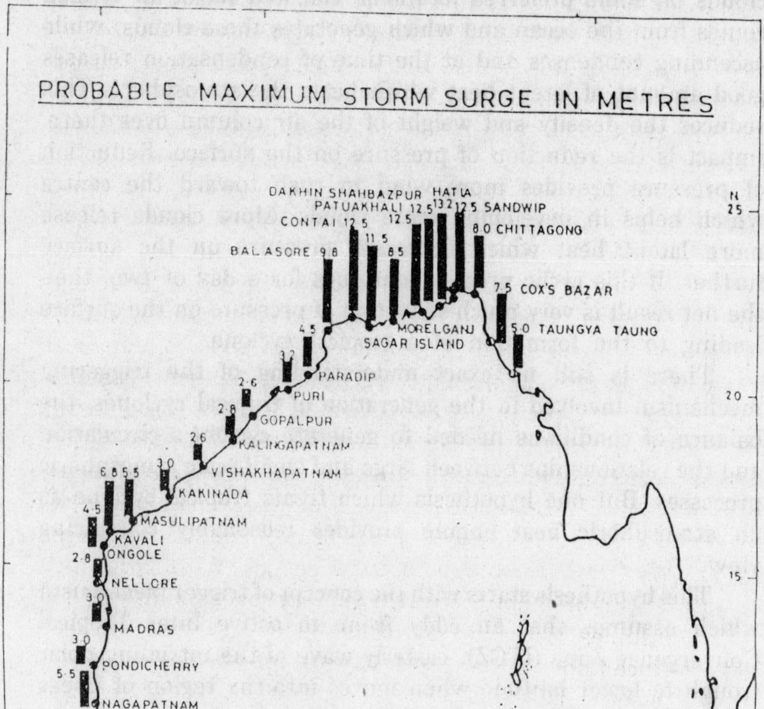
PROBABLE MAXIMUM STORM SURGE IN METRES
DAKHIN SHAHBAZPUR
HATIA
PATUAKHALI
12.5
13.2
12.5
SANDWIP
CONTAI
12.5
12.5
8.0
CHITTAGONG
11.5
BALASORE
9.8
8.5
7.5
COX'S BAZAR
MORELGANJ
4.5
5.0
TAUNGYA TAUNG
SAGAR ISLAND
3.2
PARADIP
2.6
PURI
2.8
GOPALPUR
2.6
KALINGAPATNAM
3.0
VISHAKHAPATNAM
6
6.5
5.5
KAKINADA
4.5
MASULIPATNAM
KAVALI
ONGOLE
2.8
NELLORE
3.0
MADRAS
3.0
PONDICHERRY
5.5
NAGAPATNAM
80 E
85
90
95 E
N
25
20
15

Fig. 4

"CISK". In a very simplified form the process is stated below.

At times, over the ocean the atmosphere initially creates conditions to generate a large number of cumulomibus/cumulus clouds on some preferred locations. Hot and moist air (which comes from the ocean and which generates these clouds) while ascending condenses and at the time of condensation releases good amount of latent heat which heats the atmosphere. This reduces the density and weight of the air column over there. Impact is the reduction of pressure on the surface. Reduction of pressure provides more wind to rush toward the centre which helps in developing more clouds. More clouds release more latent heat which decreases pressure on the surface further. If this cyclic process continues for a day or two, then the net result is very much reduction of pressure on the surface leading to the formation of a tropical cyclone.

There is still no exact understanding of the triggering mechanism involved in the generation of tropical cyclones, the balance of conditions needed to generate cyclone's circulation and the relationships between large and small scale atmospheric processes. But one hypothesis which treats tropical cyclone as an atmospheric heat engine provides reasonably convincing view.

This hypothesis starts with the concept of trigger mechanism which assumes that an eddy from an active Inter Tropical Convergence Zone (ITCZ), easterly wave of the intruding polar trough to lower latitude when moves into the region of upper level diverging flow (out flow), a vertical circulation is set up which might finally develop into a tropical cyclone.

The initial disturbance becomes a region into which low level air from the surrounding area begins to flow accelerating the convections already occurring inside the disturbance, leading to more organisation of the vertical circulation. But, if the inflow of air mass continues without any exhaust mechanism at a higher level (12-16 kms) over the area where the air mass surges upward, the incipient circulation may soon fill up and die. This forced ascent of warm and moist air from the ocean surface due to the cyclone system over the area of outflow can heat the atmospheric column sufficiently due to release of latent heat leading to sudden drop of atmospheric pressure at the surface. This process can produce steep pressure gradient along which wind may reach hurricane force.

It is believed that if the convergence of low level air (inflow) is more than the divergence at the high level (outflow) then the system is likely to fill up and die. On the other hand if the outflow at the top is more than the inflow in the bottom then the circulation would sustain and the system would intensify.

The view of tropical cyclone as atmospheric heat engine is necessarily a general one. The exact role of each contributor is not yet completely understood and a large number of delicate conditions must be satisfied for the atmosphere to produce a tropical cyclone. Some of the physical parameters favourable for the formation of tropical cyclones have been identified. However, these will not be discussed here.

Decay of Tropical Cyclone

Tropical cyclones loose their tropical characteristics and die when they move out of the environment of warm and moist tropical air, move over land or move under an unfavourable large scale flow aloft. Tropical cyclones after recurvature when move towards northern latitude, they generally enter cold water where normally they lose their intensity and tropical characteristics and ultimately die.

The Bay of Bengal and the Arabian Sea are land locked oceans and tropical cyclones unless die over the ocean (which is not very common) generally enter land. As soon as they enter land their primary source of energy, the transfer of sensible heat from the ocean surface is cut off. The sudden reduction of supply of moisture, the comparative cooler and rough surface of the land kill tropical cyclones when they enter land leaving the ocean. With the decrease of latent heat and increase in mean upward motion, adiabatic cooling dominates diabetic heating in the interior of the cyclone and the temperature through out the troposphere decreases leading to the death of tropical cyclones.

Tropical cyclones also die when they enter into the hostile atmosphere of very strong upper tropospheric mid-latitude westerlies or when the cold and dry winds from the higher latitude enter in the rear of a tropical cyclone in the lower levels. The large vertical wind shear associated with the westerly jet stream of the mid-latitude prohibits the accumulation of temperature in the air column due to strong ventilation at the top of the tropical cyclone. The cold air entering from the west decreases the release of latent heat, weakens the upper air divergence, decreases the temperature in the core and consequently pressure in the surface rises leading to the decay of tropical cyclones.

Cyclone Warning System

One of the short term mitigation measures against tropical cyclone disaster is the efficient cyclone warning system. Needs for an efficient cyclone warning system are (i) accurate and detailed forecasts of dangerous conditions in sufficient time in advance, (ii) rapid and dependable distribution system for the forecast/advisories and warnings to all interested parties, and (iii) prompt and effective utilisation of warnings by the government and public.

To get good forecast it is necessary to have (a) adequate data of proper type, (b) forecasters with sufficient ability, training, experience and time to prepare suitable forecast, and (c) good techniques for preparing accurate forecast of the storm's movement, change in intensity and storm tides. The communication system for distribution of the advisories and warnings should be one that can dependably deliver the advisory information to all concerned in a short time even in cyclone conditions like strong wind, heavy rain, floods, etc.

Cyclone Warning System in India

The cyclone warning service of the India Meteorological Department is now over a hundred years old and is one of the most important functions of the Department.

Present Cyclone Warning Organisation

At present the cyclone warnings are provided through the Area Cyclone Warning Centres (ACWC's) located at Calcutta, Madras and Bombay and Cyclone Warning Centres (CWC's) at Bhubaneshwar, Visakkhapatnam and Ahmedabad. The zone of responsibility of each office is clearly demarcated. Cyclone warning bulletins for All India Radio/Doordarshan, and cyclone advisories for the north Indian Ocean to Bangladesh, Burma,

India Maldives, Pakistan, Sri Lanka and Thailand are being issued from the Meteorological Office at New Delhi. This office in New Delhi also issues tropical cyclone advisories for the tropical cyclones in the southwest Indian Ocean to Mauritius.

Cyclone Tracking

In India, tropical cyclones are tracked with the help of (i) regular observation from water network of surface and upper air observing stations; (ii) Ships' report; (iii) Cyclone Detection Radars; (iv) Satellites and (v) Reports from the commercial aircraft.

In addition to large number of surface and upper air observatories, about 280 ships of Merchant Fleet are equipped with meteorological instruments for taking observations out at sea. Ships of the countries passing through our oceanic areas are also expected to provide frequent meteorological observations to the nearest Meteorological Office through Post and Telegraph Department's Coastal Radio Stations.

A network of 10 Cyclone Detection Radars have been set up along the Indian Coast. Six of them are located at (i) Calcutta, (ii) Paradip, (iii) Visakhapatnam, (iv) Machilipatnam (v) Madras and (vi) Karaikal on the east coast, while four are located at (i) Cochin, (ii) Goa, (iii) Bombay and (iv) Bhuj on the west coast. Range of these radars is 400 kms.

Satellite is one of the most dependable tools for tracking the weather systems such as cyclones. When the cyclone is beyond the range of coastal radars, its intensity and movements are monitored with the help of weather satellites. Today, the India Meteorological Department has the capability to monitor half hourly cloud pictures from the Indian Geostationary Satellite INSAT-1D and from the Polar Orbiting Satellites launched by the USA and the USSR.

Aircraft reconnaissance is another important tool for tracking tropical cyclones and measuring some important meteorological parameters from the storm field. This facility is not yet available in India.

Main Users of Cyclone Warning

The main users served by the Department are (i) Commercial Shipping and the Indian Navy; (ii) Port Authorities; (iii) Officials of the State and Central government; (iv) Fishermen and fisheries officials of the State government; (v) Special Warners, who are registered with the Department (Album Page Warners); (vi) Commercial aviation and (vii) General public.

Preparation of Forecast

The important components of cyclone warnings are the forecast of future path, intensity and the associated destructive weather. For the preparation of future position (path) of tropical cyclones and storm surges the modern computer based techniques are used in addition to conventional methods. For the intensity forecast satellite techniques are used.

Average errors of path prediction, even when modern and sophisticated techniques are used, for 24, 48 and 72 hours forecasts, are 220 kms, 430 kms and 730 kms respectively. Errors for 24 hours forecasts in India are around 150 kms. Therefore, earlier the warnings provided, greater is the landfall error. More areas are needed to be warned and evacuation of the people to safer places, which is the only solution to minimise loss of lives, becomes more impracticable. Therefore, cyclone warnings are not provided before 24 hours anywhere in the world. It is therefore necessary that the government machinery should be kept in readiness to evacuate large number of people to safer places in a short notice and in inclement weather.

Dissemination of Cyclone Warning

Warnings to the state government and Album Page Warnees are issued in two stages. In the first stage a 'Cyclone Alerts' is issued normally 48 hours before the commencement of adverse weather alone the coast. A cyclone warning is issued about 24 hours before the cyclone strikes the coast. Port and fisheries warnings start much earlier. These warnings are disseminated through, (i) Landline telegrams of special high priority; (ii) Repeated broadcasts through All India Radio in different languages; (iii) Bulletins to the Press; (iv) Posts and Telegraph Departments' Coastal Radio Stations (broadcast in code for the benefit of ship plying in the high seas); (v) Telephone, telex and teleprinters wherever available; and (vi) Wireless network of the police.

However, till today Postal Department's telegraph channels are widely used for the dissemination of cyclone warnings in

India which are normally vulnerable to disturbed weather.

Recently, to overcome these difficulties the India Meteorological Department has developed a system known as "Disaster Warning System (DWS)" to transmit cyclone warning bulletins through INSAT-DWS to the recipients. There are four elements of INSAT-DWS. These are (i) the cyclone warning centre for originating the area code of the districts and disaster warning message; (ii) the earth station located near the cyclone warning centre with uplink facility in C-band and suitable communication links with the cyclone warning centres; (iii) the C/S band transponder on board INSAT; and (iv) the INSAT-DWS receiver located in cyclone prone areas. A schematic diagram of the system is shown in Fig. 5.

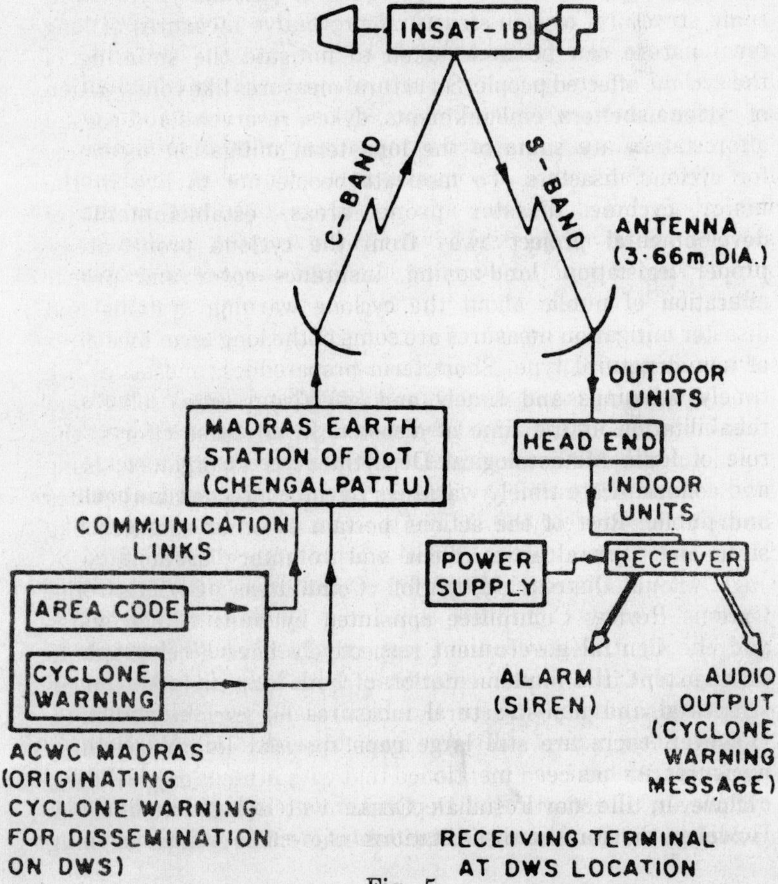

Fig. 5

Disaster Management and Mitigation Measures

The last requirement of the efficient warning system is the prompt action by the government and public on the warnings issued. It may be mentioned that accurate warnings will have no impact unless protective measures are taken by the government and affected people. It is also necessary that government must have the adequate means to evacuated large number of people in short time to safer places. Recently, the government awareness has increased manifold and proper actions are being taken on tropical cyclone warnings.

Disaster management refers to all activities connected with prevention, preparedness and relief. Prevention of formation of tropical cyclone is not in the realm of possibility. However, some structural or non-structural preventive measures of long term nature can be undertaken to mitigate the suffering of the cyclone affected people. Structural measures like construction of cyclone shelters, embankments, dykes, reservoirs and coastal afforestation are some of the long-term mitigation measures for cyclone disasters. To motivate people not to live in the major cyclone disaster prone areas, establishment of developmental project away from the cyclone prone areas, proper legislation, land-zoning, insurance cover and proper education of public about the cyclone warning systems and disaster mitigation measures are some of the long term measures of non-structural type. Short term preparedness measures are timely warnings and timely and effective rescue, relief and rehabilitation at the time of disaster. In all these efforts, the role of India Meteorological Department is to organise, issue and communicate timely warnings to the concerned authorities and public. Rest of the actions pertain to other agencies like state and Central government and voluntary agencies.

Cyclone Distress Mitigation Committees (CDMCs) and Cyclone Review Committee appointed by some of the states and the Central government respectively have accelerated, to some extent, the implementation of both long and short term structural and non-structural measures for cyclone disasters. However, there are still large gaps specially in preparedness measures. As has been mentioned that with present day facilities, cyclone in the north Indian Ocean will not go undetected. However, there are some limitations inherent in cyclone warning systems, particularly in forecasting of place and time of landfall more than 24 hours in advance and precise warnings cannot be provided more than 24 hours in advance any where in the world. In northeast coast of India, even today, the cyclone shelters have been only a few and far apart. On the other hand, this is the most vulnerable area for cyclone disaster. This is the area from where, because of the nature of the terrain, evacuation of people at short notice could be extremely difficult. Therefore, although, the planned and systematic disaster mitigation measures are necessary for all the cyclone prone areas, greater attention in needed for the northeast coast of the country.

7

Engineering of Structures for Cyclone Disaster Mitigation

J. Shanmugasundaram   T.V.S.R. Appa Rao***
*B. Venkateswarlu***

Many natural hazards such as floods cyclones, earthquakes and landslides strike every year in different parts of the world. Such disasters affect almost all the countries large or small, rich or poor. Tropical cyclónes are considered to be the most destructive among the natural disasters, when viewed in terms of their severity, duration and extent of destruction. Tropical cyclones, also known as typhoons in the pacific and hurricanes in the Atlantic region, cause considerable havoc destroying millions of houses and other industrial structures, and the most important of all killing people and livestock.

The cyclones are characterised by a revolving wind system with a mean wind speed of 33 m/s or more covering an area of more than 800 kms across[1]. The maximum wind pressure during such cyclones can be as high as 320 kg/sq m. These cyclonic winds are more turbulent than the normal winds of well behaved climate. The turbulent eddies in cyclones are capable of contributing significantly to the amplitude of oscillation of structures having natural periods that are close to the periods of cyclone eddies. Therefore, the dynamic effects of cyclonic winds on structures are considerable in many cases, and so inadequate considerations of such effects generally, leads to damage or even failure of structures.

The present level of R and D effort towards better understanding of the effects of cyclonic winds on houses, buildings and other structures and studies towards mitigation of damage

---

* Assistant Director, Structural Engineering Research Centre, Madras

** Deputy Director, Structural Engineering Research Centre, Madras to structures is inadequate. Further, it may by noted that there are complexities involved in assessing (i) probability and occurrence of extreme wind speeds during severe cyclones, (ii) wind pressure/load distribution of different types of structures (iii) dynamic response/strength of structures and (iv) types of failures/damage to structures and mitigation of damage. Science and technology can play an increasing role in improving our present knowledge in the above mentioned areas. Improved guidelines and techniques can be developed for design and construction of structures, in cyclone prone areas to mitigate damage. Even though R and D efforts have been made in this direction at the Structural Engineering Research Centre, Madras, and at other institutions in the country, more detailed studies are required in these areas. Post-disaster surveys on damage suffered by different types of structures and analysis of failures have been extremely useful in understanding the behaviour of structures in extreme winds and also in developing basic guidelines to improve the designs. The purpose of the paper in to present a critical assessment of the problem and complexities involved in the R and D work toward cyclone disaster mitigation. The areas/problems of R and D that deserve immediate attention have been identified. Emphasis is also laid on training to be imparted to design and field engineers so that the results of R and D are translated to mitigate the damage to structures.

Cyclones

Cyclones are formed due to atmospheric disturbances and they derive their energy from the latent heat released by the condensation of warm moisture picked up from the sea. Unlike tornadoes which may occur almost anywhere, cyclones originate between five and 30 degree latitudes on either side of the equator and affect island and coastal regions.

The average number of all the cyclones in the world occurring per year was estimated to be about 92[2]. The Indian ocean is one of the six major cyclone-prone regions of the world. In India cyclones occur usually between April and May, and also between October and December. The cyclones in the Bay of Bengal originate near the Andaman sea or in the south China sea, and move towards the east coast of India, whereas those in the Arabian sea usually originate near Sir Lanka and

Lakshadweep and move in the north to north-west direction hitting Konkan and Sourashtra coasts. During the period from 1945 to 1989 about 225 cyclones have occurred along the east and west coasts of India, of which, nearly 80 per cent of the cyclones were experienced along the east coast[3].

Such cyclones occur every year with wind speeds of about 260 kmph accompanied by storm surges of about 4 m to 5 m high. They cause considerable damage to crops, different types of buildings/dwellings and other structures, power transmission, communication systems, etc., resulting in heavy loss of life and property. The annual average cost of damage in India caused by cyclones has been estimated to be around Rs. 200 crores, which at times has exceeded even Rs. 400 crores[4]. The United Nations Disaster Relief Organisation (UNDRO) has reported that the total cost of damage caused by storms and cyclones in various developing countries, during the year 1987 is over Rs. 1,800 crores[5]. Thus it is imperative that immediate and adequate attention has to be paid to develop scientific/ rational methodologies and techniques tc mitigate the losses due to natural disasters.

Damage to Buildings and Structures due to Cyclones

Seldom a sever cyclone passes without inflicting damage to houses, buildings and other structures. The cyclones cause damage to structures ranging from non-engineered type, such as huts, tiled houses, and boundary walls to well-engineered structures like microwave towers, elevate water tanks, and chimneys. Typical damage observed during severe cyclones including rearing of rolling shutters, failure of industrial sheds, yielding of foundation anchor bolts, blowing of roofs in low-rise residential and industrial buildings, and failure of masonry structures such as freestanding compound walls and gable-end wall. A few examples of failures caused by the fury of the past cyclones are given below :

(a) Collapse of a 300 cubic metre capacity reinforced concrete elevated water tank in Sriharikota, Andhra Pradesh due to the 1984 cyclone (Fig. 1).

(b) Total failure of the bus depot (at Kavali, Andhra Pradesh) belonging to the Andhra Pradesh State Road Transport Corporation during the 1989 cyclone (Fig. 2).

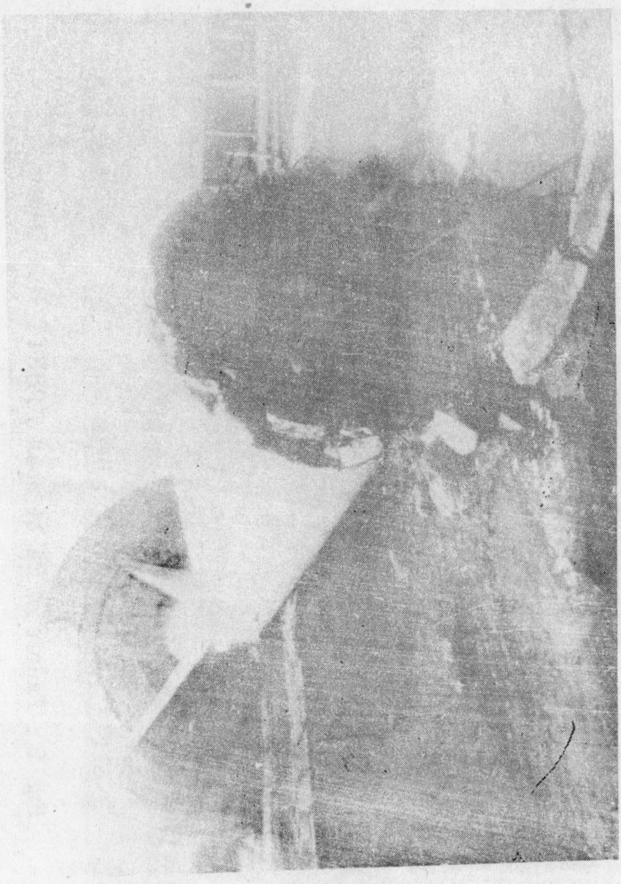

Fig. 1 : Collapse of a 300 cubic metre capacity elevated water tank

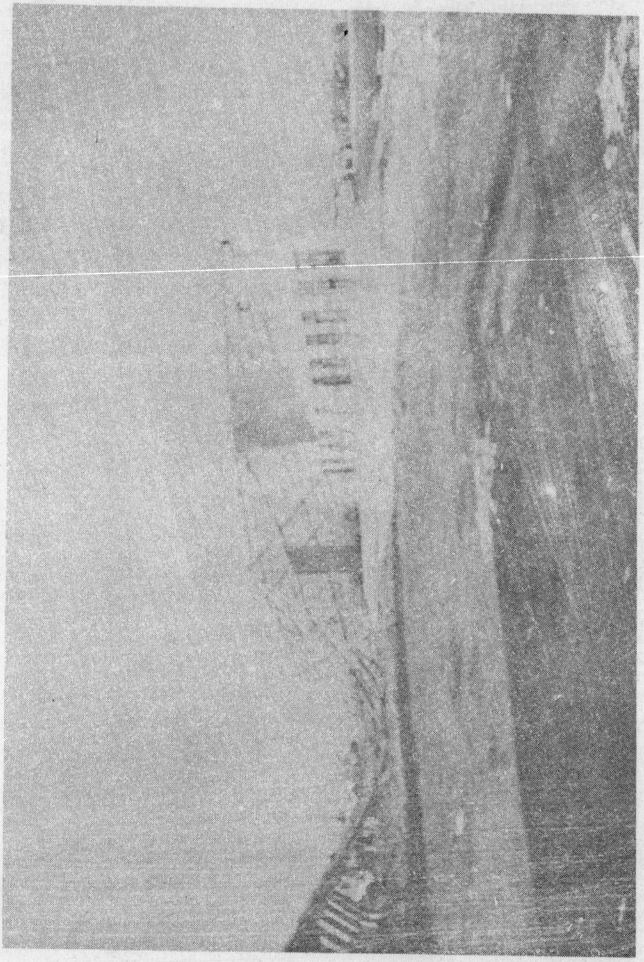

Fig. 2 : Failure of 22 M Span APSRTC Bus Depot

(c) Failure of the storage structure at Machilipatnam port due to the 1990 cyclone at Machilipatnam, Andhra Pradesh (Fig. 3).

Similar damages to various buildings and structures due to cyclones have been reported in other coastal regions of India.

However, it may by mentioned here that the resistance of the structures to withstand extreme winds without sever damage is dependent on the type of material and methods of construction adopted and by the degree of engineering attention bestowed during the design and construction stages.

Standards for Cyclone Resistant Design and Construction

One of the important measures to mitigate cyclonic wind disaster is to improve upon the wind loading standards for design of buildings and structures. The recent revision of the Indian Standards on Wind Loading, IS : 875 (Part 3)-1987[b] adopts specification of three sec basic wind speed map for different zones in India. The reported values of maximum wind speeds during the cyclones in the coastal regions of India, were found to be always higher than the values specified in the above code. In order to determine accurately the cyclonic wind loads acting on various structures there is a necessity to carry out risk analysis of cyclonic wind speed data and to compute characteristic cyclonic wind speeds corresponding to different mean return periods.

Two of the major areas of work which would further contribute towards improving the standards for design and construction of buildings in cyclone prone areas are discussed in the following section.

Risk Analysis of Cyclonic Wind Speeds

Connection of cyclonic wind speed data, assessment of vulnerability of different zones based on frequency of occurrence and intensity of cyclones, and determination of characteristic wind speeds for different zones and for different life periods of structures are important for accurate estimation of cyclonic wind pressures on structures.

Fig. 3 : Failure of Storage Structure

At present, only a limited number of anemographs are installed in India to measure wind speeds. Due to failure of measurement systems during cyclones, wind speeds greater than 50m/sec could not be recorded in many cases. The cyclonic wind speeds in the coastal regions are now estimated from the barometric pressure differentials obtained from the on-shore meteorological stations, radar observations, satellite pictures and the off-shore ship observations. Investigations were carried out at the Structural Engineering Research Centre, Madras, on risk analysis of cyclonic wind speeds for the coastal regions of India. The limited cyclonic wind speed data pertaining to the east and west coasts of India were collected from the India Meteorological Department and were later augmented using the Monte Carlo simulation technique. Only wind speeds exceeding 62 knots (115 kmph) which are known to cause damage to structures have been considered in this analysis. Based on the Gumbel (Type I) extreme value distribution, which was found to fit the field data closely, the characteristic cyclonic wind speeds for different mean return periods were computed[7]. Thus a cyclonic wind speed map of India covering the coastal regions of Tamil Nadu, Andhra Pradesh, Orissa and West Bengal in the east coast and Konkan and Sourashtra in the west coast, has been developed and is given in Fig. 4. The characteristic wind speeds specified in the above figure correspond to normal structures of 50 year life period with a risk level of 0.63 (i.e., 50 year mean return period).

The maximum basic wind speed recommended in the Indian standards on wind loads for the coastal regions in east and west coasts of India, where severe cyclones are frequently occurring, ranges from 44 m/s to 50 m/s, whereas the maximum cyclonic wind speeds specified in Fig. 4 are more than 60 m/s. Hence it is suggested that a cyclone factor of different coastal regions, to account for the increased intensity of cyclonic winds, as given in Table 1 may be adopted for structures of considerable importance[8].

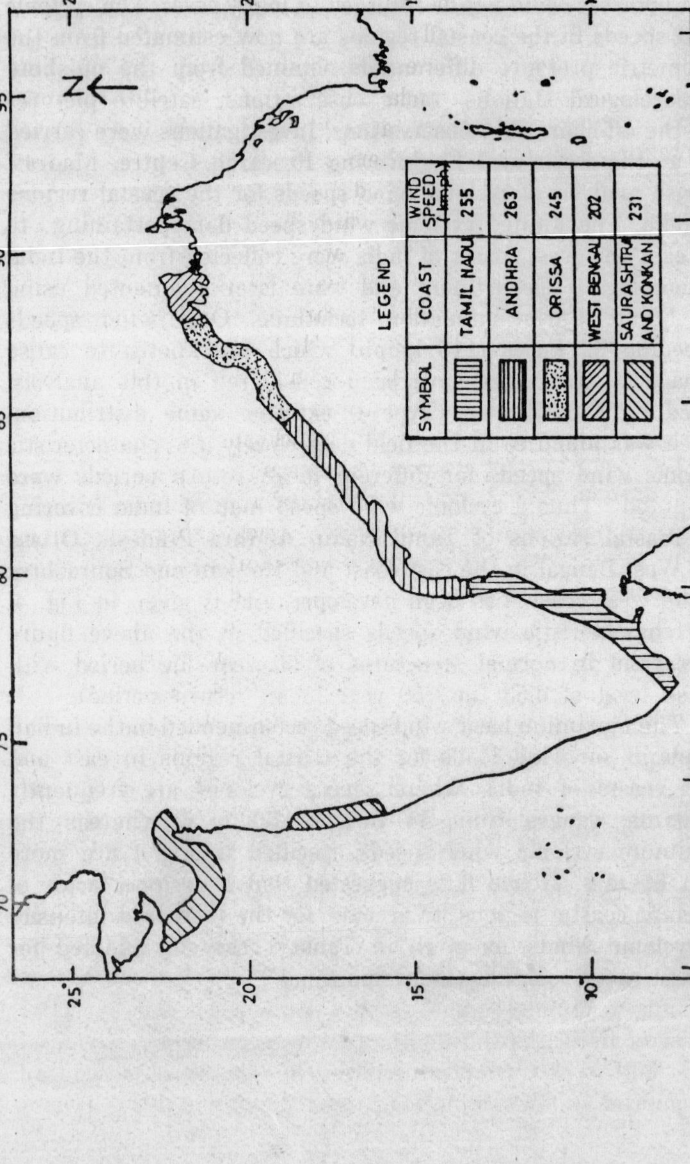

Fig. 4 : Cyclonic Wind Speed Map of Coastal India

Table 1

Recommended Regional Multiplying Factors For Cyclonic Winds

SL. No.	Coastal Region	Basic wind speed as per IS : 875 (3)-1987 (m/s)	63% characteristic wind speed (kmph)	(m/s)	Regional multiplying factor
1	2	3	4		5=(4/3)
1.	Tamil Nadu	50	254.85	70.8	1.42
2.	Andhra Pradesh	50	262.79	73.0	1.46
3.	Orissa	50	259.00	70.3	1.41
4.	West Bengal	50	215.48	59.9	1.20
5.	Konkan	44	223.51	62.1	1.41
6.	Sourashtra	50	223.51	62.1	1.24

Besides development of cyclone resistant designs of structures, the concept of providing cyclone resistant core units in the houses of rural/low-income groups in the coastal regions has been experimented. At the request of the Town and Country Planning, Government of Tamil Nadu, SERC, Madras, has developed cyclone resistant core units in ferrocement and the details are shown in Fig. 5.[9]

Post Disaster Cyclone Damage Survey and Analysis

Engineering of structures to resist cyclonic wind forces required interdisciplinary and integrated efforts including the areas of meteorological, structural engineering and numerical modelling techniques. The present knowledge and expertise in disaster mitigation have to be improved to develop advanced design and construction procedures for increased resistance of structural systems subjected to cyclonic winds. Post-disaster

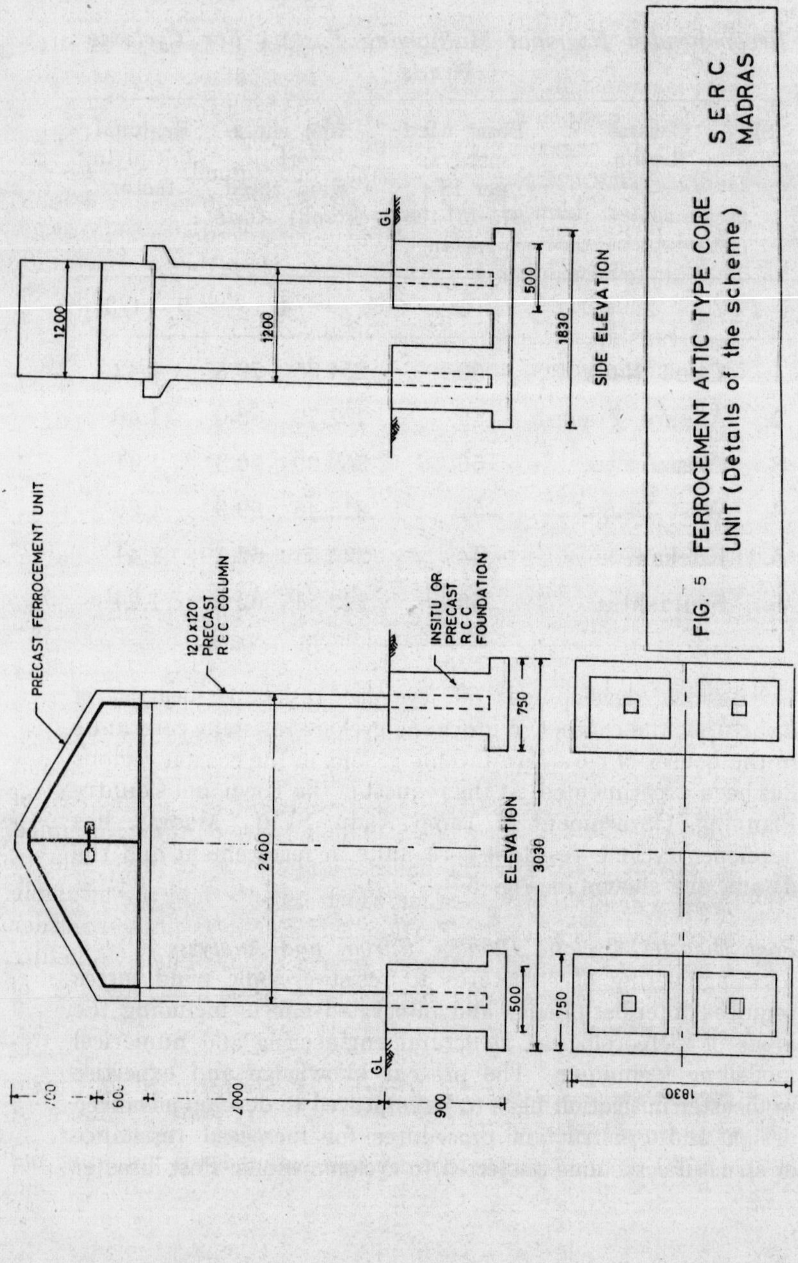

Fig. 5 : Ferrocement Attic Type Core unit

field surveys on damage suffered by buildings and structures enable one the identity the tropical failures of structures and the factors influencing the damage. Observations on failures made during such survey and subsequent analysis of failures provide an insight into the mechanisms of failures of materials, structural components and systems.

Various organisations around the world including SERC, Madras, have been actively engaged in conducting surveys on post-disaster damage due to cyclones and in analysing the behaviour of structures subjected to resist extreme wind forces.[10] The data to be collected in these surveys include type of structural system, materials used, joint/connection details, quality of workmanship, etc., besides the details of actual failure. Based on the information collected during the post-disaster surveys conducted in India and abroad, suitable guidelines have been suggested for achieving improved resistance of structures against cyclonic forces.

In India, the available field data in the performance of structures during cyclones are limited, and their is a need to conduct detailed post-disaster surveys and document the damage to different structural members and the structure as a whole.

By analysing the type and extent of damage suffered by trypical structures, it is possible to reasonably assess the maximum cyclonic wind speed that could have caused the failure[11]. The accuracy of the above type of analysis in back calculating the maximum wind speed from the damage depends on various factors such as the type of the structure, construction material, gust sensitivity of the structure, influence of surrounding structure, if any, and the terrain conditions assumed in the analysis. For the failure analysis it is preferable to select a suitable structure for which reliable data are available to compute its strength. Further it is also desirable to consider a severely damaged structure with a simple mode of failure so that it is amenable for analysis with least number of assumptions.

Recommendations to Minimise Structural Damage due to Cyclones

From the studies on damage suffered by building and

structures in various parts of the world, the following typical failures may be identified:

(i) blowing off of roof sheets due to poor connections between structural elements in pitched roof buildings;
(ii) failures of tiled and A.C. sheet roof system due to uplift forces owing to their light-weight compared to R.C.C. roof system;
(iii) collapse of boundary and gabled walls due to inadequate strength in resisting lateral high wind forces;
(iv) collapse of low-rise industrial structures, due to lack of roof and wall bracing system; and
(v) failures of a few well-engineered structures due to design inadequacies and poor quality of construction.

The above types of failures can be minimised and the resistance of such structures against cyclones can be increased by adopting simple, improved design and construction techniques. Anchorage, bracing and continuity are the prime factors influencing the structural integrity.[12] To ensure structural integrity the following measures may be adopted:

(i) every part of a structure should be firmly tied or anchored to a secure point which can safely resist all the forces acting on it;
(ii) roof and end walls must be properly braced to prevent overturning, sliding and rotation; and
(iii) each part of the structure must be properly connected to every other member along the strength chain from cladding to foundation.

For example, failure of compound walls during cyclones is common. Guidelines for their design have to be improved. By anchoring them to the concrete foundations through the use of tie-down bolts/rods as shown in Fig. 6, their resistance to cyclonic wind pressure can be increased.

It may be noted that most of the dwellings in coastal regions of India are constructed using thatch material of tiles.

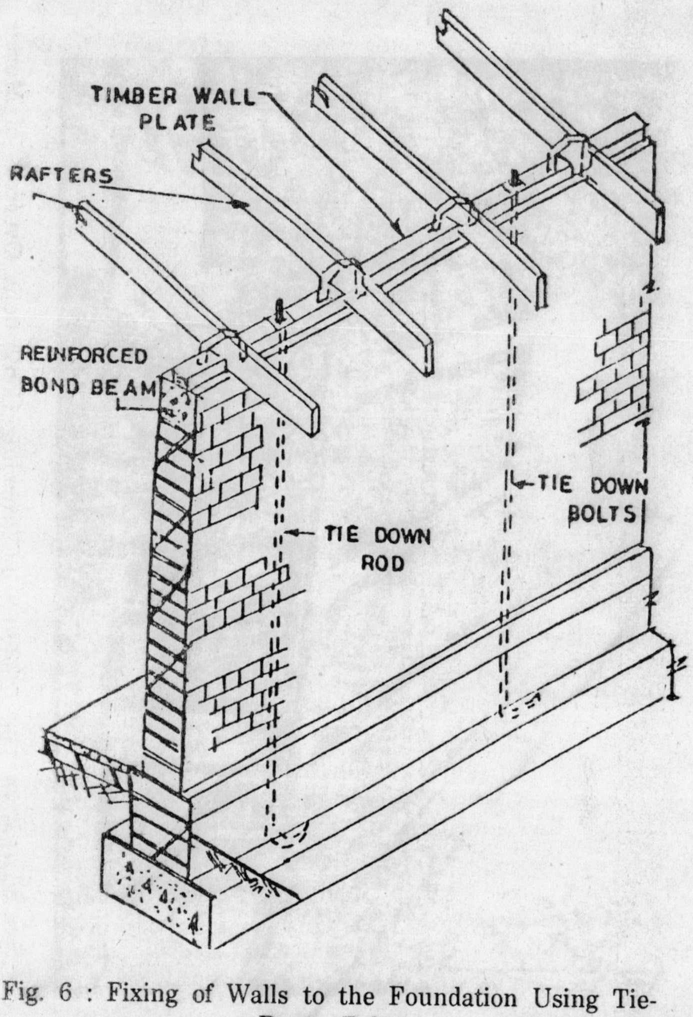

Fig. 6 : Fixing of Walls to the Foundation Using Tie-Down Bolts

In view of the poor quality and strength of thatch material, collapse of such houses in cyclone-prone regions occurs and hence such types of house construction can be avoided upto about 100 kms from the coastal line. In the case of tiled houses, their resistance to cyclonic uplift forces can be improved by providing a continuous mortar bands over the cladding (Fig. 7)

Fig. 7 : Protection of Tile Cladding by Providing Continuous Overcoat of Mortar.

or by providing closely spaced concrete restraining strips in the critical regions of ridges, eaves, corners as shown in Fig.8 and by tyingdown the roof tiles to the main rafter using G.I. straps as shown in Fig. 9.

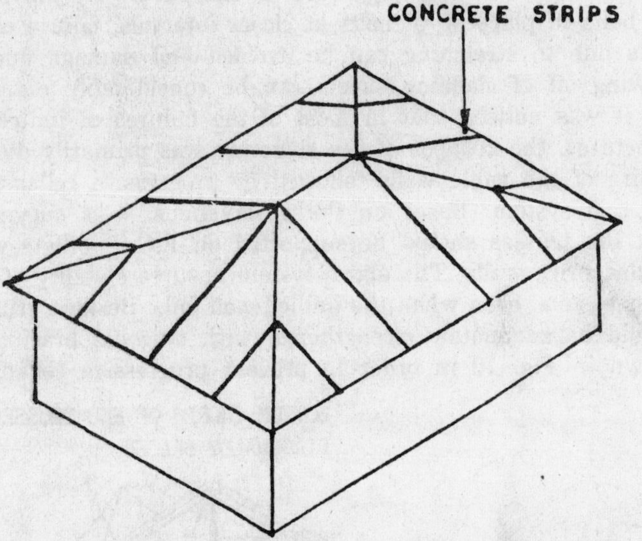

Fig. 8 : Cyclonic Wind Speed Map of Coastal India

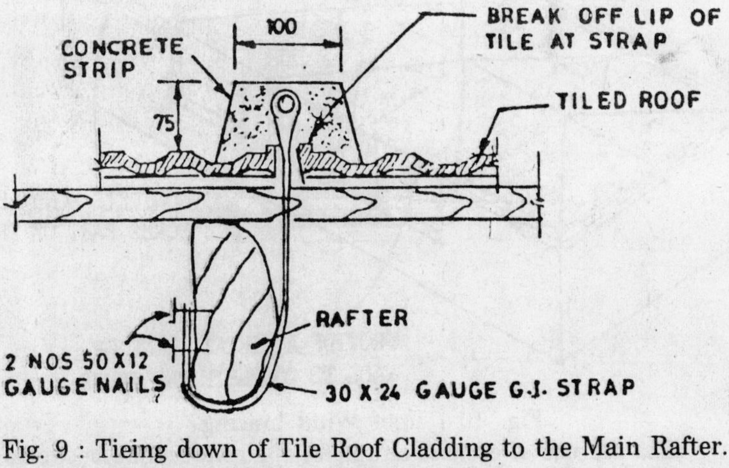

Fig. 9 : Tieing down of Tile Roof Cladding to the Main Rafter.

In pitched roof residential and industrial structures 'J' bolts are conveniently used to tie down the roof cladding to the purlin. Due to dynamic action of cyclonic forces, the hook of the 'J' bolt is flattened, weakening the connection ineffectively holding down the cladding sheets to the purlin. By providing 'U' bolts in place of 'J' bolts at closer intervals, failure of 'J' bolts due to stretching can be avoided and damage due to blowing off of cladding sheets can be considerably reduced.

It was noticed that in most of the failures of industrial structures, the collapse of the structure was primarily due to failure of the gable walls followed by progressive collapse of the roof system. Based on the observations, it is suggested that the trusses should be supported on R.C.C. pillars with infilled brick walls. The above system ensures stability of the truss system, even when the infilled wall fails. Besides, trusses should be adequately strengthened with diagonal bracing as shown in Fig. 10 in order to prevent progressive collapse.

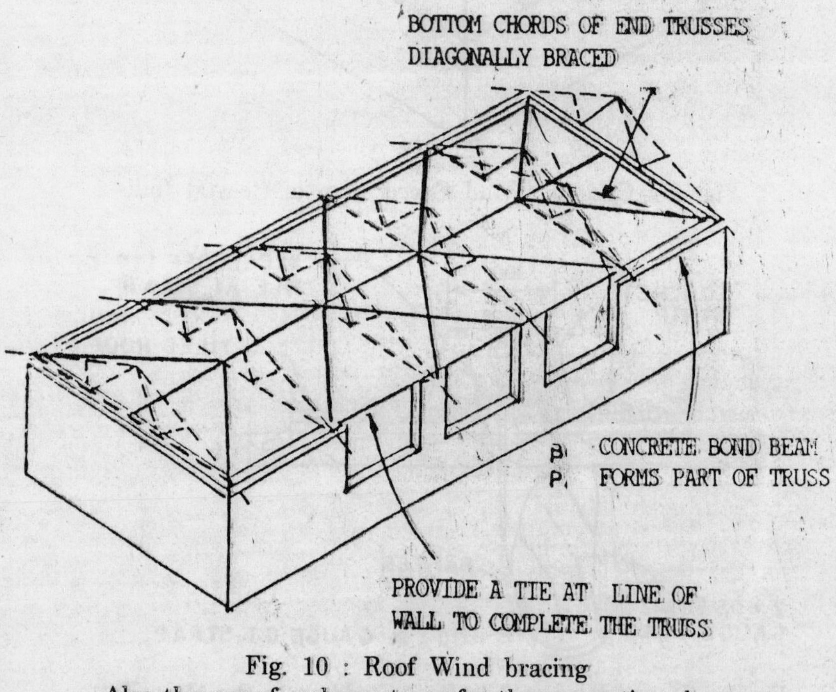

Fig. 10 : Roof Wind bracing

Also the use of cyclone straps for the connections between

different structural elements of the roofing system as shown in Figs.11 and 12 is recommended.

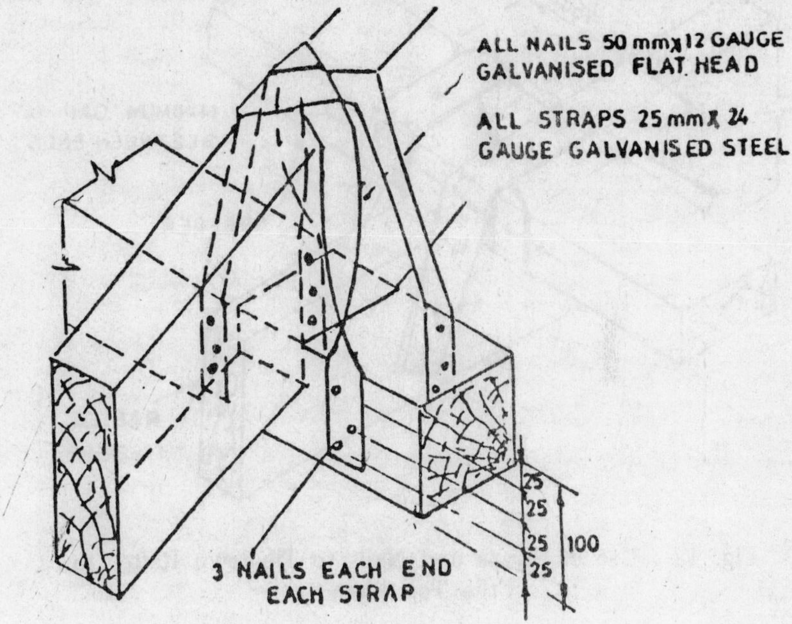

Fig. 11 : Connection Detail between Reeper and Rafter

Some of the well engineered structures, such as tall communication towers, chimneys, also collapsed due to severe cyclones. It was noted that these failures were due to inadequate design considerations and construction practices. It is suggested that for such structures a detailed analysis taking into account the dynamic response of the structure and the effects of height, terrain and topography on wind speed has to be carried out. Besides, buffeting, torsional effects should also be considered in the design.

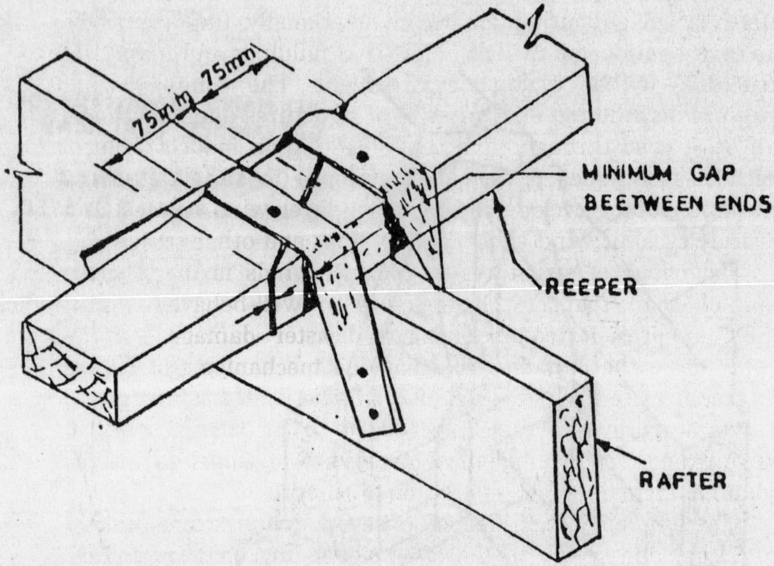

Fig. 12 : Use of Straps and Nails to Tie-down Rafter to the Top Plate

Future Research Towards Mitigation of Damage to Buildings and Structures

Even though many investigations have been carried out around the world on the characteristics of cyclones and on the causes of failures of buildings and structures due to cyclones, there are many aspects requiring further studies to improve our present understanding on the behaviour of various structures to resist cyclonic forces.[13] For example, at present there is a growing demand for construction of tall, slender, flexible and wind-sensitive structures, but there are many uncertainties in estimating the dynamic characteristics and response of structures subjected to cyclonic winds. Hence there is a need to develop reliable analytical models to predict the dynamic response of different types of structures. This can be achieved by detailed studies on analytical modelling and by conducting field experiments to validate the analytical models. Studies on aeronautic models in wind channels are also required to understand the dynamic response of structures including the effects of neighbouring environment. Equally important are the investigations on models of low-rise buildings and industrial structures in the cyclonic environment. The complex wind pressure distribution and response of structures due to cyclones can be studied through wind tunnel testing on models. Hence, methods/techniques have to be developed to simulate severe storms including cyclones in boundary layer wind tunnels and to study cyclonic wind effects on buildings and other structures.

Behaviour of structures in cyclonic winds is much more complex than that of the structure in well-behaved winds. Thus, at present, conducting post-disaster damage surveys seems to be the only way to study the mechanisms of failure of structures in cyclones. Detailed surveys and documentation of typical failures of structures have to be carried out till accurate and realibale analytical models are developed to analyse dynamic cyclonic wind effects on structures.

The frequency and intensity of severe cyclones considerably vary from one region to the other depending on geographical conditions. Microzoning of cyclonic wind speeds will help in better estimation risk of structures in different zones. Hence it is suggested that detailed cyclonic wind speed contour maps delineating different risk zones in the east and west coasts of India may be developed.

While the problem of risk assessment can be well addressed using the probabilities approach, the problem of future damage prediction and assessment of risk of structure against cyclones often depends on information which is vague, qualitative, and incompetent. several factors such as type of structural system, quality of workmanship, strength of connections, and the assumptions made in the design influence the extent of damage to a structure. However, due to uncertainties involved in the above mentioned factors, a crisp and clear description is seldom possible. Hence in recent times there is a new school of thought to incorporate the qualitative information based on wide knowledge and experience of experts into the analysis and design of a structure in a more rational manner using fuzzy logic methods. Application of theory of fuzzy sets to civil engineering problems is of recent origin. Since risk assessment of buildings and other structures prone to cyclones is essential for mitigation of effects of the natural hazards, it is necessary and useful of develop a knowledge-based risk analysis/ methodologies incorporating the experience gained from the field damage surveys and the data collected on response of structures.

Training Courses on Cyclone Disaster Mitigation

Many national and international workshops, seminars and conferences have been organised in India and elsewhere to discuss the problem of natural disaster mitigation. Realising the importance of the problem, the Structural Engineering Research Centre, Madras, has organised the following workshop/ courses between 1985 and 1990:

(a) Indo-U.S.Workshop on wind Disaster Mitigation sponsored by Department of Science and Technology, Government of India and National Science Foundation, U.S.A.;

(b) UNCHS-SERC Workshop on Cyclone Disaster Mitigation; and

(c) Course on Wind Disaster Mitigation of Structures, sponsored by Department of Science and Technology, Government of India.

The expertise acquired and the results/information obtained/generated based on the work/research done by various organisations have to be passed on the building industry, civil construction companies in public and private sector, and to the state and the central public works departments to realize construction of cyclone-resistant structures. Such dissemination of information and transfer of techniques may be carried out by conducting training courses and workshops in which a large number of design, and field practising engineers can participate.

Concluding Remarks

For safety of structures against cyclonic wind speeds, it is necessary that the cyclone-prone areas must be designed for the characteristic wind speed shown in Fig. 4. However, it may be uneconomical to consider such high wind speed of cyclones at service condition for designing all types of structures. But the failures of structures due to cyclones indicate that the effect of cyclones on structures cannot be completely disregarded. The structures should be designed and constructed to resist the cyclonic wind forces in such a way that neither complete collapse causing severe risk to human lives nor damage to an irreparable extent occurs.

It is necessary to carry out detailed post-disaster field surveys on damage to different buildings and structures and to document details of typical failures of structures. This will help in further understanding of the structural behaviour and in improving the designs of structures to resist cyclonic forces. The data/information would also help in developing analytical improved models to predict/assess damage by making use of advanced methods/theories such as fuzzy set theory.

Further R and D work is required to improve the methods/ techniques of design and construction of structures in cyclone prone areas to mitigate losses. Studies on the following topics are suggested :

(a) Wind speeds/characteristics in normal and extreme wind climates;
(b) Development of cyclonic wind speed contour map for the peninsular India (microzoning of cyclonic wind data);
(c) Analytical and field investigations on structural response of wind-sensitive tall structures in different wind exposures;
(d) Post-disaster cyclone damage surveys and failure analysis;
(e) Wind tunnel testing on models for dynamic response of structures subjected to extreme wind loads; and
(f) Development of knowledge-based systems to assess risk of structures in cyclone-prone areas.

References

1. Sharma M.C., "State-of-the-Art Report on Wind Zoning in India." Proceedings of the Indo-U.S. Workshop on Wind Disaster Mitigation, SERC, Madras, 1985.

2. Venkatesarlu, B., M. Armugam, and S. Arunachalam, "Risk Analysis of Cyclonic Wind Data," Proceedings of the National Seminar on Tall Reinforced Concrete Chimneys, New Delhi. 1985.
3. Shanmugasundaram, J., S. Arunachalam, G. Annamalai, and M. Arumugam, "Cyclone Hazards to Structures and Methods of Mitigation," Proceedings of the Symposium on Preparedness, Mitigation, and Management of Natural disasters, Vol. 1. New Delhi, 1989.
4. Rakshit, D.K., "Some Aspects of Community Preparedness Plan against Cyclone." Proceedings of the US-ASIA Conference on Engineering for Mitigating Natural Hazards/Damage, Bangkok, 1987. Rao, V.R. L. Lalitha, Nageswara Rao., A.K. Gupta, and G. Vijayalakshmi, "Disasters in India, Can Remote Sensing do Something," ISRO, Bangalore, 1984.
5. Disaster News in Brief, January 1-December 31, 1987 UNDRO News Bulletin, 1988.
6. Indian Standards, "IS-875 (Part-3) 1987, Indian Standard Code of Practice for Design Loads for Buildings and Structures, Wind Load," Bureau of Indian Standards, New Delhi.
7. Venkateswarlu, B., and J. Shanmugasundaram, "Probabilities Estimate of Cyclonic Risks for Indian Coasts," Proceedings of the Third Indian Engineering Congress, Institution of Engineers (India), Madras, 1989. Also see, Shanmugasundaram, G. Annamali, and B. Venkateswarlu, B., Probabilistic Models for Cyclonic Wind Speeds in India." Proceedings of the Second Asia-Pacific Symposium on Wind Engineering, Beijing, China, 1989.
8. Shanmugasundaram, J., "Engineering of Structures to Resist Cyclonic Winds", Proceedings of the Indo-U.S. Binational Workshop on Advances in Construction Materials, Techniques, and Management, IIT., Madras, 1990.
9. Madhava Rao, A.G., "Cyclone Resistant Core Units," Course on Wind Disaster Mitigation of Structures," SERC, Madras, 1990.
10. Mehta, K.C., J.E. Minor, and T.A. Rainhold, "Wind Speed Damage Correlation in Hurricane Fredric," Journal of Structural Engineering, ASCE, Vol. 109, No. 1, 1991. Chiu, A.N.L., L.E. Esclante, J.K. Michell, D.C. Perry, T.A. Schroeder, and T. Walton, T., "Hurricane Iwa, Hawaii, 1982, National Research Council, National Academic Press, Washington, D.C., 1983. Krishna, P., and P.K. Pandey, "Failure of the AIR Transmission Towers in the Delhi Tornado of March 1978," Journal of the

Institution of Engineers, (India), Vol. 60, Pt CI. 3, 1979. Venkateswarlu, B., and K. Murlidaharan, "A Report on Structural Damage due to Cyclone in Andhra Pradesh," SERC, Madras, 1978.

11. Shanmugasundaram. J., S. Arunachalms, T.V.S.R. Appa Rao, "Post-disaster Cyclone Damage Surveys and their Impact on Design of Structures," Proceedings of the International Symposium on Wind Loads on Structures, New Delhi, 1990.
12. Ministry of Local Government, Housing and Construction, Design of Buildings of High Winds, Colombo, Sri Lanka, 1980.
13. Appa Rao, T.V.S.R. and S. Arunachalam, "Considerations in Design of Structures for Disaster Mitigations," Proceedings of the International Seminar on Mitigation Technology for Storms and Floods, Japan, 1989.

8

Impact of Cyclones on Transport in Madras : A Case Study

S. Ponnuswamy and C. T. Sriramulu***

Disasters can be caused either by natural phenomena like hurricanes, typhoons, cyclones, storms and heavy downpour or due to errors and omissions of people, e.g., fires, structural failures and accidents. In all these cases, some part of the humanity or other is affected and they need measures for saving lives and belongings. Urban areas suffer relatively higher damages. The availability of immediate transport facility for rushing aid to such areas is the first need. The entire transport system should be available expeditiously. But in times of natural disasters, and accidents on road or rail the transport infrastructure itself becomes the major victim. This paper describes how the natural disasters affect the Madras metropolitan area with special reference to transport facilities in the city--the fourth largest metropolis of India. It covers action plans available, cost of implementing them and need for long term measures. These are considered with particular reference to cyclonic storms of 1978 and 1985, which are of recent occurrence, since Madras is not an area known to be affected by other types of disasters.

The Study Area

Madras Metropolitan area has a population of 5.34 million persons. The city area covers 172 sq km and urban area of

---

* Research Scholar, Traffic and Urban Systems Engineering Division, Anna University, Madras.

** Professor and Head, Traffic and Urban Systems Engineering Division, Anna University, Madras.

1,167 sq kms. It is a Port city located at longitude 80.18°E and latitude 13.05°N. There are two small rivers and a canal passing through the city. The rivers Coovum and Adayar run east-west and have seasonal flow only. The catchment areas of Coovum is 290 sq km (including 140 tanks) and of Adayar 857 sq km (including 219 tanks). Both the rivers have confluence with the Bay of Bengal within the length of the city area. They thus divide the city into three parts, in fact Coovum almost bisect the city. The mouth of both the rivers are blocked by sand bars and hence their waters flow into sea only during sever floods and flood waters which cause inundation in low lying neighbourhoods.

The Buckingham Canal runs north-south, parallel to the coast (about 1 to 2 kms away from the sea). It cuts across Coovum and Adayar and locks are provided at its crossing with Adayar. Over four decades ago, it was a major navigation canal plying country craft, carrying firewood, salt, etc., Now it is in disuse and mostly serves as a major collector drain; particularly during rains. There is another drainage canal, Otteri, running for 12 kms east-west and originating from west of Villivakkam. It serves as a drainage outlet to some of the most congested and low lying areas of the city and carries the spill of Coovum during very major storms.

Apart from these there are four major water bodies near the city in the form of man-made lakes, *viz.*, Red Hills (71 mcft capacity), Chembarampakkam (90 mcft), Poondi (80 mcft) and Sholavaram in the outskirts of the MMA, which are used for storing water during rains and supplying to the city. In addition, the city had a number of small tanks which formed part of an irrigation system before city building activities covered these.

Transportation System in Madras

Fig. 1 shows the major road network and railway system which crisscross the Madras Metropolitan areas.[2] The city is served by three rail corridors which are radiating from the city centre (i.e., CBD including the Port) in three directions. Two of them (north and west) are broad gauge lines and one towards south is a metre gauge line. All are inter-city lines

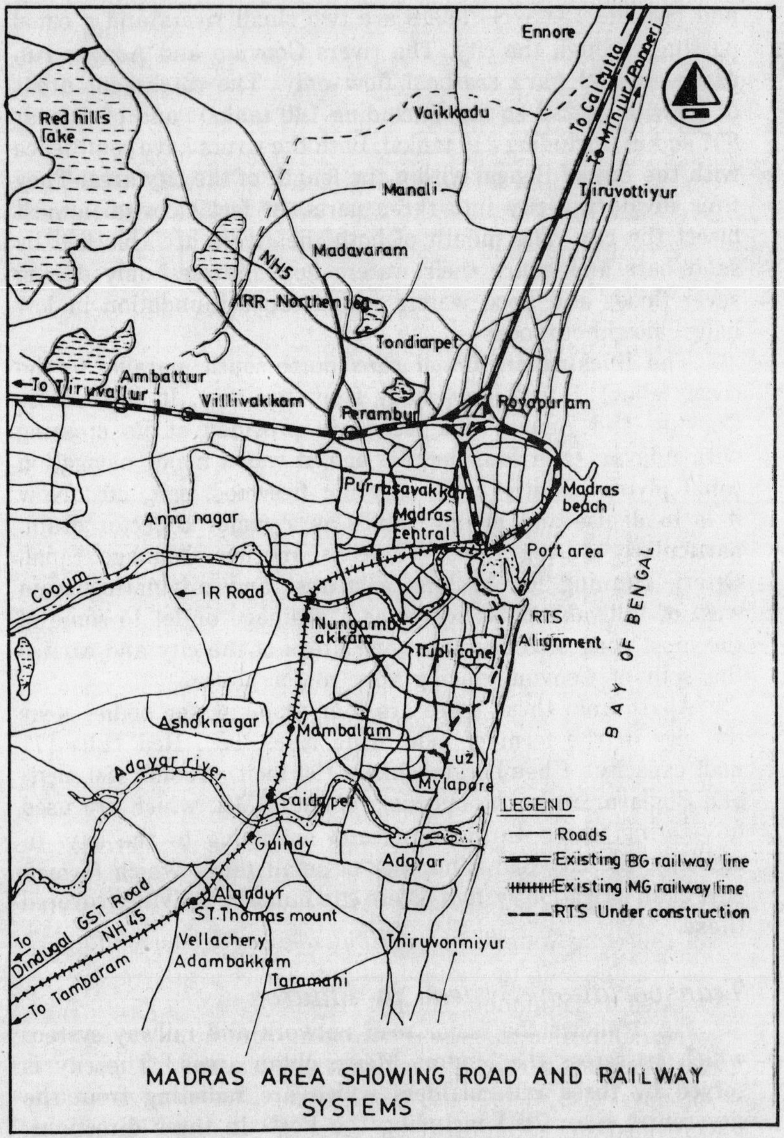

Fig. 1 : Madras Area Showing Road and Railway System

but there are suburban rail services provided to them. The western line and southern line have separate dedicated tracks for suburban services over the busy stretch (25 kms on BG and 29 kms on MG respectively). The road system comprises five radial arterials. Three of them which run more or less parallel to the three rail alignments are part of national highways and the two others connect CBD to major residential belts. They are linked by a large number of lateral arterials and collector roads. Only the inner Ring Road partly completed is a continuous link which connects all five radials. The other rings of laterals are disjointed. Many of them serve both as arterials and commercial service roads. The total road length in MMA comprises 90 kms of arterials and 470 kms of collector and distributor roads. A study conducted in 1984 showed that 93 per cent of their length are deficient in surface conditions and drainage. The net work within the city bus route roads are 288 kms long and all other roads are consisted of 305 road links and 127 nodes.

All the radials cross the main water courses mentioned in the previous section at one place or the other. Many laterals are also crossed by them at a number of points. There are four road bridges on Adayar, 13 on Coovum, 16 on Buckingham canal and many on Otteri, nallah of which 11 are narrow ones. There are a total of 71 bridges within the city. The three railway lines are crossed by roads at 32 locations spread over different locations within MMA. The subways have been constructed at many locations and they need less headroom. They turn out to be more economical and have been formed with minimum visual intrusions. In an area where there are only a few rainy days in a year these should cause comparatively less trouble in maintenance. The drainage in these are by way of collecting water in a sump at midlength and pumping out or leading out to natural drains as in the case of the one located at Perambur. Though regular pumping is provided for, when abnormal rains take place, they are inundated and cause interruption to traffic for hours and sometimes for a couple of days also. The most troublesome that way are subways provided at Perambur, Rajaji Salia in CBD and Kannammapet and Doraiswamy Road (T' Nagar). These are all on busy roads and during cyclones and heavy storms call for diversion of traffic to adjacent crossings which are one to two kms away. Bus transport is very much affected on routes passing through these roads. One remedy is to widen the adjacent crossing and also make more efficient pumping arrangements by keeping heavier duty portable emergency diesel driven pumps which can reach the site on receipt of warning of forecast of heavy rains.

Storms and Cyclones

The south-eastern part of India receives its major rains in the north east monsoon season, i.e., from October to December but some sporadic storms occur in the south-west monsoon period from June to September also. These rains, particularly the one in north-east monsoon are accompanied by cyclonic storms. There is not a single year which passes of without one or two major cyclones hitting the east coast of the Peninsular India. The location, however, differs. They hit anywhere between latitudes 50N and 15°N. In 1891-1984, there were 234 storms in Bay of Bengal as against 32 in Arabian sea. Average cyclonic disturbances are 13 per year of which 35 per cent (4 to 5) develop into cyclonic storm and one or two per year become severs storms which cross the coast. They result in gales and winds which can exceed 120 kmph sustained velocity, torrential rains and high tidal waves. Though Madras is a vulnerable spot, more often the eye of the storm hits the coast at locations about 50 to 150 kms in the south (Nagapattnam-Vedarnayam) or 100 to 250 kms or beyond in the north (Nellur, Ongole area). There is however a probability of 0.05 to 0.1 of very severe cyclonic storm hitting the city or environs. Even if the eye of storm does not cross Madras, the effects of the crossing nearby are quite severe. For example the major storm effects have been in years 1884, 1903, 1937, 1943, 1976 1985 and 1990.

The annual rainfall in the city is of the order of 120 cms Two-thirds of which is received during NE monsoon in six to eight spells with about five cms rainfall on a single day. The maximum one day rainfall in Madras was 20.3 cms (on 7th October 1943) preceded by 15.5 cms on the previous day, the total rainfall in seven days of that week being 84 cms. In that year the Adayar flood was 985 cumecs at Adayar bridge and spilled by 0.8 m over old bridge at Saidapet and Coovum flood was 1000 cumecs at Aminjikarai. Though beyond this it started going down due to spill, drainage from city area added to it and at lowest point it was again 1,000 cumecs. Otteri Nallah absorbed some spill of Coovum, which had a discharge as high as 445 cumecs.

During heavy rains, the water supply lakes mentioned earlier serve as rearing basins, e.g., in 1943, the peak inflow in the Chembarambakkam lake was 1,180 cumecs and outflow 490 cumecs. Thought at these times, they cause concern on what would happen in the case of any mishap, the lakes served this secondary purpose of flood absorption very well.

The next major depression was in 1976 when maximum one day rainfall was 45.2 cms and week's rainfall was 51.3 cms. At Adayar bridge the river discharge was 2110 cumecs, but at Saidapet the water was 0.6 cm below the road level. This was due to increase in water way from 123 to 238m during the construction of the bridge in period intervening. In Coovum, on the other hand, flood was lower, i.e., 750 cumecs at Napier bridge near the sea. In Chembarambakkam lake, the inflow went as high as 2,310 cumecs with outflow 890 cumecs and water level rose 1.5 cms above M.W.L. In 1985, rainfall over a 10-day period was 94 cms of which maximum one day fall was 32.9 cms.

Fig. 2. shows areas inundated and vulnerable during storms in Madras. Such heavy rainfalls as in 1943, 1978 and 1984 and spill from rivers and hillocks cause heavy damage to roads. As already mentioned, the city itself has three major railway lines passing through it towards CBD and out of road crossings over these lines are in from of subways. Of these three subways get inundated and, though constant pumping is resorted to, they become unpassable for some hours. These cause dislocation to road transport. The railway line and yards in Madras are generally above the ground and get inundated at only a few places whereas soft spot develops in others. These cause dislocation to rail traffic also. Inundation of rail track in Madras area, however, is much less in extent, compared to what happens in Bombay over its suburban lines. In order to meet such problems certain management measures are adopted. They

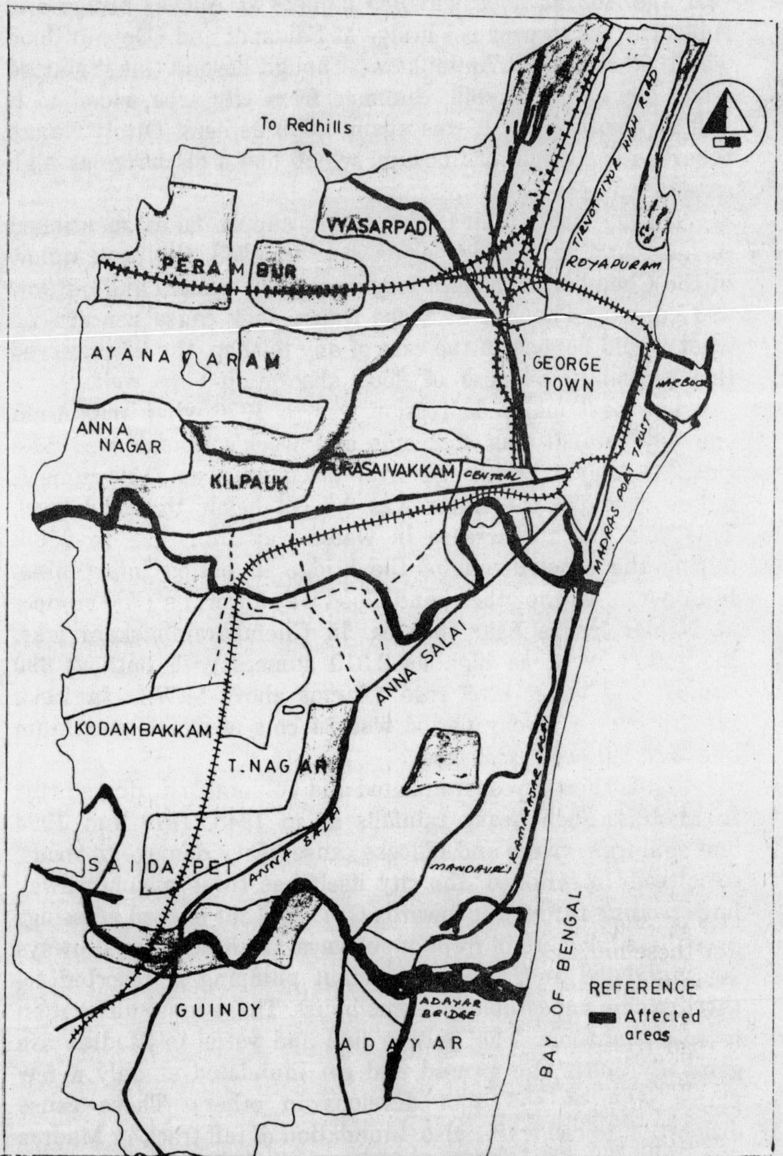

FIGURE 2. APPROXIMATE AREA SUBMERGED DURING NOV. 1976 FLOOD

Fig. 2

involve keeping watch on communication and contact with Meteorological Department, action for alleviating sufferings of people, meeting the emergency situation, monitoring and follow up of repair works. Unusual floods and cyclones being considered as disasters arising out of fury of nature, form part of Disaster Management Action plan of the railways and civil authorities. This paper briefly describes salient parts of such plans.

Emergency Management

There is no separate disaster management organisation available in Madras. However, departmental instructions exist on what action is to be taken and who will assume various responsibilities. Railways have a well laid procedures and responsibilities devolving on various officials. Similar procedures exist in the Madras City Corporation also.

During the emergency, the Meteorological Department issues warnings to the State government, Port, Railways and Corporation and also to public through Radio and TV. Immediately depending on gravity of situation, the Chief Secretary to the State government initiates action for holding consultations and issues instructions on general lines of action. Details are left to various civil, railway and military officials to work out for their respective organisations. Coordination is again done by the Chief Secretary. So far as the city is concerned, the Collector of the District stations at Saidapet directs the actions.

Rail Transport

The Railways' Disaster Management Action Plan forms part of their scheme for prevention of accidents. They have a well set safety organisation which is the permanent co-ordinating agency for action during accidents and disasters. There are control units in railway headquarters and the divisional offices (e.g., one at Madras) which monitor and control train movements round the clock. The Civil Engineering department and the control offices receive the forecast and warning messages from the Meteorological department regularly and whenever an emergency situation is feared the action plan is put into effect. First is to augment the staff in control offices and post duty officers round the clock to monitor the position, advice concerned authorities and convey instructions down the line.

In fact, railways have a regular line patrolling scheme which requires that the railway lines are inspected by foot by one or a pair of patrolmen during nights all through the rainy season. These patrolmen take spot action to warn any trains likely to pass the affected section and prevent mishaps as well as advise the station master on either side to stop traffic in the case of breached to track, submergence of track, boulder or tree falling across track, etc., The station master keeps the control office immediately informed about such situation. During cyclones these units may be strengthened as necessary. Prior to monsoon, they have regular schemes of clearing up all drains and checking up cross drainage works for safety and proper functioning of tracks and structures. In the case of any disasters occurring and traffic getting paralyzed, or delays and dislocation being caused due to heavy storms, the railway action plan envisages

(i) regulation of trains by slowing them or holding up at suitable stations;
(ii) relief to passengers of trains stranded due to line breach on one or both sides; and
(iii) carrying out repairs expeditiously and resuming normal traffic.

The emergency organisation functions till the normalcy is restored. For attending to these activities, suitably equipped relief trains, medical vans and emergency building/track materials including emergency bridge components are kept in readiness all the time. In urban areas and major stations, they have to deal with some additional problems like :

(i) attending to flooding and damages to structures mainly in workshops, sheds and staff colonies (neighborhoods);
(ii) arranging alternative accommodation to staff whose residences are affected due to flooding or heavy wind;
(iii) attending to drainage and water supply and protecting health in staff colonies; and
(iv) ensuring proper communication and power supply in offices, stations and railway colonies.

Apart from laying down instructions regarding procedures for action, they have fixed line of commands, as well as provide for communication and monitoring at higher levels. The railways carry out periodical training programmes for staff in executive, supervisory and field positions on disaster management aspect either as part of their training courses or as special courses.

Road Transport

On the road transport side, the disasters affect the basic road infrastructure, drains and the transport vehicle operation. Arterial roads form part of national highway and the Inner Ring Road is under the State Highways Department, while all other roads are under local authorities. The metro bus transport is under the Palavan Transport Corporation (PTC). The Special Officer of Corporation, local collectors and the Chief Engineer, highways and heads of metro water (for water supply and sanitation) have to set up their own *ad hoc* organisations to deal with the situation.

The PT has a control room which looks after day-to-day operations. This keeps it in contact with local depots and bus terminals and based on feedback on conditions of roads, bridges, underpasses and low lying areas they reorganize their schedules by either cancelling some services of rerouting them. They also have to come to the aid of railways for supplying buses to clear any stranded passengers in sections and to avail of the services of civil authorities for relief work.

City Corporations

There is an Action Plan laid down by the Corporation of Madras for meeting any emergency situation during the rainy season. This is updated every year. It lays down duties of every senior official during emergencies. There is no separate organisation for this purpose. The Special Officer of Corporation is the Chief Coordinator for the relief work in the city area. The plan is brought into effect immediately after receiving 24 hour warning message any impending cyclone, storm, etc., from the Meteorological Department.

In the city there are 454 kms of store water dreading for a road length of 1,800 kms. These include seven arterial drains.

The storm water drains are being added only at the rate of 30 to 40 kms per year due to the paucity of funds.

As a premonsoon arrangement, control offices are set up in September every year in the Secretariat, with Advance Disaster Warning System connected to the Regional Meteorological Office. The Corporation also arranges to have the storm water drains cleared before monsoon (which includes seven arterial drains). The desalting of Buckingham canal and Otteri nallah is to be done by the Public Works Department.

The Action plan of the City Corporation envisages setting up of five relief camps under the charge of a senior officer administration grade lays emphasis on :-

(i) relief to people by shifting them from flood prone areas to public buildings like schools, colleges, and relief camps like Gandhi Mandap, etc.;

(ii) supplying food and medicines to the affected people;

(iii) pumping out water from flood areas specially subways and roads;

(iv) ensuring water supply and proper drainage; and

(v) taking action to restore disrupted transport and communication.

Examples of Impact

The major recent disasters in the form of cyclonic storms followed by heavy rains which struck Madras in 1943, 1976 and 1984. No detailed statistics are available about how transport was affected. Suburban trains were completely disrupted for two days in 1976 and badly affected for two days in 1984. Road transport over some lateral links was affected for two to three days badly. The inter-city services on railways were badly affected in all cases and they had consequent impact on local trains. Working in the railway marcelling yard was also affected.

In 1976, the cost of damage to roads was estimated at Rs. 55 million--equivalent to about Rs. 150 million. A sizeable city area was inundated by spill water due to delay in drainage through available underground drains. Most areas do not have adequate storm water drains. Vysarpadi, Pulianthope, Chintadripet, Kotturpuram and parts of Perambur were most affected and in Vyasarpadi the depth of water was over 80 cms and boats had to be used for rescue purpose.

In November 1985, when rains extended for over a week with two days of concentrated fall, over half of the length of bus route roads and 44 per cent of other roads were affected causing damage to about eight million sq m of surface. Repair costs were estimated at Rs. 329 million, 51 kms out of 454 kms of drains were damaged costing Rs. 51 million, five per cent of street lamps and 10 per cent of cables were also damaged. Total cost of all damages and relief works was around Rs. 450 million. Low areas were again inundated but rivers did not swell so high as in the previous disaster years.

Measures Required to Mitigate Losses

Being located in a cyclone prone area, the natural occurrences cannot be combated. But the adverse consequences to the people and properties can be minimized. In order to reduce the impact of winds on buildings, specially tiled and thatched huts of medium height, trees can be grown on sides of wide roads, neighbourhood avenues and in the residence compounds depending upon the availability of space. This will help the environment also. Madras was known as garden city. It had a lot of avenue trees and most of individual houses used to grow coconut, mango and neem tress in their compounds. But with the rapid growth of apartment type buildings and need for parking space around residences, for growing number of vehicles, this practice is on decline. With priorities shifting towards various aspects of social commitments by the government, the civic authorities by themselves are not able to spend much on planting and protecting avenue trees on roadside. The citizens' awareness to this aspect has to be rekindled and encouragement is to be given to them by the civic authorities initially by planting trees with gabions on road side and encouraging the nearest resident of house owners or Residents' associations to 'own' trees and nurture them.

The drainage condition in general needs improvement, if period of inundation of roads and verges is to be reduced. Longer the water stands on road or verge, deeper it penetrates into the base through cracks in the pavement and makes it weak. Some research is needed to find out most suitable base preparation, pavement design as well as verge protection for roads in the Metropolitan area so that they could become impermeable.

Earlier the areas of storm water drain work is completed, lesser will be the extent of damage to roads. This applies to improvement of arterial drains and cleaning of silt in Bunkingham Canal and Coovum from the MG Railway crossing to outfall. Keeping both Coovum and Adayar free to flow into the Bay by doing periodical dredging of the mouths can help reduce period of inundation of low areas and consequently reduce period of running relief camps. A cost benefit study would clearly show the extend to which the heavy initial investment on these two aspects can be more recumerative than the present periodical expenditure on relief measures.

Improvement of drainage and pumping arrangement at locations of sub-way crossings specially near Reserve Bank, Kannamampet Road and Perambur needs attention.

The railway lines planners have laid railway lines generally high enough to be free from inundation except in the case of a few locations like Guindy-Saidapet, Park and Tondayarpet. No remedial arrangement like lifting of tracks with yard under use can offer a practicable solution. Relocating outside the MMA and using released land for other commercial/residential purposes can be looked into, specially in view of another satellite port being developed to handle coal in Ennore area.

A better control and prewarning system can be adopted by PTC for planning of there bus rescheduling and rerouting at the time of such disasters, so that public may be put to less inconvenience as is done by them in the case of Bandhs at present. A better inter-model transfer and ticketing arrangement between suburban rail system and PTC will be helpful in such cases as it would facilitate commuters in availing of alternative facilities more easily in cases of emergencies.

Conclusion

The impact of disasters caused due to cyclones and storms in Madras is commensurating with the growth of the city. Though their impact on transport system in Madras is felt less than other hardships, reduction of such impact will have indirect benefit in other directions also. Some major capital intensive works like expansion of storm water drains and river outlets, better road designs, relocation of some transport facilities improving water ways in some narrow bridges across Coovum by rebuilding them early have to be accorded priority if frequent dislocations and costly relief measures are to be reduced.

A Select Reading

Sethuraman, A.S., "Flood Plain Management in Central Urban Areas-A Case Study of Madras City". M.F. Thesis, Anna University, 1982.

"Madras Metropolitan Area Traffic and Transport Study" Kirloskar Consultants Report for Madras Metropolitan Development Authority, 1986.

"Disaster Management-An Action Plan"-Southern Railway Safety Organisation, 1990.

"Contingency Plan to Mitigate Floods and Cyclones in Madras City", Corporation of Madras, 1989.

9

Sustainable Development of Groundwater Resources : Lessons from Amrapur and Husseinabad Villages in Junagadh District*

*Tushaar Shah***

This report presents an analytical narrative on groundwater planning and management issues in two villages of Junagadh district, namely, Amrapur in Malya taluka and Husseinabad in Mangalore taluka which represent two classes of implications of the over exploitation of groundwater resources.

Amrapur and Husseinabed represent the conditions that obtain in much of the coastal belt of Saurashtra which, until a decade ago, was so green and agriculturally prosperous as to be popularly called 'Lili Nagher' (Green Creeper). Intensive groundwater irrigation with the onset of the modern pumping technologies in the mid-1959 was all along central to this rural prosperity. Under an encouraging government policy which made subsidies and credit freely available for intensive private groundwater development, the installation of wells with diesel engines or electric pumps increased at a rapid pace especially since 1960; in many area, water loving crops such as sugar cane, banana, fruit orchards, etc., began to replace traditional

---

* The report is based on fieldwork conducted by Dr. Daniel Bromely and the author during 2-9 June 1989 and draws upon discussion with farmers, local leaders, Anil Shah and other members of the AKRSP staff, particularly, Parmesh Shah, Appoorva Oza, Leena, and others who worked closely with us. The analysis benefitted from the author's discussions with Daniel Bromley builds upon and uses the results reported by William Barber's recent inquiry into the geological and other physical characteristics of the aquifers underlying areas.

** Director, Institute of Rural Management, Anand.

crops. Three crops a year became quite common with the help of motorised wells. The amount of water lifted from the coastal aquifers between any two monsoons increased over 10-15 times. As a result, by the late 1960's, the fragile coastal groundwater balance began to develop cracks; in some of the unplying areas, such as Amrapur, separated from the sea by a natural ridge, wells began to dry up in late rabi and summer seasons as happens in the hard rock areas of the south-Indian peninsula; more seriously, in low lying areas closer to the sea, large and increasing areas experienced intrusion sea water into their wells.

The socio-economic backlash that salinity ingress in an area created and the misery it caused especially among the poor have been documented by several authors (Shukla 1985, Menon 1985, Shah 1988). The government responded to the challenge by mounting a programme to construct check dams, bandharas, tidal regulators, and such physical structures with the aim of increasing fresh water recharge and to stave off the pressure of intruding sea water. It was soon found that farmers quickly used up the 'slack' so created as a free 'open access' resource and brought larger areas under well irrigation. The inefficacy of this 'hardware' based strategy to fight saliently ingress has emphasized the need to introduce a more effective common property management of the aquifer at village of sub-region level as the only sustainable method of preserving groundwater intensive rural prosperity.

The main purpose of fieldwork was to explore the possibilities of this happening; and to understand the conditions under which the present open access groundwater use regime could be replaced by a better regulated management regime. This paper describes the experience of raising some of these issues with the people of Amrapur where conditions are somewhat better than in Husseinabad and the scope for cooperative management strategies good. It also presents a somewhat speculative analysis for Husseinabad; this analysis offers some guidelines and ideas of action but falls quite short of an action plan. The last section is essentially an apology for this inadequacy and argues strongly for experimentation and adaptation through a flexible plan of action that involves the two village communities in planning and managing the use of their groundwater resources.

Amrapur

Village Profile and Social Structure

Amrapur is a largish multi-caste village in the Malya taluka of Junagadh district (Fig. 1.); Ismailies, Karadias, Sagars, Lohanas, and lower caste minority communities including Harijans, Rabaris, Bharwads, Mumnas, and Khat Darbars account for over 95 per cent of the village's 2,000 strong population. The bulk of the farm lands are, however, owned and cultivated by the Ismailies, Karadias and the Sagars.

Some of the Harijans and Rabaris got some Sathani land from the Government of Gujarat in 1969; however, this land used to be government wasteland or poor quality; almost all of it is unirrigated and therefore useful only for a kharif crop.

Farming, dairying and trade in agricultural outputs and inputs are major sources of income. Amrapur is the hub of a major trading outfit serving 17 neigbouring villages; this entire trade is controlled by the Lohanas of Amrapur. In agriculture, the bulk of the surpluses are generated on irrigated lands; over half of the irrigated land in the village is owned by Ismailies who account for 25 per cent of the households; Karadias and Sagars claim the bulk of the remaining irrigated land. About 60-70 per cent of the land has some mitigation facilities; almost all Sathani land and the land belonging to marginal farmers have no irrigation and can be used only for the kharif crop. The land holdings of those who own wells are quite large ranging from 15 to 80 bighas (acre=2.5 bighas) with a modal value of around 20 bighas. For non well owners, the modal value would most likely be around five bighas.

The Origin of the Problem

Open, dug wells are the primary source of irrigation in the village; some farmers also lift water from river Magherdi and river Vrajmi when they have water. There are about 320 wells (although the number registered with the talati in 1979-80 in only 210). Over half of these use electrically powered pump sets; the remaining use diesel engine driven pumps. Almost all the framers used five hp motors or engines; 7.5 hp

Figure 1

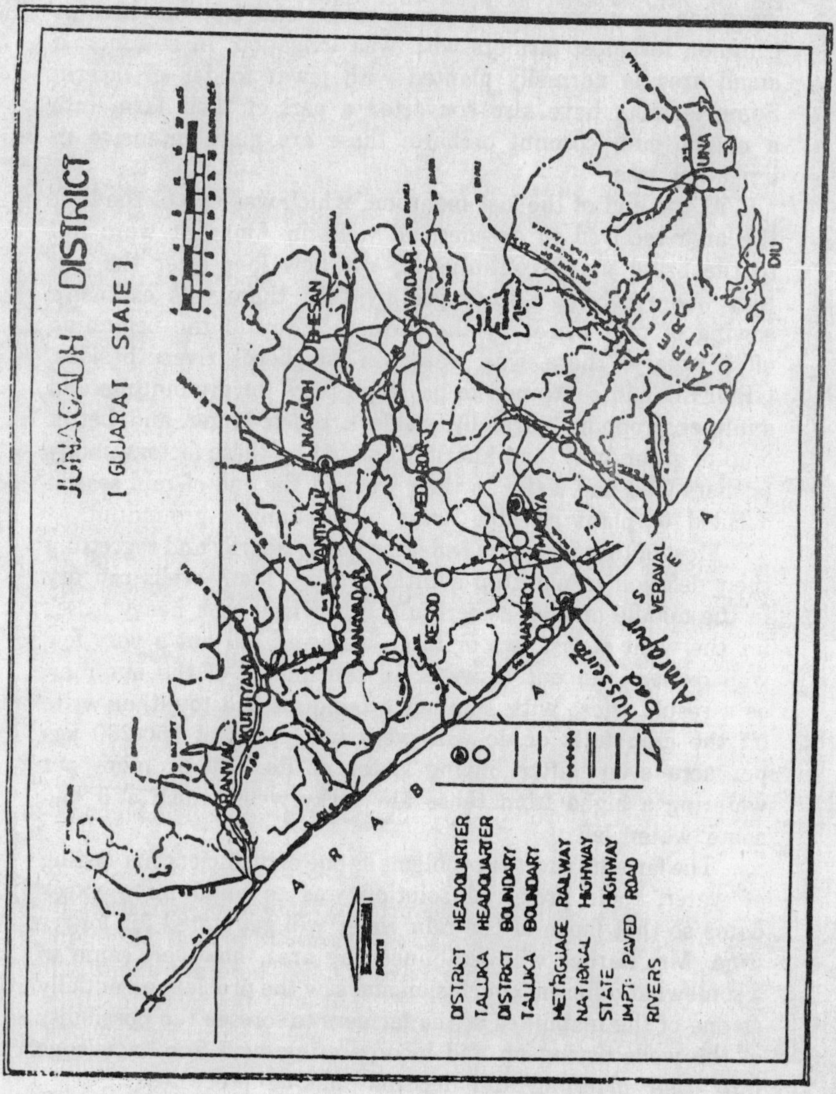
JUNAGADH DISTRICT
[GUJARAT STATE]
DISTRICT HEADQUARTER
TALUKA HEADQUARTER
DISTRICT BOUNDARY
TALUKA BOUNDARY
METRGUAGE RAILWAY
NATIONAL HIGHWAY
STATE HIGHWAY
IMPT: PAVED ROAD
RIVERS
JUNAGADH
BHESAN
VISAVADAR
MENDARDA
VANTHALI
MANAVADAR
KUTIYANA
RANAVAV
KESOD
MANGROL
MALIYA
TALALA
VERAVAL
UNA
DIU
AMRELI DISTRICT
A R A B I A N S E A
Hussain Amirali Road

motors were exceptional.

The monsoonal rainfall in the area ranges between 750-1000 mm. The kharif crop, mostly of groundnut, continues to be the most important crop despite extensive access to well irrigation. In more recent times, a rabi wheat crop has become common for most farmers with well irrigation. In summer, a small area is normally planted with jawar fodder of lucern. Some farmers have also converted a part of their farm into a mango cum coconut orchard; these are quite intensive in irrigation use.

At the end of the last monsoon, which was one of the best the area received in decades, all wells in Amrapur were full to the brim; many continued to overflow long after the last rain was received. Encouraged by this, there was extensive sowing of rabi wheat by the farmers. Even at the beginning of February, there was water in Magherdi river; besides, GROFED had continued to pay high price for groundnuts and summer cropping normally yields a much larger and better crop of groundnut than kharif. Tempted by these factors, many farmers who had water in their wells at the end of rabi season decided to plant sizeable areas with summer groundnut.

Most of these farmers ended up losing heavily and regretting their decision to plant an additional crop. Many wells ran dry in the middle of rabi; as a result, rabi wheat took heavy losses for the want of last two or three watering. All but a very few well owners ran out of water in the middle of the summer; as a result, those with summer groundnut had to either write off the crop fully or do with very low yields of 150-200 kgs per acre even after buying water at Rs. 200 or more per watering a bigha from those few lucky wells which still had some water left.

The farmers saw the problems as one of inefficient harvesting of water; their preferred solution was to build more check dams so that move of the rain water will get stored for longer time. Mr. Barber who examined the area, however, came to a somewhat different conclusion and saw the problem essentially as one of the inabilities of the farmers to foresee the possibility of the wells drying up and incorporating such fore-knowledge into their planning and decision making processes.

Aquifer Characteristics

Fig. 2 presents a map of the village. The village is in a valley; and is surrounded on all the sides by either uplying plains or hillocks. Magherdi, a seasonal river cuts across the village and is met by three small rivulets called Vrajmi, Rakhodio and Jarado. All these then flow into Dadhichi reservoir where water is stored to provide drinking water to several villages of Mangarol taluka. In fact a number of 50 hp pumpsets constantly pump water from the reservoir and borewells; the water is transported several kilometres away through underground pipelines.

The entire valley constitutes the catchment area for the aquifer. In addition, the rivers bring more water which recharges the aquifer. The AKRSP had built two check dams which further increase the recharge and storage (Fig. 2 shows the command areas of the two check dams). Check dam I which was ready by the 1988 monsoon brought considerable benefit to the wells. Enormous storage was provided by check dam II after the first shower of the 1989 monsoon (in Fig. 3, compare (a) just before the shower with (b) just after).

Mr Barber has proposed that the village is underlain by a 'trap' aquifer whose boundaries coincide with the village boundaries; that the aquifer is like a bowl so that the wells located at the center will always have more water and for longer period than those at the rim; that the bowl has a hole in the bottom, as it were, so that conserving water is not a virtue but a great folly since all water not used is lost to the village. In his analysis, thus the aquifer and the wells provide no inter-year storage; the key problem then is (a) to capture as much of the rainfall and river recharge as possible, (b) schedule its utilisation so that water loss to the village from the 'hole in the bottom' is minimised while at the same time ensuring that alkali water is used up before the monsoon, and (c) organise most efficient and equitable use of the available water through suitable community groundwater management system.

We visited about 30 wells and met the owners of some more wells which we could not visit. The wells we visited covered all major topographical zones within the village; for instance, we met well owners in the valley and along the rim,

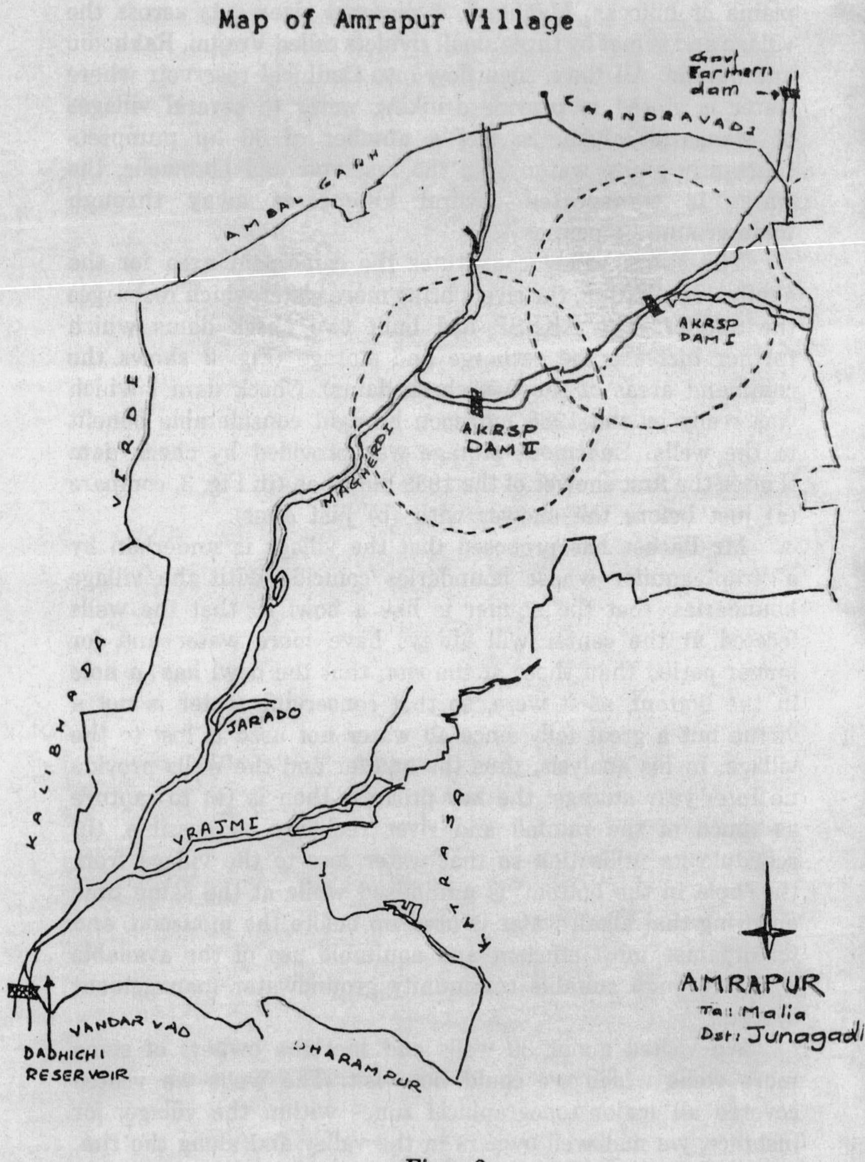
Map of Amrapur Village
Govt
Farmern
dam
CHANDRAVADI
AMBALGADH
AKRSP
DAM I
AKRSP
DAM II
MAGHERDI
VIRDI
KALIBHADA
JARADO
VRAJMI
KATASA
VANDARVAD
DADHICHI
RESERVOIR
DHARAMPUR
AMRAPUR
Ta: Malia
Dst: Junagadh

Figs. 2

Fig. 3

within the river bed, near the river and away from it; near the check dams and away from them; near the Dadhichi reservoir and away from it, etc. These interviews suggested evidence contrary to Mr Barber's theses; many wells on the rim had good recharge even just before the monsoon with some being able to pump almost continuously; on the contrary most wells in the center, including many near the river and the dams and one or two within the river bed had no water at all. Indeed no pattern seemed to emerge which would explain why some wells had water and others did not. We visited wells less than 50 feet apart with one having plentiful of water and the other completely dry suggesting independent sources of recharge for such wells. In contrast, in some areas, there was a major element of well-interference among neighbouring wells with the attendant problem of externality. In one such case, we came across, the owner of the well which suffered reduced yield due to the pumping of the neighbouring well upstream purchased water from the latter at Rs 10/- hour.

We inquired if the farmers had a theory of their own to explain how the aquifer of the village behaved; several were offered but most turned out to be piecemeal though credible. Farmers operate under conditions of uncertainty right from the point of decision about digging a well. Striking water at the first attempt was uncommon; we met a farmer who had spent over Rs. one lakh digging five unsuccessful wells. Even if one struck water, there was no way of being sure as to how long will it last during the year. If over years of differing rainfalls, one developed some working knowledge of the well's behaviour, that too would be invalidated as more new wells come up in the neighbourhood, check dams are built, and more deep bores are sunk behind the Dadhichi tank which would 'steal' water from underneath the village wells.

Farmers are found to respond to this uncertainty in a variety of ways. Most make sure that they make several (2-4 being common but several having more than 5) vertical and horizontal bores at the bottom of their huge well so as to capture all possible sources of recharge. Those who have resources dig two or three productive wells at different locations in their farms; in a few such cases, we found that if one wall did not have water, the other did.

Each farmer seemed to have identified, from experience, some kind of 'leading indicators' which help them to predict, in some sense, the likely direction of the behavior of their wells. For instance, a series of well owners along the river suggested that as soon as the river begins to dry and water level drops below a certain level, they know that it would not be long before their wells begin to suffer major declines in yields. All these farmers begin to pump furiously from this point on trying to claim as much of the remaining water as possible presumably wasting a good deal of it. This competitive pumping' must, to a great extent, hasten the pace of depletion of the acquifer. Horse power linked power tariff accompanied by reasonably good electricity supply has further encouraged this behaviour.

Though our interviews were unstructured, we collected for each well information on (a) diameter of the well in feet (b) depth to the bottom and the number of vertical and horizontal bores inside the well (c) current depth to the water level in the well (d) hours of pumping needed to empty the well and (e) hours taken for the well to refill. These unstructured interviews also provided us some clues about the pumping behaviour of well owners especially towards the end of rabi and through the summer.

Normally, during and after a good monsoon, most wells can be pumped continuously since the rate of recharge to the well far exceeds the rate of withdrawal; in some well, the water table would not fall at all while in most it would fall but only by a few feet even after a full day's pumping and would be restored in a few hours. During and after the middle of rabi season, this situation would begin to change somewhat; water table would fall by several feet after a day's pumping. In summer, continuous pumping becomes impossible in most wells; our interviews suggested that the well would be emptied after pumping between 10 minutes to six hours depending on the well; and it would take between six to 48 hours before the well can be pumped again for the same duration.

Individual and Group Strategies

From our discussions with farmers, there seemed four district conditions of recharge in the wells: first two are situations in which 'continuous pumping' is possible; in the first of these, the rate of recharge clearly exceeds the rate of discharge so that the other level in the well in not affected at all by pumping; in the second, the rate of recharge is marginally less than the rate of discharge so that is would take several days and nights of continuous pumping before the well begins to get emptied and pumping would need to be discontinued for some hours before the well is full.

The next two are 'wait and pump' phases ('uleri uleri' in local language) in which the rate of recharge is much less than the rate at which water is extracted. In the third phase, the well can be pumped through out the day and will get recharge during the night; in the fourth phase, recharge becomes so small that the well can be pumped only for a few hours, often for a few minutes, before the well gets emptied and needs a day or several days to recharge. In these later two phases of 'wait and pump', water use programming becomes important. It is also largely during these phases that farmers become aware about the well interference externality and indulge in 'strategic behaviour'. All the wells in the village can be classified according to their conditions of recharge at any time point. Fig. 4 maps the sample wells in the village according to their recharge condition at the time of fieldwork.

Given the location of a well with a recharge source, the static storage in the well S can be written, in a simplified form as

$$S = \pi.\ (d/2)^2.\ h$$

where d=diameter of the well below the highest recharge point and h=H*-Ho with H*=depth to the besalt layer and H0=depth to the water level in the well.

If x defines the rate of discharge of the pump and r, the rate of recharge, both in cubic feet per second, then the hours for which the well can be pumped continuously can be written as [S/(x-r)]/3600 and the time the empty well will take to recharge to the pre-pumping water level will be [S/r*3600].

We can also define the four sets of recharge conditions as:

Phase I r>>>x : continuous pumping
Phase II x>r; but [S/(x-r)]/(3600x24) = several day
Phase III x=(1.5 to 2.5) r and/or S = large;

so that $[S/(x-r)]/3600 = 8$ to 12 hours

Phase IV $x = (10 \text{ to } 30)r$ and S = small;

so that $[S/(x-r)]/3600 = 0.5$ to 3 hours

The options available to individual well owners, especially in Phases III and IV, and to the community as a whole are:

a. increase the value of r, the rate of recharge to their wells and/or of S, storage of their wells below their recharge points.

b. suspend summer cropping all together and/or adapt their cropping plans so that they can do with less water especially in rabi and summer thereby reducing the required x.

c. develop better understanding of the behaviour of their wells so as to be able to do better crop planning.

Some of the ways in which these can be done are presented in Fig. 4.

There are large variations in the individual responses to the water conditions. Kamabhai, and Ismaili small farmer, for example, followed a two-pronged strategy which was different from other farmers. Most well owners have 2-4 bores at the bottom of the well; Kamabhai made 15, most of them horizontal, to capture greater recharge. Whereas most wells are large in diameter at the top and become progressively smaller as they go down, Kamabhai's well was much bigger inside (especially below what he thought were the recharge points) than at the top. Kamabhai's well could be pumped continuously for days when we visited it and is well known in the village as one of the most productive and dependable wells and he attributes it to the two changes he made in the design.

The explanation he offered made sense in terms of our simple analytical framework of recharge conditions; the static storage S is largely determined by the recharge rate and the storage space available below the points where the well receives horizontal recharge. Since his well affords greater storage during the night when pumping is discontinued, he can pump through the day uninterrupted. He also argues that one of the problems of the wells which reduces to 'wait-and-pump' status early in the summer is that they get smaller in area as one goes down and therefore offer less scope for storage to build up when the well is not pumped

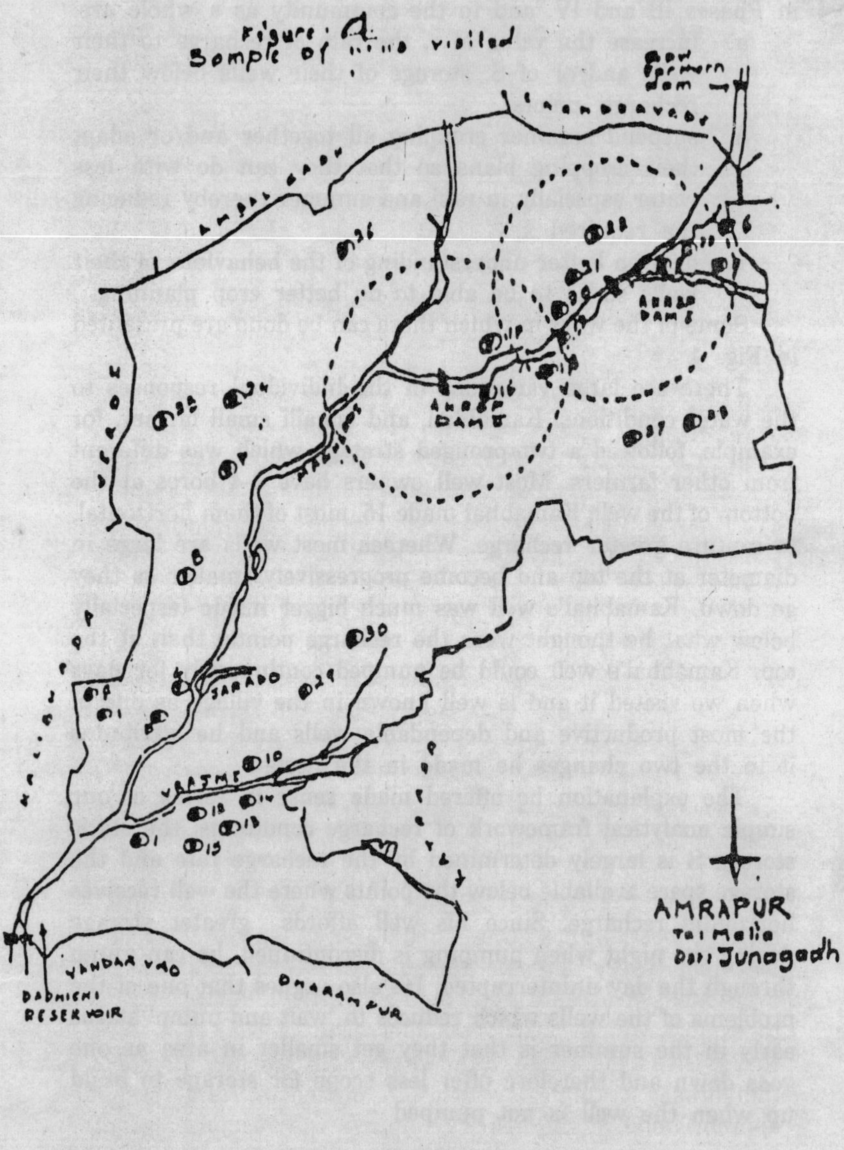
Figure: A
AMRAP DAM
AMRAP DAMS
JARADO
VRAJMI
VANDAR VAD
DHARAMPUR
DADHICHI RESERVOIR
AMRAPUR
Tal Malia
Dist Junagadh

Fig. 4

Individual and Group Strategies for Groundwater Management

	Individual strategies	Group strategies
1. Increase r, the rate of recharge	Farm pond (lined?) as recharge source; exploit deeper aquifer; more bores; bigger diameter below the recharge point	More check dams; reduce pumping from beyond Dadhichi tank;
2. Reduce x, the requirement of water	Reduce summer cropping; use piped conveyence and sprinklers.	Group decision on extent and mix of summer cropping; socialisation of ground-water
3. Better crop and water use planning	Better understanding of one's well and its interaction with the aquifer	Better understanding of interaction between wells; effecient water markets.

Anoth · unusual decision Kamabhai took was to leave a part of his farm unirrigated and intensively apply his scarce water to only a part of his land which he has converted into an orchard.Kamabhai was happy with the outcome and his orchard looked quite good. This is something no other farmer had done; every one was applying water (perhaps too) thinly over extensive areas and it would be worthwhile for the AKRSP to explore which of the two approaches is superior. We felt that wise farmers like Kamabhai might provide elements of individual strategies which, if presented and extended appropriately, might help to improve the responses of other farmers.

For viable group strategies, the most important condition is a shared and improved understanding among well owners of (a) aquifer conditions, (b) interaction between one's well and the acquifer, and (c) interaction among different wells. In the contest of Amrapur, creating such understanding would imply, among other things, mapping of all the wells over the year according to the four sets of conditions discussed earlier. Such mapping would then form the basis of all discussion, extension and negotiation on water use strategies within the village fora. Hypothetically, the mapping for a typical year can be developed over weeks by individual well owners wishing to understand their wells better. Each well owner may be provided studying the ways of enterprising and a proforma which he may complete and turn in to the Gram Vikas Mandal (GVM) every fortnight or month; his main incentive in completing the proforma can be a periodic analysis of his own well to be prepared and furnished to him by the GVM. The GVM will store information on each well and construct analysis for each well as well as all the wells together. Increased and shared understanding of water management issues will get generated by the very process involved in such analysis; at the same time, once, one or two years' analyses become available, they will form stronger basis for community water management strategies.

Husseinabad

Village Profile

Husseinabad village of Mangarol taluka is about the same size as Amrapur with a population of about 2,000 but has just over 1,200 acres of cultivated area. Unlike Amrapur, Husseinabad is predominantly Muslim; the village was settled at the beginning of the century by Sheikh Hussien of Mangarol; hence the name Husseinabad. The village is situated on the bank of river Noli. The river is seasonal and the government has built a series of dams to conserve and store water just before the river flows into the sea. The Sheikh had built a large dam near the neighbouring village of Shaikhpur. From the reservoir of the dam, a canal was built to transport water to Husseinabad. The village elders informed us that before Independence and even until 1965, the canal was used for irrigation by farmers. Over years, however, due to siltation, water was not able to flow easily into the canal. In 1967, the government decided to repair and enlarge the dam; further, the government installed a 100 metres pipeline to convey water to the canal. This fix never worked; and after the renovation of the dam, whatever little water earlier flowed into the canal stopped.

Mango and coconut orchards have dominated the land use pattern in the village and are a major source of income. Some crops are also grown. In kharif, most farmers grow groundnut; in rabi, many grow wheat and mung. Wells are the only source of irrigation although on the river bank, a few farmers are able to pump water directly from the river.

Salinity Problem

Unlike Amrapur which is over 10 kms away from the sea and at a higher altitude, Husseinabad is much closer to the sea. Indeed, one can see the sea from some fields of the village. As a result, while the three-year drought that lasted till 1987 left Amrapur with only a relative water shortage, it left Husseinabad in deep trouble. A third of Husseinabad's wells located on fields closer to the sea become saline. Except for some days during the rains, all water pumped from these wells now is unfit for irrigation. The fields in these parts have suffered major decline in the yields of all crops except kharif groundnuts. In the next two or three years, it will no longer be possible to take any irrigated crops on these lands. Coconut yields have declined by 30 to 70 per cent; coconuts mature faster on these lands but that does not help as the size of the coconuts has shrunk; the bulk of the coconut output has jelly instead of water and therefore fetches only Re 0.50 to 0.80 per piece as compared to Rs. 1.50 it fetched earlier.

The conditions of the farmers located in the saline zone is desperate; and that is true about large as well as small farmers. We met two owners of large orchards close to the sea some distance from Husseinabad; both earned most of their income from coconut; their earnings have, over the past decade, declined to 10-12 per cent of their pre-salinity levels. We also met several small holders who were in a more miserable state. One young farmer out of these had already reached the phase where he had begun to live off his assets; he had sold off his buffaloes last year and his pair of bullocks only last week.

Three Zones

These farmers are located in that part of Husseinabad where groundwater and land have become fully saline; somewhat further inland is another district zone where well water has just begun to turn saline; salinity levels are low and it is still possible to use well water for irrigation. Soils in this middle zone have not been affected by salinity. However, it is commonly understood that it is only a matter of a drought year or two before the saline zone extends itself to engulf these lands (Fig. 5).

In inland areas, farmers from the sea are still completely unaffected by salinity. The wells here have fresh water during and after the monsoon and in the rabi and summer seasons. These farmers are not yet alive to the salinity problem; their problem is the quantity of water. Rough estimates provided by a group of well owners suggest that about 50 wells are in the saline zone close to the sea, some 100 are in the middle zone with mild salinity levels and another 100 in the inland zone which has still not been affected by the salinity.

The quality of water and its quantity are found to be inversely related in Husseinabad. In the saline zone, where water has high salinity content, the wells abound with water. As one moves inland the water quality improves but the well yields decline. If the records of other such villages in the area are any guide, in the next few years the entire village will suffer from acute salinity problem. Barber's view has been that the salinity can be pushed back and the productivity of the lands restored completely over a period of 30 years but only when all the well owners restrict their pumping to the wells to the fresh water recharge alone.

Farmer Responses on Restricted Pumping

We asked individuals and groups of people about what they thought ought to be done to retrieve the situation. The first stock answer received was that only the government could do something about it; and that all feasible solutions were

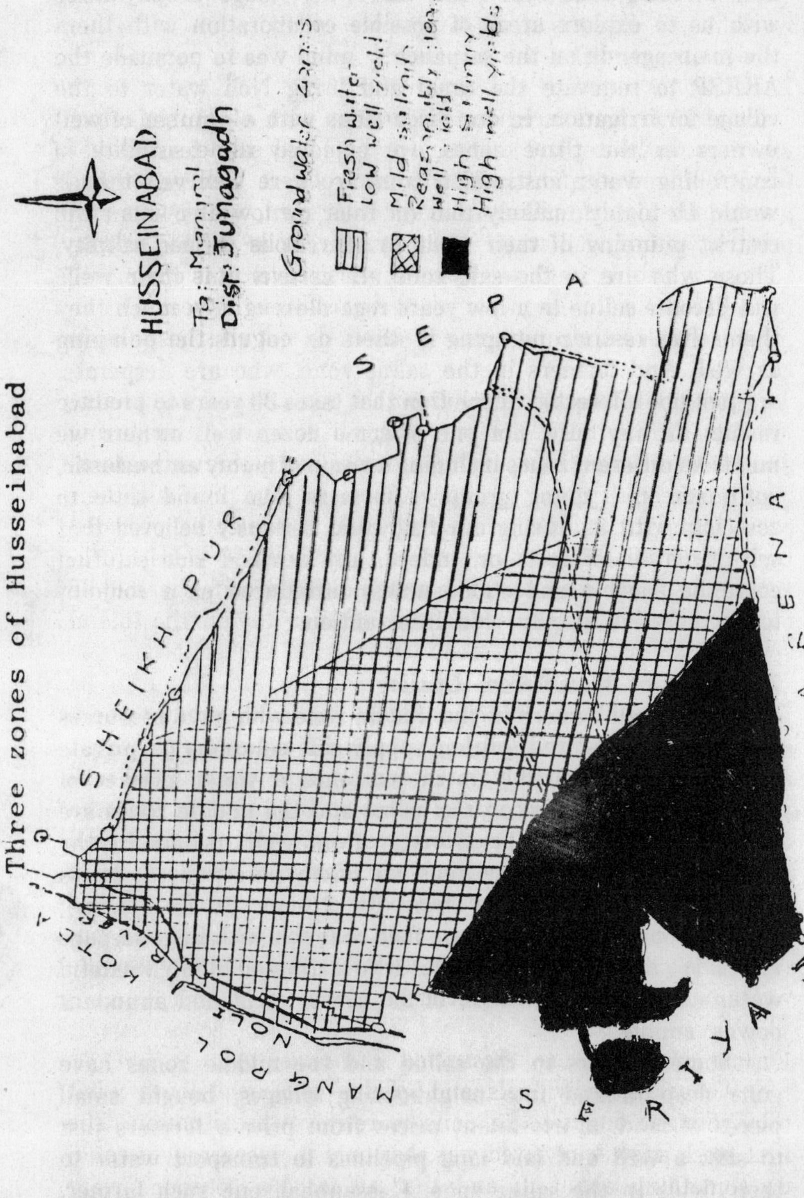

Fig. 5 : Three Zones of Husseinabad

those which had something or the other to do with increasing the supply of fresh water brought from outside. Indeed, in the first meeting that Anil Shah had with village people along with us to explore areas of possible collaboration with them the main agenda on the sarpanch's mind was to persuade the AKRSP to renovate the canal and bring Noli water to the village for irrigation. In our discussions with a number of well owners in the three zones, we explored the feasibility of controlling water abstraction from wells; it emerged that is would be highly unlikely that on their own, well owners will restrict pumping of their wells to prevent or reduce salinity. Those who are in the safe zone are certain that their wells will become saline in a few years regardless of how much they themselves restrain pumping if others do not restrict pumping as well. And farmers in the saline zone, who are desperate, are just not interested in solution that takes 30 years to produce results. In any case, not one of some dozen well owners we met from different zones including a group of highly enthusiastic, optimistic and young group of farmers who found time to associate with us during our fieldwork, seriously believed that self-regulation of sorts or, indeed, any demand side solution could be feasible and stable unless introduced as a conjoint to an effective supply side intervention.

Transport of Water from Outside

Many well owners in the middle zone who have resources have already explored quicker supply side solutions on private initiative. There already is in existence a water market of sorts in which farmers in the saline and the middle zones are buying limited amounts of water from well owners in the inland zone. These transactions are highly personalized; prices charged vary a great deal (from Rs. 2/hour to Rs 8/hour); water is conveyed through open field channels with huge seepage losses. We met an old well owner who attributed highly wasteful water use to the imposition of flat power tariff and abundant power supply.

Some farmers in the saline and the middle zones have gone deep in-land into neighbouring villages, bought small pieces of land at exorbitant prices from private farmers just to sink a well and laid long pipelines to transport water to their fields in the saline zone. Hassanbhai, one such farmer, paid Rs. 6,000 for a one guntha piece (1/40 the of an acre) to dig such a well whereas the market value of irrigated land is Rs. 40-50,000 per acre. In a way, in profiteering from land sales for wells, the farmer who sold this piece is imposing a high cost on his village since, if this trend gathers momentum, it must either result in progressive spread of salinity in inland areas or, in any case, the depletion of the inland aquifers.

There are elaborate contracts, formal as well as informal in laying pipelines for long distance (1 to 3 kms) transport of water. It the pipelines pass through government lands, special permission has to be secured and rent paid. If the pipelines pass through private fields, consideration has to be offered normally in the form of assured irrigation service. In one such case, the well owner had to offer 12 hours irrigation every week at a price which was slightly below the market. In one case, the farmer with his field under which the pipeline passed broke off from the group and dismantled the pipes passing from his field thus ruining the farmers further away from the well.

One of the best known efforts to transport fresh water into saline zones is offered by the Lohej Irrigation Cooperative in Mangarol taluka which transports water from village Kantasa through a 10,000 pipeline to serve 150 members of the co-operative. Lohej became saline as far back as in the 1960's. Arjanbhai, a remarkably brave and intelligent man, who was the Sarpanch of the village at that time thought up the scheme and secured government assistance to install the Rs. 1.5 lakh project. In 1978, when the first well turned saline, he got an SFDA grant to go further inland and sink another well in Kantasa village. The old well too continues to function; however, it can be pumped for fresh water only during kharif and rabi. The new well is a large well--some 25' in diameter and 50' in depth; a horizontal pipe bored into the wall of the well links it to a pond which must be serving as a good recharge source. Two 7.5 hp motors pump water non-stop into a 25' high chamber from where water is conveyed through underground pipes. There are also two eight hp diesel engines as standby. A secretary, a water clerk and two machine drivers constitute the team paid by the co-operative to manage its affairs. The cooperative has also invested in a tractor which it hires out to members as well as non-members.

The area served by the system has declined by half since 1978; as soils become more saline, farmers need more fresh water to flush the salts out. The area served in a typical year recently has been as follows :

Area Irrigated by the Lohej Irrigation Cooperative

Season	Main crop	Area served (in bigha)	Pumping hours
Kharif	Groundnut	300	1200
Rabi	Wheat	100	2000
Summer	Bajri	100	2400
All		500	5600

Only a fraction of the village farm households are members of the cooperative; further, the co-operative can serve only a fraction of its own members' land. While deciding on a season's irrigation schedule, priority is accorded to the needs of the farmer with less than five acres; if there is spare capacity left after their needs are met, additional irrigation is offered on request. Nonmembers take only a rainfed kharif crop; so do members on their land falling outside the command of the system. During the drought year, many members found their relatives from saline areas camping with them in search of fodder. The cooperative decided to suspend normal cropping schedule and every one grew only fodder; the cooperative also provided water to non members to grow fodder. This helped the village and many other families from the saline areas to survive the drought.

Members have their own private wells on their fields within the command; Arjanbhai gave us to understand that although there are no formal restrictions on their pumping their wells, most members of their own avoid pumping their wells especially in summer. In kharif and early rabi when there is some fresh water charge, framers pump their own wells but that is safe. In summer, no member pumps his well since everyone knows that it will affect his soil. If this is indeed true, it established at least one point: that self regulation can be generated with an effective supply side intervention.

Options

There are two ways Husseinabad and other villages in the area suffering similar condition will go first, without a major initiative to change the current trend, it would take between three to 10 years or 2-3 drought years before the entire village land becomes saline; in this event, the farm output and employment would decline to about a 10th of the present level; and majority of the population will get pauperised and have to shift elsewhere for livelihood. The second way it can go is for a new ecological equilibrium to be established in the village through: (a) effective enforcement of checks on the withdrawal and wasteful use of groundwater; (b) planned efforts to increase recharge and harness rainwater in surface structures; (c) import of fresh water from points further inland without disrupting the groundwater balance there; and (d) changing cropping patterns and plans which can be sustained either with modest amounts of fresh water of which can tolerate saline water.

Of these, (b) and (c) and, to some extent, (d) which would require extensive interface with agricultural research establishment can be undertaken with ease by institutions like the AKRSP; these will, no doubt, delay the doom by a few more years, however, as current experience with government programmes has suggested, the slack created by (b) and (c) will most likely get used up by farmers to increase their irrigated area rather than for establishing a new ecological equilibrium. For this, the village community needs to evolve demand side interventions which involve making and enforcing new rules of the game.

The responses we received to suggestions about demand side interventions was usually lukewarm and often outright negative. Those whose wells have fresh water still would have no part of it ; those whose wells do not, just do not care. Professor Bromley suggested that compliance to some rules and norms be the precondition to AKRSP involvement in the village. This would work if the village community believes that AKRSP can deliver something substantial for each of them; it might also work if someone people believe in succeeds in helping all or the majority of the community members to share the vision of the new equilibrium which would leave everyone better off and commit themselves to the action and sacrifice needed now to realise that vision.

Lessons

Our study of Amrapur and Husseinabad (and the work that the AKRSP intends to do in these villages) is significant only to the extent that they represent two typologies of conditions; as a result, lessons drawn too will be useful largely to the extent they relate to the typology of conditions rather than the specificities of each village. For the next ten years of so, the Amrapur problem can be largely resolved by an assortment of physical structures that AKRSP can put up to retain and increase the recharge to wells; likewise in Husseinabad, conditions can by temporarily improved by the AKRSP rehabilitating the old canal and using it as a source of fresh recharge. But what would be more important and useful is to understand what would it take the village communities themselves, with some outside support, to develop their own internal capacities to cope with such problems and to institute self-correcting mechanisms (SCMs). What would also be important and useful to understand are ways in which macro-level policies--legal, infrastructural, and others might support the development of such localized self--correcting mechanisms.

All the SCMs one can think of in this particular context would involve either enforcement of internal mechanisms for equitable regulation of water use or developing new sources of fresh water or both. In either case, some form of community organisation would be needed with a widely acceptable authority structure.

Present experience suggests that, on their own, it is highly unlikely that such SCMs will evolve except where leaders like Arjanbhai chance to apply themselves to such problems. Although all such studies which ascribe local successes to capable local leaders seem to lead one to a blind alley, in our field work we came across several young people who might well be the 'Arjanbhais' of their respective villages if only being a leader did not impose a high personal cost in terms of resources, time and effort. This cost means that besides being willing and able to assume the leadership role, the potential contender must be so well off and ably supported that he can afford to neglect his personal affairs. In course of our discussion,

Bromely mentioned the importance of restoring traditional local authority structures in better management of common property resources. It is doubtful if this is possible in these villages; but it certainly seems within the realm of possibility to draft more potential leaders into the task of creating SCMs by reducing the personal cost of assuming leadership. Experimentation alone can help us identify how best to do this; and NGOs like the AKRSP might take a lead in this regard.

Given the presence of good local leadership, the process of community organisation around water management issues can be best started by involving water user groups in understanding the technical relationships between the location and pumping of wells, recharge sources, aquifer characteristics and interaction between different wells. Such shared understanding can form a sound basis for community planning and management of water resources. The involvement of individual well owners in such a process can be strengthened if such involvement also helps them understand their own well better and to use it more creatively. In the process, mechanisms should be created for the well owners to share their new knowledge and understanding with other well owners. Over time, such a process would heighten the awareness among well owners of the various inter-dependencies and the opportunities for better community management of water resources. Such a process would also be essential to community initiatives in (a) identifying new sources of recharge and surface water and using resources to develop them; (b) evolving and enforcing mechanisms for equitable regulation of water extraction and use; and (c) optimal water use planning. The scheme such as the one outlined earlier for Amrapur may eventually result in such community initiatives which may help in macro level policies. Such macro level policies can support or discourage the emergence of SCMs and the individual behaviour that accentuates the problem. For instance, throughout our fieldwork, we were told that flat charge for power encourages profligate use of water because the incremental pumping costs under flat power tariff become very low. In principle, the options here are two fold : (a) to switch to pro-rata power charge based on meter readings as before June

1987; while this will make water costlier to lift on the margin, it will by no mean guarantee regulation of water use to the desired level and (b) continue with the flat power price regime but use judiciously planned restrictions on power supply for pumping so as to limit water extraction to desired levels. There are many operational and political issues involved in this; however, it needs to be stressed that power supply and pricing policies can be a potent instrument of groundwater regulation in the typologies of areas represented by our two villages.

Legal interventions too can, in principle, help. In Burma, for example, a 1930 Groundwater Act is believed to have effectively regulated the rate of establishment of wells in areas with precarious groundwater balance through a system of licensing. In India, however, most researchers and development practitioners have serious reservations about the enforcement of groundwater laws. Experience with the implementation of siting and licensing norms, in force in most states, support these doubts. Political opposition is likely to be another factor that may reduce the effectiveness of legal interventions; in Gujarat, for example as groundwater Act passed in the assembly over a decade ago is yet to be made into a law.

In the long run, aggregate planning of water resource development in the State and the regions would have to take into account the high pay-offs of bringing surface water to coastal areas with fragile aquifers. It is somewhat irony that mega--projects like the Narmada should increase surface water supplies in areas like Kheads, Baroda, etc., which already have large groundwater recharge and surface water resource while additional surface water supplies could avoid so much misery in coastal Saurashtra.

A Select Reading

Menon, Rs (1986) Saurashtra: Teras f Salt *India Today*, February 15, Bombay

Shah, Tushaar (1988) Externality and Equity Implication of Private Exploitation of Groundwater Resources *Agricultural Systems* 28 (1988) : 1-21

Shukla, S (1985) Salinity Ingress in the Coastal Areas of Katch and Saurashtra (Gujarati) *Gujarat*, 16(8), June 21-27, Gandhinagar

10

Landslide Correction Techniques

*P. Jagannatha Rao**

Every year, hill regions of the country sustain damages at hundreds of locations, due to incidences of landslides and other slop process, high and small. Extensive damages are caused to the roads, buildings, forests, plantations and agricultural fields. Damages may be partial or total, requiring costly remedial measures to restore the damaged facilities to the original or usable state. Often, the damaged facilities may have to be abandoned and new ones created at a great cost. Loss of life as well as loss of property have occurred as a result of landslides. Figs. 1 and 2, show bridges and houses damaged by landslides. Fig. 3 shows subsidence of road due to mass movements in the hill slope.

Landslides are primarily triggered by natural causes including heavy or substantial rainfalls, sudden cloud bursts, earthquakes, etc., and have a random nature both in time and location and thus are difficult to predict. The slope movements may occur relatively rapidly or may take the shape of slow subsidence. On the other hand, landslides caused primarily by human activities arise many a times due to inadequate consideration given to the stability of natural slopes affected by such activities. Hence such landslides can be controlled and damages minimised by taking precautionary or preventive measures in the shape of proper surveys, sampling and testing, design and evaluation of slopes, so that adequate stability of slopes is maintained and no adverse effects arise.

---

* Deputy Director and Head, Geotechnical Engineering Division, Central Road Research Institute, New Delhi.

Fig. 1 : Collapse of bridge due to landslide in clayshale stratum adjoining the abutement.

Figs. 2 : Extensive damage to building due to landslide.

Frequency of Landslide Incidence in Various Hill Ranges of India

The severity and frequency of landslide incidence can broadly be grouped as below, for different hill ranges of India:

(i) Himalayas	Very high to high
(ii) North-Eastern hill ranges	High
(iii) Western Ghats and Nilgiris	High to moderate
(iv) Eastern Ghats	Low
(v) Vindhyas	Low

Economic and other Losses from Landslides

Statistics concerning the number of landslides and the monetary losses occurring therefrom are not available at a single place and the data are also probably not collected in a systematic manner. It is therefore, difficult to have a representative figure for even the direct losses arising from landslides. However, based on general experiences concerning the frequency and magnitude of the incidence of landslides, and the cost required for the restoration works, a rough estimate of the monetary loss of Rs. 100 to 150 crores per annum at the current prices, for the country as a whole, is probably on the conservative side.

From consideration of defence, economy, trade, commerce and safety of the people, the development and adoption of effective technologies to mitigate and manage the landslide hazards, is a national need that should be accorded high priority.

Some Catastrophic Landslide Occurrences in India

Some examples of extensive damages arising from landslides due to heavy rainfall, cloud bursts, earthquakes, etc., are given in Table 1.

Table 1

Case Histories of Some Landslides (in brief)

Place	Date	Damages
A. *Landslides due to heavy rainfall and cloud bursts.*		
(i) *Eastern Himalaya*		
Sikkim and North Bengal	1968	Wide spread mass movement of soil in the form of slides caused death and devastation due to cloud bursts of the order of 160cm. in 36 hours. River bed rose by 10 mt at places resulting in destruction of large number of bridges including the famous Anderson bridge at Tista Bazar.
Darjeeling	1973	Heavy rains resulted in numerous slides and subsidence resulting in disruption of road and rail communication on Siliguri-Darjeeling sector for considerable periods.
North Bengal	1975	Tista, Jaldhaka and Diana rivers were flooded. Wide spread landslides and floods rendered 4500 people homeless.
Sikkim and Darjeeling	1976	Landslides in Sikkim and Darjeeling area due to heavy rainfall and consequent floods in Tista valley due to which several people died.

North Sikkim	1983	Wide spread incidence of landslides and damages occurred. A number of bridges were washed away and highway was blocked. Traffic could not move for two months on the affected stretch. Extensive loss of property and life also occurred. The army camp belonging to Border Roads Organisation was completely washed away.
(ii) *Kashmir Himalaya*		
Jammu and Kashmir	1971	Wide spread landslides caused disruption of traffic and communication systems.
Jammu and Kashmir	1972	Wide spread landslides caused damage to life and properties.
Jammu and Kashmir	1973	Landslide cut off Kashmir valley from rest of the country.
Jammu and Kashmir	1975	Landslide caused death of people and disrupted transportation system for three days.
Jammu and Kashmir	1977	Srinager-Leh road was blocked due to landslides.
Jammu and Kashmir	1979	Extensive damages due to landslides created problems to the traffic.
Jammu and Kashmir	1986	Landslide incidences created severe problems in Jammu and Kashmir area along NH-1A.

(iii) *UP Himalaya*

Uttar Pradesh	1952	The Kaliasaur landslide, initiated in 1952, occurring almost every year, damaged the road considerably. The area suffered a major landslide on 19th Sept. 1989, which had blocked three-fourth of the river flowing about 100m below the road level.
Uttar Pradesh	1970	Alaknanda river caused considerable loss of life. Many bridges, houses and entire villages were washed away. More than 223 people were killed.
Uttar Pradesh	1971	Heavy rainfall and erosion of hill slopes caused damming of river and burst involving loss of life, property and disruption of communications. One village Belakuchi was completely washed away. Due to the vast devastation it is termed as Alaknanda Tragedy.
Uttar Pradesh	1976	Slide on Mussorie bypass (Mussoorie-Chamba Road) creating disruption of communication and many houses suffered extensive damages.
Uttar Pradesh	Frequent	Kathgodam-Nainital state highway and Kathgodam-Almore state highway are both affected by landslides during the monsoons.

(iv) *Western Ghats and Nilgiris*

Kerala	1985	Extensive landslides in the hilly areas of Kerala took place.
Western Ghats	1978-1979	The unprecedented rain caused more than 100 landslides with in area of 250 sq km. Nearly 200 landslides were recorded in Niligiris. Such severity of disastrous landslides has not been felt in any part of the country so far.
Western Ghats	1983	A major length of NH-17 in the western ghats was damaged by landslides.

B. *Landslides due to earthquakes*

Kashmir	1885	Large scale landslide took place due to which about 6,000 people were killed.
Himachal Pradesh	1905	Massive landslides and rock fall, etc., took place and about 2,000 people were killed.
Assam	1950	Extensive landslides and rock fall, collapse of buildings, roads, bridges and loss of life took place.
Himachal Pradesh	1975	Severe earthquake disturbed the stability of the area permanently due to numerous landslides, subsidence, cracks, etc., along Hindustan Tibet road.

Landslide Hazard Zonation

During the last two decades, the use of landslide hazard zonation maps has gained wide spread currency in different parts of the world. Basically, the methodology of landslide zonation mapping classifies different areas of the hill slope according to the degree of potential stability or instability. This enables the identification of zones having equal degree of risk of failure. Such zones could then be plotted on a map depicting the landslide potential of the hill slope. With the help of such maps a road alignment passing through zones of high stability rating can be chosen, thereby minimising the risk of landslide incidence or an area for development of housing estate may be identified or other uses specified. It is strongly emphasised that hazard evaluation data should be available before planning of a project is taken up, so that safe and economical solutions can be formulated.

Broadly speaking, landslide zonation maps are prepared on the basis of extensive and intensive surveys of the slopes. The relevant geological, geotechnical, geomorphological and hydrological factors that control the stability of the slope and kind of paragenetic associations have to be considered, often semi-quantitatively. Various parameters and the associated sub-parameters affecting the slope stability are given a numerical rating and the cumulative numerical rating is used as an index of the degree of stability. Large amount of data would have to be handled, storing and processing of the data on a computer would be of advantage.

The complex and subtle interaction of a large number of factors affects the stability of a slope. As a result, the factors included for the preparation of zonation maps and the relative weightages accorded, have varied from country to country and sometimes within the country as well. through familiarity with the area under study for zonation is essential if a successful hazard zonation map is to be prepared. As a word of caution, it may be stated that the overall accuracy of hazard maps has to be evaluated over a long period of time. Only with the help of very close and detailed monitoring, it is possible to quantify the probability of failure of a specific slope to a high degree of accuracy. The practice of landslide Hazard Zonation mapping has gained currency in a large number of countries, *viz,* U.S.A.,

France, Switzerland, Hongkong, Newzealand, etc.

Organisations such as CRRI, CBRI, GSI, University of Roorkee and IITs, etc., have been involved in landslide zonation studies in India. In 1984, CRRI carried out landslide zonation studies with a view to develop highway alignments to bypass chronic unstable slope stretches. The following factors were considered in evaluation of potential slope stability in this area (Table 2). These factors were tailor made to the slope and ambient condition in the study area. It is emphasised that for a different area it may be appropriate to omit some of the factors and include some other factors that may be of more relevance. Three zones of varying stability were identified with the ratings, good, fair and poor. The highway alignment was chosen so that it passes mostly through zones rated good and through the zones rated fair if unavoidable. Bypasses have since been built for two landslide areas along the alignments developed on the basis of the above studies. These bypasses have been observed to be stable for the past two to three years and further monitoring is continuing. Fig. 4, shows one such realignment selected by CRRI, based on the principles of zonation to bypass a chronic landslide. Fig. 5 shows landslide hazard zonation map prepared by CRRI, wherein, instability risk rating has been given.

National Data Base of Landslides

Data concerning landslide occurrences are presently not available at a single location. The information available is scattered in the files of the departments under whose jurisdiction the areas of landslides are situated. The information may not be complete, nor it might have been collected and recorded in a standard fashion. The lack of standardisation makes it difficult for the data to be used and interpreted properly by various specialists as well as agencies concerned with the work of landslide hazard mitigation.

Some stretches of highways, such as the Kathgodam-Nainital highway have an excellent record available giving basic data regarding slide incidence, remedial measures taken, etc., covering a large number of years. However, other data, such as the relevant geological, and geotechnical information and rainfall data are scarce. Thus mostly the data base is incomplete. It

Fig. 3 : Subsidence of roads due to mass movements in the hill slope.

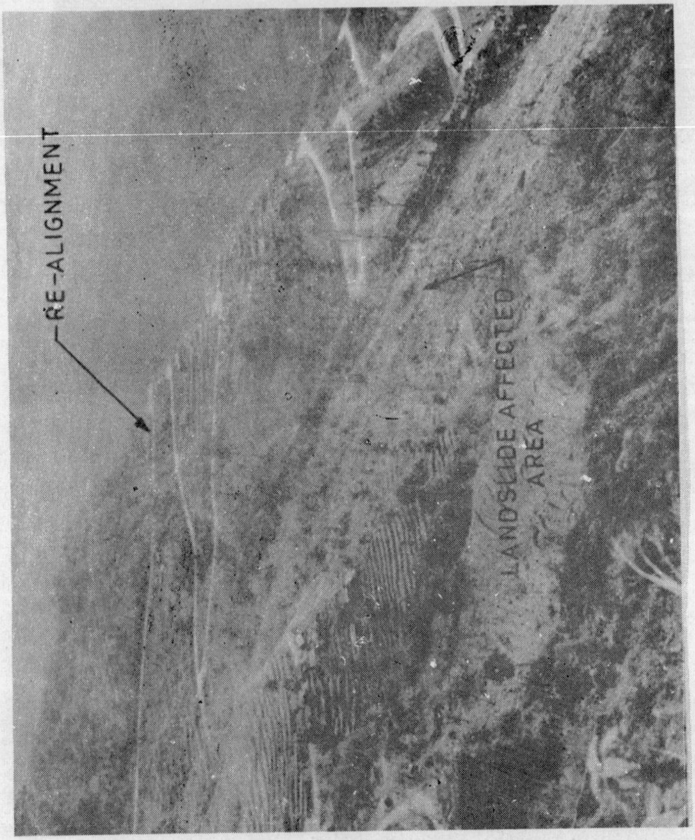

Fig. 4 : Alignment selected on principles of zoantion to bye pass a chronic landslide. The selected alignment has been found to be stable for over 5 years.

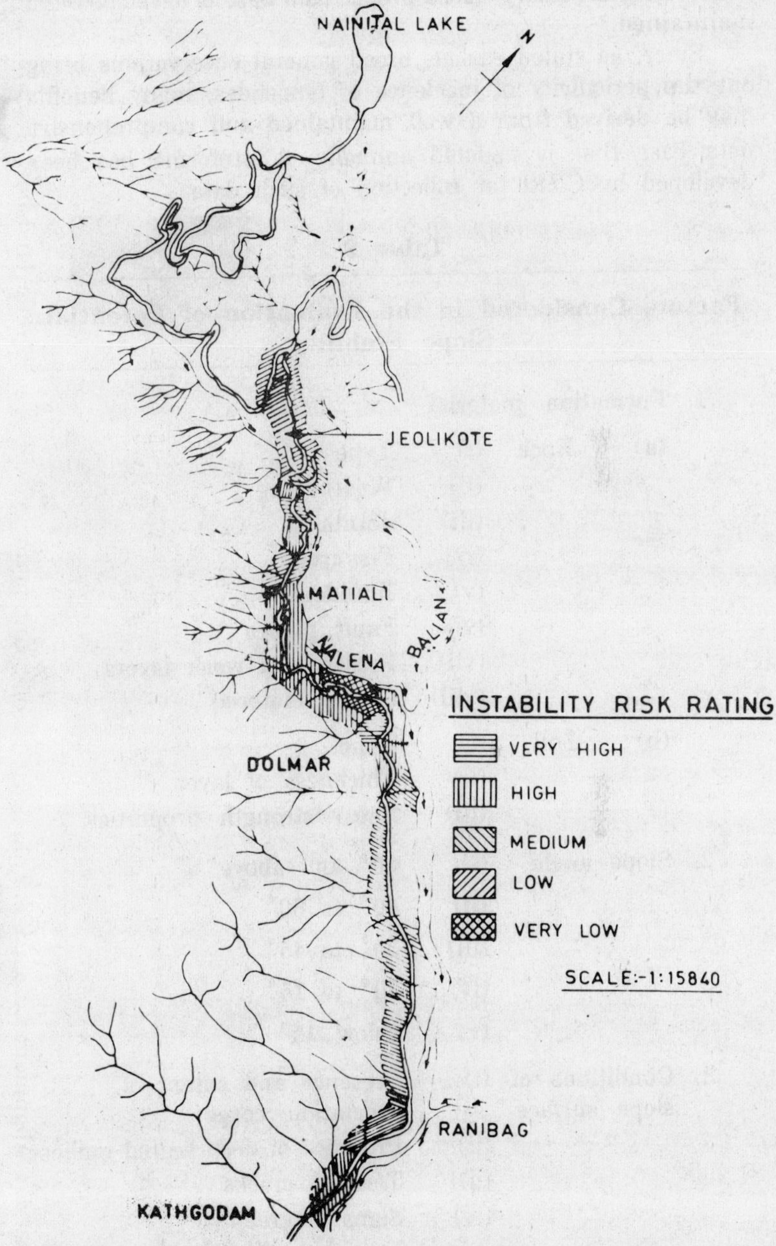

Fig. 5 : Zones showing instability risk rating

is therefore necessary that a proper data base is developed and maintained.

Since, as stated earlier, broad general observations bring out the periodicity of incidence of landslides, many benefits may be derived from a well maintained and comprehensive data base that is updated annually. A proforma has been developed by CRRI for collection of such data.

Table 2

Factors Considered in the Evaluation of Potential Slope Stability

Factor		No.	Item
1. Formation material			
(a)	Rock	(i)	Type
		(ii)	Weathering
		(iii)	Joints
		(iv)	Fissures
		(v)	Boulders
		(vi)	Fault planes
		(vii)	Presence of weak layers
		(viii)	Gouge material
(b)	Soil	(i)	Type
		(ii)	Thickness of layer
		(iii)	Shear strength properties
2. Slope angle		(i)	60° and above
		(ii)	40° to 60°
		(iii)	30° to 45°
		(iv)	30° to 15°
		(v)	below 15°
3. Conditions of slope surface		(i)	Presence and extent of vegetation cover
		(ii)	Presence of deep seated gullies
		(iii)	Tension cracks
		(iv)	Signs of creep

4.	Toe-erosion	(i)	Possibility and extent of toe-erosion
5.	Hydrological features	(i)	Presence of streams in the hill slope
		(ii)	Catchment area and pattern
		(iii)	Run-off characteristics.

Simple and Labour Intensive Landslide Control Techniques

Back Cutting of Hillsides

The most simple and commonly adopted practice of tackling slope stability problems arising out of a landslide is to back cut a new road in the hillside (Table 2). Depending upon the site conditions, the disposition of the debris, slope geometry, and related factors, the newly cut formation may still be located partly on the slid-out material itself or may be cut through the exposed hillside or located beyond the scarp of the slided area. Efforts should be made to ensure that the new cut is a stable part of the slope. In general, the formation width made by the back-cut is left in a temporary state till the surrounding area shows signs of improvement over a period of years. subsequently, when the stability of hill-side increases significantly, the road surface is improved to the required level of riding comfort.

This approach results in

(a) low initial expenditure, but significant continued recurring expenditure, to keep the stretch open to traffic.

(b) Poor quality of riding surface in the affected stretch. Reliance on manual labour for the landslide clearing work has its basis in the prevailing socio-economic conditions. Available unskilled labour has limited avenues of other employment. This has created a societal obligation on the highway departments to make maximum use of unemployed labour pool in various highway works. This situation, as well as the lack of adequate financial resources, form major constraints against adoption of technologies requiring increased mechanisation in landslide correction works.

Construction of Breast Walls, Check Walls, etc.

Another commonly adopted remedial measure consists of building breast walls and check wells at different points on the slope. These walls have only shallow foundations. Occasionally, a remaining wall with a deep seated foundation may be built but retaining walls designed for the earth pressures anticipated and located on suitable foundations are expensive in the hilly terrain and are built only at unavoidable spots. Due to heavy rainfall, backfill would be in a saturated condition for a greater part of the years and retaining walls show signs of severe distress. It is therefore essential to keep backfill to be in a well-drained condition. Breast walls and check walls also are of more flexible construction and are inherently capable of withstanding larger deformations than the relatively rigid retaining walls. Breast walls and check walls are suitable for controlling slaughbing of slopes and minor failures.

Surface Drainage

Water is the major cause for instability of slopes. Accordingly, removal of water and prevention of its ingress, rank as the most important of landslide control measures. Presence of water increases the weight of material. Any planes of weakness in the hill slope material are adversely effected by the presence of moisture. Effective system of surface drainage is needed to intercept the surface runoff, to minimise percolation of water into the slope material and to establish a stable moisture regime. Drainage enables a reduction in the weight of the mass tending to slide, as well as, leads to increase in the strength of the slope forming material. Reduction of infiltration and seepage also prevents the build up of high pore water pressures within the slope.

Hill slope drainage systems are designed to collect and dispose off the surface water, flowing on the slopes, to the nearest available natural water course. Surface drainage can be achieved by the following :

(a) Contour drains
(b) Catch water drains
(c) Drainage chutes
(d) Road side drains

Surface drainage is some times supplemented by

(a) reshaping of the slopes

(b) installation of drain pipes

(c) paving or bituminous treatment of slopes,.

Surface drains should be located very carefully, based on the study of topography of the slope area. The provision of surface drainage should ensure that surface run-off does not enter or percolate a potentially unstable area. Provision of surface drains along the outer periphery of the potentially unstable area is particularly desirable.

Surface drains serve to intercept the run-off from higher ground above the scarp and thereby divert it away from the slide area. If surface drains are likely to be clogged by debris from above, a drain pipe should be placed to ensure that water will not be trapped. Regular maintenance measure should be taken up to ensure the efficiency and effectiveness of the drainage system. A dislocated or broken surface drain may sometimes cause damage to the slope more than that due to lack of any drainage. Surface drainage may also be used in conjunction with other types of treatment of slope such a seeding, sodding, riprap, rockfills, etc.

Control of Surficial and Deepseated Slides

Extensive experience of CRRI developed from study, analysis and correction of landslides in the Himalayas as well as other hill ranges of the country has shown that it is advisable to group the landslides into two categories :

(a) shallow surficial erosion type landslides

(b) deep seated landslides

Some of the remedial techniques for both the types of landslides are briefly discussed.

Vegetation Cover for Control of Surficial Erosion Type Landslides

There exists a general consensus that the incidence of landslides has gone up due to hydrological problems arising from widespread denudation of hill slopes. Hill side slopes that are denuded of grass or vegetation cover, have been found to experience cumulative erosion which may ultimately grow to a slide involving a greater degree of slope instability. Majority of slope stability problems in the Western Himalayan areas have their origin in a cumulative erosion of hill slopes. It has been repeatedly observed that the combination of rainfall, type of slope material and conditions in these areas favours the occurrence of shallow erosion type landslides. Plantation of grasses and shrubs to restore the vegetation cover has been found to be successful in arresting this type of mass movement. The presence of vegetation cover is beneficial to the stability of slope in a number of ways, as enumerated below :

(a) Surface erosion is checked. If surface erosion remains unchecked, there is a high probability that the erosion may extend deeper and wider, and eventually endanger the stability of the slope.

(b) Infiltration of water into the slope is reduced.

(c) The root network extends to a depth of about 0.5m to 1.0m into the subsoil and binds the soil, thereby imparting to the soil an added component of cohesive strength. This cohesive strength improves the overall stability of the slope significantly.

Since a high proportion of landslides are of erosional type, the need for providing a vegetation cover on denuded slopes is an urgent task. However, experience shows that plantation has been resorted to as a landslide corrective measure only sporadically, but deserve to be used on a much wider scale. Such techniques as (i) the use of asphalt mulch (ii) use of coir netting (iii) use of jute netting, have been found to be significantly helpful in promoting and sustaining the growth of a vegetative cover over denuded slopes. Fig. 6 shows stabilisation of shallow surficial landslide induced by surface erosion, using coir-geogrid for promotion of vegetative growth over the denuded slope.

Landslides and Environment

Landslides have often been attributed as a cause of environmental degradation. The converse is also observed to be true. Especially degradation of environment in terms of denudation of slopes from cutting of forests and loss of vegetative cover, has also been observed to induce not merely erosion of the hill slope but also mass movements. In either case, the slopes fall prey to the destructive potential of the flowing water which washes away the soil cover. The debris often damages slopes downhill or may even choke the streams below. A significant part of the eroded soil is carried into the stream system causing siltation problems. The environmental damages caused by landslides as well as landslides induced due to degradation of environment have a tendency to feed on each other and provide a multiplying effect. Consequently, mitigation of landslide hazard is attracting increasing concern from the point of view of improvement in the environment.

Majority of slope stability problems in the Himalayan and other hill areas have their origin in a cumulative erosion of hill slopes. Hill area environment can be preserved and upgraded whenever called for, by proper planning and care, concerning slope stability aspects. Particular attention needs to be paid to promotion of vegetative cover on denuded slopes, as well as for ensuring that water flow on hill slopes does not cause heavy erosion. Concerted action on these aspects is being increasingly recognised as a vital aspect of hill area management.

Sealing of Tension Cracks

Tension cracks are usually present in all slopes affected by instability. Cracks have been observed with widths ranging from a few millimeters to as much as 30cm or more. The cracks constitute a sure sign of the unstable nature of the slope and as such should be read as forewearingness of impending slope movements. Further, open cracks serve as direct paths for the infiltration of surface run-off water, enabling it to reach deep into the slope mass, thereby further decreasing the factor of safety of the slope.

It is, therefore, of foremost importance to seal the tension cracks effectively to prevent any ingress of water. Such a treatment has been of immense help in restoring the stability of slopes on the verge of instability.

The procedure to be adopted for sealing the tension cracks is as follows :

All along the length of the cracks, a trench of about 50cm depth and 50cm width should be cut. The trench width should normally extend 25cm beyond either edge of the crack. The excavated material, if predominantly soil, should be mixed with water to make up to the optimum moisture content for compaction purposes. The consistency of the soil at this moisture content would normally be such that the soil can easily be manipulated to form a lump when pressed in hand but does not wet the hand.

Deeper parts of the cracks should be filled up at first by rolling and tamping thoroughly with crow bars. Filling the trench should be done by spreading the wet soil at O.M.C. to about 15cm depth and compacting by hand rammers. The top layer should be finished such that the original shape of the slope is retained to the maximum extent possible. The filled up surface over the tension crack should then be made waterproof by evenly spraying it with bituminous cutback of following composition :

Bitumen	: 1.0 kg
Kerosene	: 0.6 kg
Paraffin wax	: 0.01 kg

The bitumen should be first heated to about 110 C and removed from near the flame and the other two components added. The mixture may be sprayed with a garden sprayer, at an average rate of 0.2 kg per sq m.

Sealing of tension cracks should be done periodically, as a maintenance measure. The slopes should be inspected before the onset of monsoons and tension cracks present should be sealed. The experience at Central Road Research Institute has shown that the sealing of tension cracks is an inexpensive measure and the improvement in slope stability is very high.

Sub-surface Drainage for Control of Deep Seated Landslides

In the case of deep seated slides, the failure surface is located at a significant depth below the slope face and remedial measures, to be effective over a long period of time, must reach the failure plane or be adequate enough to counter the force of instability acting on the failure plane. Pore pressure action on deep-seated planes is one of the major causes leading to failure of deep seated masses. Figs. 6 and 7 show a massive deep-seated landslide in clay hale formation.

Fig. 6 : Stabilisation of shallow surfacial landslides induced by surface erosion. Use of coir geogrids to provide vegetative growth.

Fig. 7 : A massive landslide in clayshale formation.

In such cases, unless the pore pressures acting on the failure planes are relieved, the stability of the mass will not improve. Provision of any number or types of remedial works near the surface at shallow depth is bound to remain infructuous. Such slides require drainage of slope layers extending deep into the surface. Two methods of achieving such drainage are available. These are (a) use of horizontal drains and (b) use of deep subsurface trench drains. Horizontal drains consist of perforated plastic (PVC) or GI pipes driven into the slope so that the subsurface water flow is intercepted and the water drained out. Typically these drains may have a diameter of about 5cm and may be driven to depths of 15 to 20m into the slope. Drains are given a downward gradient of five to six per-cent. Spacing of the drains could range from 2m to 5m in a grid pattern depending on the quantity of seepage. The number of points at which the drains should be located would need to be determined on the basis of a careful site investigation to establish the ground water depth and flow patterns in the slide area.

Deep trench drains consist of rectangular trenches cut into the slope and backfilled with clean well graded rubble. Normally, a deep longitudinal trench running down the slope, with feeder trenches connecting to the main trench is the usual pattern adopted. The depth of these trench drains may extend from 3m to 15m depending on the hydrogeological conditions. Trench drains serve to intercept ground water flow and depress the level of water table thereby causing a sustained and significant decrease in the pore water pressure. Trench drains have been found successful in stabilising landslides beset with persistent instability problems even in situations where horizontal drains were not found adequate or successful.

Field trials using horizontal drains have been carried out by CRRI in the Niligiri hills area and were found to be successful. Fig. 8 shows hillslope at Nilgiri hills stabilized using horizontal drains.

Use of Restraining Piles and other Restraining Structures

Restraining piles of different types, such as cast in-situ concrete piles, or steel piles, driven or placed in premade boreholes to depths sufficiently below the surface of sliding, are effective in preventing mass movements. At any location where a deep-seated slide may be expected to take place or might have already taken place, the stability of the roadway can be restored or ensured by the use of restraining piles. The stability of the slope involved should be analysed from data obtained by site investigation and testing, and the location and number of such piles required should be determined to ensure the required degree of stability. Restraining piles have been used at number of locations in many countries to prevent hillside slips. It is possible to adopt this technique for use with a wide range of equipments from simple to sophisticated. For instance, cast institute concrete piles can be installed using a simple tripod, any boring equipment to make the boreholes and a mixer for preparing the concrete mix. On the other hand, sophisticated drilling equipments can be used to carry out the project work speedily. The adaptability and flexible nature of the technology, is thus an added advantage.

Restoration of Slopes using Reinforced Earth Technique, Geogrids, etc.

The advent of the reinforced earth technology in the late 60's followed by the development of different types of synthetic geogrids has placed, in the hands of the engineers a tool to build embankments of significant height with steep or even nearly vertical side slopes. This technology can be used to restore a hillside where significant damage due to sliding has occurred. It can also the be used in constructing a highway fill along the existing hill slope in a fashion to ensure stability of the highway fill as well as of the existing slope.

Reinforcing strips of steel, galvanised iron, grids of synthetic materials such as netlon and tensar serve to improve the frictional strength of the soil thereby enabling a retention of soil slope at steep angles.

Rockfall and Rockslide Protection Measures

On some of the freshly cut hill faces, rock exposures occur. If the exposed rock surfaces are in a shattered condition and are prone to lose strength due to weathering, rockfalls will occur periodically. Such rockfalls pose a hazard to the travelling

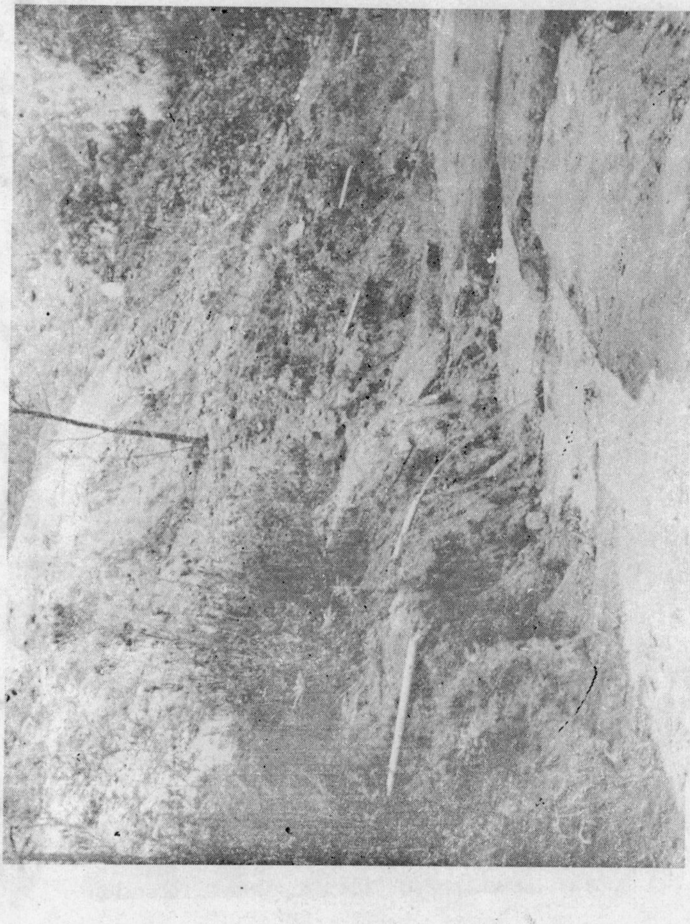

Fig. 8 : Horizontal drains to stabilise hillslope.

Fig. 9 : Rockfall control using Netlon geogrid

public as well as to workmen on the roadway. In general, not much attention has been devoted in India to protection against rockfall hazard. It is only at a handful of locations that any protection works against such hazards exist. It is considered essential that on slopes where it is identified that a rockfall problem exists, adequate protective measures be installed. These may consist of providing a cover of either G.I. or synthetic mesh over the affected area or rock fences, etc. The cost of these structures is only low to medium, but dividends in the form of safety to travelling public are appreciable. Fig. 9 shows a hillslope protected against rockfall using netlon geogrids.

Depending upon the state of the slope a few other protective measures such as rock bolting, prestressed anchors may be used to strengthen unstable block or beds of rocks. Rock bolts are normally used to stabilize shallow layers of rock. Prestressed anchors are used to stabilize a rock slope against deep seated failure. It is an expensive remedial measure and is used only where there is no alternative solution available.

To sum up, developmental activities in hill areas have focussed attention on landslide problems and their mitigation. The paper summarises the present status concerning landslide problems and landslide hazard mitigation activity in India. Some of the common landslide control techniques and those that have been developed and propagated in India, are briefly discussed.

In the context of the International Decade on Natural Disaster Reduction, work on landslide hazard mitigation has received a greater impetus in India. Preparation of a Natural Data Base on landslides, work on development of economical and effective control measures, instrumentation of landslides, etc., are on the anvil.

A Select Reading

Bhandari, R.K. (1987), "Slope Instability in Fragile Himalaya and Strategy for Development', 9th Annual IGS Lecture, *Indian Geotechnical Journal,* Vol. 17, No. 1, January, 1987.

Chowdhury, R.N. (1978), *"Slope Analysis"*, Elsevier Scientific Publishing Co., New York, 1978.

CRRI (1991), State-of-the-Art Report on Landslide Correction Techniques (Under Preparation for IRC).

Mehra, S.R., T.K. Natarajan, and S.C. Gupta, (1967), "Practical Lessons in Landslide Correction", *Journal of I.R.C.*, Vol. XXX-3, New Delhi, 1967.studying the ways of enterprising and

Mehra, S.R. and T.K. Natarjan, (1966), *"Handbook on Landslide Analysis and Correction"*, C.R.R.I., New Delhi, India.

Natarajan, T.K., R.K. Bhandari, and V. Sreenivasulu, (1975), "Prestressed Anchors to Prevent Slides in Rock Slopes', Vth Asian Regional Conference on Soil Mach. and Found. Engg., Bangalore, 1975.

Proceedings of International Symposium on Landslides, New Delhi, 1980. (Vol. 1 and Vol. 2).

Proceedings of IVth International Symposium on Landslides, Toronto, July, 1984 (Vol. 1 and Vol. 2).

Proceedings of IVth International Conference. and Field Workshop on Landslides, Tokyo, Japan, 23-31 Aug, 1985, (Vol. 1.).

Proceedings of 5th International Symposium On Landslides, Lauzanne, 10-15 July, 1988, (Vol. 1 and Vol. 2)

Rao, P.J. and D. Mukerjee, (1988), "Rockslope Protection Using Geogrids", Proceedings 1st India Conference on Reinforced Soil and Geotextile, Bombay, December 1988.

Rao, P.J. (1988), "Some Geological and Geotechnical Factors Influencing Landslides in Himalayas", Vth International Symposium on Landslides, Lausanne, Switzerland, July 1988.

Rao, P.J. (1989), General Report on Landslides, Symposium on "Preparedness, Mitigation and Maintenance of Natural Disaster", New Delhi.

Rao, P.J. and J. Bhagwan, (1989), "Use of Geosynthetic in Slope Protection", State-of-the-Art Report on Use of Geosynthetic in India-Experiences and Potential, by CBIP, New Delhi, 1989.

Rao, P.J. J. Bhagwan, and O.P. Yadav, (1990), "Slope Stability Problems in Semi-Arid Hillslopes", ALPS-90, Alpine Landslide Practical Seminar, 6th International Conference and Field Workshop Landslides, 1990.

Rao, P.J., O.P. Yadav, and S. Saha, (1991), "Prestressed Anchors for Rockslope Stability Improvement-A Case Study", 7th International Congress of ISRM, Aachen, West Germany, 1991.

Rever, R.B. (1982), Application of Walls to Landslide Control Problem, published by ASCE, 1982.

Schuster, L.R. and R.J. Krizek, (1978), Landslides Analysis and Control, National Academy of Science, Washington, D.C., Special Report-176, 1978.

Varnes, D.J. (1985), "Landslide Hazard Zonation", Review of Principles and Practice, UNESCO, Paris, 1985.

Voight, B. (1978), **Rockslides and Avalanches,** Natural Phenomena Vols. 1 and 2, Elsevier Scientific Publishing Co., New York, 1978.

Walker, B.F. and R. Fell, (1987), "Soil Slope Instability and Stabilisation", Balkema, Rotterdam, Brookfield, 1987.

Zaruba, R. and V. Mencl, (1982), Landslides and their Control, Elseviever Scientific Publishing Co., New York, 1982.

11

Education to Fight Against Natural Disaster

*B. Ganguly**

From time immemorial, the human beings are experiencing various natural hazards like storm, gale, cyclone, earthquake, volcanic eruption, flood, drought, landslides and forest fires. These have been taken as nature's anger and accepted as destiny or fate. When one or more of these hazards disrupt human ecology beyond normal recovery capacity, it is termed as natural disaster. The result of natural disaster has been loss of life, health hazards, loss of agricultural products, interruption of economic development and creation or lack of confidence in the minds of planners and investors. The results are aggravated in an unprepared community which is unnecessarily exposed and not able to either provide or use warning signals. With the growth of science and technology, it is possible today to minimise these results. For this purpose, it is necessary to have well thought out pre-disaster and post-disaster planning in which education constitutes an important component.

How Can Education Help?

Education has an important role to play in the planning of both pre-disaster and post-disaster stages. One component of education would be to train the volunteers and social workers who will be involved in the tasks of carrying out relief works and communicating messages and warning signals. Another group will have to be sufficiently educated to act as experts who will be in a position to handle various sophisticated equipments and gadgets to cope with the situation. They will

* Professior-Head, Department of Education in Science and Mathematics and Dean (Academic), National Council of Educational Research and Training, New Delhi.

constitute the expert group to collect and interpret the data and forecasting the hazards. But, the most important need is to educate all citizens who will be ultimately responsible for implementing the pre-and post-disaster plans. Such education must begin at the early stage of schooling and is justified for the following reasons :

1. It Provides Education which is Contemporary and Relevant

Relevance to environment and contemporary nature are the two important criteria for including any topic in the curriculum. 'Natural Disaster' is a subject which fulfils both these criteria.

2. It Prepares for Participation

Although a natural hazard may occur only in certain part of the country, its after-effect is felt across its length and breadth. Therefore, all citizens must have adequate knowledge, awareness and skills to participate in both the pre-and post disaster activities.

3. It Combines Past Experience with Recent Trend

Previous experience of hazard (in the country and abroad) and advances of science and technology to tackle them are the two basic principles for imparting education of natural disaster. Each individual citizen must learn about these two basic principles as a part of his education.

4. It Helps to Develop Effective Domain Abilities for Collective Work

The success in the natural disaster programme lies in the cooperative activities of a large number of individuals, agencies and countries. For this reason, it is necessary to learn how to work together. Thus, instead of only cognitive knowledge and psychomotor skills, it is necessary to develop certain effective domain abilities like compassion, hard work, persistence, tolerance, commitment, concern, amenability, etc., through education.

5. It Promotes Informed Decision Making Abilities

The natural disaster education is not an effort to mitigate some hypothetical, localised and infrequent events. On the contrary, it is a means to sustain economic development and improve the quality of life. It becomes possible only through the application of contemporary knowledge about disaster reduction in enhancing the security of different economic development enterprises. This increases the immediate cost but proves to be beneficial in the long run. It calls for properly informed decision-making ability in experts and general citizens which should be a major goal of natural disaster education.

What would be the Objectives for Educating Children of School-going Age Group?

The selection of objective should be based on four major ideas (1) types of natural hazards, (2) disaster management to minimise the impact of disaster, (3) usual impediments to natural disaster reduction, and (4) need to participate in various natural disaster reduction activities. Table 1 gives the details of the list of minor ideas to be developed in students. This suggested list is for the consideration of curriculum developers to formulate objectives according to the levels of the students and teaching-learning situations.

Table 1

Major and Minor Ideas for Selecting Objectives

Major Ideas	Minor Ideas
1. To understand the different types of natural hazards which cause disaster.	Nature of each hazard; relationship between natural hazards and disaster; causes, vulnerable areas and immediate impacts; long term impacts: factors which influence disaster.
2. To understand different disaster management activities to minimise the impact of a natural disaster.	Pre-disaster action is better than post-disaster reaction. Four major categories of preventive measures are prevention, preparedness, relief and

	research; different scientific and technological break-throughs and their application.
3. To understand the usual impediments to natural disaster reduction.	Impediments at the level of decision makers and planners; impediment due to the non-availability of physical resources and manpower; impediment due to unchecked population growth and crowding of short term measures.
4. To understand the need to participate in the various on-going and future activities for natural disaster reduction.	Changed approaches to natural disaster reduction programmes; experience of one disaster helps in facing other disasters; disaster management is a global responsibility; regular refresher training is important.

What would be the Content for the Children of School-going Age Group?

Despite its importance, it would not be advisable to introduce Natural Disaster Reduction as a separate subject in the school curriculum. Some of the ideas about natural hazards have already been presented in the science and geography textbooks. It is necessary to strengthen these ideas. It is not feasible to teach everything through the textbooks and that too within a specified period. Alternate methods of instruction would be necessary. A few hints that are given in Table 2 are only suggestive. The curriculum developers will have to keep in mind the age-group of the children, their background and transaction facilities before selecting the content. It may be necessary to replace some "dead woods" from the existing curricula by something which is vital for the country. The contents must give a clear idea about the following four aspects :

(a) types of hazards, (b) disaster management activities, (c) impediments to disaster reduction and (d) linking of disaster management activities with other on-going programmes of the community.

Table 2
Selection of Content

1. Types of disaster	Different hazards-past experience, causes and impact (Global and Indian examples) New scientific and technological findings for detection, warning, relief and control.
2. Prevention	Scenario of imaginary disaster; government policies and regulations; detection and warning systems-installation and maintenance in functional state; documentation of activities and messages; educating the public; land use restriction; environmental management; structural engineering measures.
3. Preparedness	Operation of detection and warning infrastructures; dissemination of warnings and instructions; communication to and from communities before, during and after disaster.
4. Relief	Provisions required for search rescue, health services and life line construction; requirement of long term rehabilitation.

Types of Hazards

The common natural hazards are landslides, earthquakes, volcanic eruptions, wind related hazards, floods, tsunamis, wild fires, drought, locusts and industrial disaster. For each disaster, it is necessary to discuss causes, well known examples, precautionary measures and extent of damages done. The well known detection technique needs to be mentioned and factors which increases the occurrence and magnitude of the disaster should be told. The hazards which come together like cyclone followed by heavy rain and flood or drought accompanied by locust invasion should be discussed with examples. Compared to different natural disaster, the industrial disaster is man-made and occurs within a short period. These disasters have established themselves as grave threats to human beings and his environment.

Disaster Management Activities

All the disaster management activities fall under four categories-(1) Prevention, (2) Preparedness, (3) Relief, and (4) Research. But most important is to give examples, where adoption of Disaster Management activities have reduced the intensity of damage. Both the emergency teams and general public are to be trained for all the four categories of disaster management activities mentioned above. For this purpose, relevant information must be well documented and important messages should be permanently displayed at a prominent place in the community. It should also be regularly updated. Besides, it is necessary to involve all levels-global and local, and exchange the latest knowledge on methods of training and information transfer.

The activities under the category-"Prevention" include (i) installation of detection and warning systems and ensuring that they are in working condition, (ii) communication of all government policies and regulations to all the members of the community, (iii) development of a total plan to face an imaginary disaster, (iv) advanced understanding of the risk by hazard mapping and vulnerability mapping and (v) to undertake well-known preventive steps like land use restriction, environmental management and application of structural engineering measures.

Linking with Ongoing Programmes

The ongoing programmes of disaster management operate according to the following flowchart :-

Collection of information	→	Examination of data by team of experts	→	Prediction of forecasts by the experts	→	Prediction issued to the community through A-V media	→	Reaction of the community as per earlier instructions

As new information is constantly coming in each of these areas, it is necessary to incorporate it in the ongoing activities.

What would be the Teaching-learning Strategies?

We are living a in a period when inumerable ideas are available towards the creation of teaching-learning situation. The trained teachers learn these methods in the pre-service and in-service training programmes (Table 3). But most teachers are untrained and physical facilities in schools are not encouraging for the trained teachers to try any innovations. Moreover, only purpose of education being examination, educational system is geared to rote-learning of bulk of facts, figures and data of different disciplines. The understanding, comprehension and skills, which are much desired from education are rarely attempted to be achieved.

Table 3

Some Teaching-Learning Techniques

1. Lecture cum demonstration
2. Student activities
3. Child to child education
4. Team teaching
5. Group discussion
6. Seminar
7. Role play
8. Debate
9. Project
10. Bulletin
11. Wall magazine
12. Exhibition
13. Mock exercises
14. Video film show
15. Audio cassettes
16. Television programme
17. Microcomputer
18. Field trip
19. Popular lectures

Many topics are already present in the existing syllabi followed in schools. It would be necessary to include a few concept related to weather, earthquake, earth's crust, soil, etc.

There is no reason why everything should be taught within the framework of time table of a class. Popular lectures, discussions, seminars and exhibitions may be organized in the school for creating interest of the students. The development of a project helps a child to learn more than the conventional textbooks. It would be necessary to present some facts, figures and data in education, but important purpose should be to convince the children that it is possible to reduce the harmful effects of a hazard by following a careful worked out natural disaster.

The training is required for three distinct target groups: (1) all citizens, (2) workers of volunteers and (3) experts or specialists. It is necessary to take up different strategies for different target groups. The training of all citizens should be a part of general education where attainment of awareness and ability to participate should be the main focus. From this group will develop volunteers of the emergency team and experts. The main task of the volunteers would be to communicate between expert group and the community, distribution and orderly management of relief works, and collection of data for researches. The volunteers may also have to function in managing and operating gadgets and equipment, in the hazard monitoring centres. The experts will be required for setting up and maintenance of equipment in such hazard detection centres. They will have to evaluate the message received and impart instruction in a very clear language. Experts are required also for relief and research. For this reason, they must be trained for the use of different gadgets including their maintenance and use knowledge about the new developments further updating, laws and rules of the country and culture of the affected people.

The ability to take decisions in a proper way should be developed during the training of all the three target groups. For this purpose, during the training, repeated exposure should be given to simulate situations so that the trainees develop the habit of thinking. The vulnerability studies and planning for imaginary disasters should be individually and collectively attempted.

12

Significance of Training and Education in Managing Natural Disaster

*D. P. Singh**

Natural disasters are of common occurrence now-a-days, and affect everyone without any distinction between the rich or poor. The devastating floods, cyclones, earthquakes, droughts and other disasters have brought not only untold misery to the people, irreparable damage to property and environment but have seriously affected the progress of our country. Every year in India, natural disasters kill thousands of people. Millions are rendered homeless, property worth crores of rupees is destroyed. Each year thousands of crores of rupees are spent by the government in mitigating the effects of these disasters which could otherwise have been utilized for development activities. The devastating toll of natural disasters is rising each year in spite of our increased understanding of hazards and how to mitigate them. The situation calls for serious rethinking and proper analysis.

It may not be possible to prevent the occurrence of these natural disasters totally but the resultant disastrous effects can be reduced considerably through proper planning and effective preparedness. Vulnerability associated with the hazards of natural disasters can be controlled to a satisfying extent by accurate and timely prediction and by taking counter measures to reduce their impact.

Management of natural disaster is a multi-disciplinary, interrelated and coordinated work and thus, requires inputs and involvement of experts from different disciplines as well as governmental, non-governmental and voluntary agencies. Combined and coordinated efforts from all the corners, can only develop attitudes and capabilities to deal forcefully with

* Officer on Special Duty, Disaster Management Institute, Bhopal.

the natural disasters. Although disasters have been a part of the life since time immemorial; the concern for planning, preparedness, mitigation and management of these disasters has been of quite recent origin.

Disaster Prevention and Preparedness

Disaster prevention and preparedness consists of a wide range of measures both long-term and short-term, which are designed to save lives and limit the losses to minimum. Prevention is concerned with long-term policies and programmes to prevent or eliminate the occurrence of disasters.

Disaster preparedness is the detailed planning for prompt and efficient response once a disaster strikes. It is concerned with operational planning, education and training of the population especially of the disaster prone areas, and technical as well as management training of the personnel who will be required to help in a disastrous situation with respect to relief operation, stock pilling of supplies, and other arrangements. The more effectively these tasks are carried out well in advance, the more readily will it be possible to take the required action during emergency phase and later on during post disaster phase such as relief, rehabilitation and reconstruction.

Disaster prevention and preparedness involves a wide variety of different services and skills all of which must work harmoniously aiming to get right things to the right place in the right quantity and in time for managing a disaster and hence, interdependence on each other is necessary.

Disaster Management

Disaster management means a planned and systematic approach towards understanding and solving problems in the wake of disaster. The science of disaster management involves a systematic observation and analysis of measures relating to disaster prevention, preparedness, mitigation, emergency response, rehabilitation and reconstruction.

Prevention and reduction of natural disaster require close collaboration of a diversity of people and organisations, within a comprehensive management programme. This requires the allocation of wide ranging tasks and development of specific skills for different persons and agencies to assume complementary roles in disaster management. In other words very large and carefully structured training programmes are needed to be organised for development of competence and skills.

Training and Education for Natural Disaster Reduction

In managing natural disasters promptly and effectively, training and education are areas of utmost importance. Amongst the goals of the IDNDR and for achieving them effectively, the proposed innovative approaches had specific contents pertaining to training and education. Thus, training and education have been recognized as important activities to achieve disaster reduction in the coming years.

Following three elements of training and education in relation to disaster preparedness are important :

(i) Technical training for utilizing specialized skills to a great extent.

(ii) Management training and education for disaster managers and planners to make them aware of the types of risks, key roles expected from them and difficulties in managing the disastrous situations.

(iii) Education for general public.

What is Training ?

Training is a means to improve performance and problem solving capabilities of people in difficult situations. It is also a continuous process to build capability, in sufficient number of concerned individuals, to bring about planned changes in the system. The changes may be small adjustments or major deviations from the existing system. Training, therefore, should be defined in the context of a desired change in the individual as well as the system they are responsible for. The goals of a training programme must be specifically set and changed from time to time according to the changing needs of the system.

Training Needs

The importance of training and education in managing natural disaster during IDNDR has to be properly assessed.

Following objectives should be kept in mind while identifying training needs :-

1. Taking the existing system for granted, how can training of people in various skills at various levels improve their decision making, problem solving and survival capabilities in disaster situations?
2. What should be the approach of an ideal training programme with a view to bring about the desired change in the existing system?

Intensive and extensive training of concerned people in disaster management will contribute heavily towards more effective disaster preparedness and response at various levels and thereby help bring about the necessary changes in the entire system in due course of time.

Target Groups

There are three distinct categories that need to be trained in disaster management, *viz.*, community groups, voluntary agency personnel, and the governmental officials. It will not be out of place to reiterate here that the affected communities will have to take upon themselves most of the responsibilities for rehabilitation and reconstruction. This observation emphasizes that training for community groups could be most effectively given at the community level itself. Training at this level would mainly focus on various skills considered essential in a disaster situation. It should be extensive rather than intensive. Training for voluntary agency personnel must take into account the diversity of their academic background, professional experience and competence. A more systematic training module, based upon their special role in disaster management in India, still needs to be evolved. Training of government officials will have to be both intensive and extensive because they are the key persons responsible for disaster management in all aspects. Regulation alone can never provide a substitute for commitment in either government or community. The important target group for training, therefore, should be the policy makers and decision takers with whom one has direct contact and to whom one is responsible. There can be three clearly demarcated levels for their training--the state, the district and tehsil or block level.

Training and education programmes should be organised frequently at the local level. At village and block level, joint programmes should be organised, besides, the development of individual capabilities and skills. These should be designed to develop mutual understanding and confidence, so that people learn to operate together, to delegate and to accept changed roles. This is the level where one really needs imaginative, instructive and also testing training. The training must follow simulation exercises to test the decision making, communication and coordination systems.

Communities in the threatened areas are expected to play key role in managing the disaster because the outside assistance always arrives late. Thus, community awareness is an important area and for this, awareness campaigns need to be organised with materials developed in native languages.

Mostly natural hazards are specific for certain regions. The impact and nature of various disasters differ widely and general disaster preparedness training is often limited to the emergency control aspects of disasters rather than to disaster prevention. Disaster prevention is an hazard specific activity because it is related directly to local conditions. Hence, local conditions should always be kept in mind.

Basic Elements of Training

Disaster prevention and preparedness training is based mostly on general principles. The protection of human lives is the most basic objective of disaster reduction and for each of the main disaster types specific steps must be developed to achieve this. It should, however, be realised that disaster management is still not a well-defined discipline. Our knowledge in this field cuts across wide professional areas such as environmental sciences, management, engineering and agricultural sciences, social sciences, public health, etc. In each of these areas there is good knowledge and experience of relevance to disaster reduction. Elements from each of these areas is, therefore, essential in disaster reduction training.

More important is to concentrate on action-oriented training. The training should increase the ability of the target group to use the sills and information from the course for fulfilling specific tasks within a joint disaster management programme.

The basic disaster cycle and related general principles must be fully understood by all, but then each trainee must be prepared for a specific task. The objective of training, therefore, differs for each target group and for each disaster type.

Personnel from the government and voluntary agencies need to be trained in rescue and relief operations so that sufficient manpower is available to carry out the task. Training should also condition them to work as a team in the context of a disaster. Relief administration is also a specialized area. An understanding of the local conditions is necessary to regulate and rationalize the flow of relief provisions and materials Training programmes can highlight the steps to be taken to meet the special needs of the most vulnerable categories of people.

Policies and Strategies for Training

Disaster preparedness training should be based on the following policies and strategies :

Training of Trainers

Preparing a national cadre of experienced trainers in various fields of disaster management would be the first positive step. This will be an ongoing process, given the variety of disciplines that disaster preparedness encompasses and the ever expanding scope of issues it addresses. Training of trainers will also ensure the multiplier effect of training.

Training Courses, Workshops, etc.

To create awareness and developing skills necessary for disaster preparedness, variety of training courses, workshops should be organised for general and specific target groups.

Institutionalisation of Training Efforts

Training efforts should be institutionalized nationally for long-term survival. For this, there should be an apex National Institution along with Regional Centres through which training can be imparted regularly and sustainably. Efforts should be made to include significant aspects of disaster preparedness in the curriculum of school and college education system.

Developing of New Areas of Technical Expertise

After establishing a mechanism for transmitting general skills, efforts should be concentrated on developing new areas of technical expertise. Because, the field of disaster preparedness is ever expanding, training programmes and materials must also be dynamic and up-to-date.

Development of Training and Educational Material

Training and educational material should be developed by reputed agencies, institutes, experts on various types of disasters and their management in the form of pamphlets, monographs, books, video cassettes, etc. This material should be made available either at no cost or low cost basis to qualified institutions, NGOs and individuals, which in turn should be used for various training programmes to make the multiplier effects of training a success.

Resources Available for Training in India

Following institutions/organisations are imparting training in the field of management of natural disasters, in India.

Disaster Management Institute, Bhopal was established by the Government of Madhya Pradesh in November, 1987. Besides others, one of the main activities of the institute is to organise training programmes on various aspects of natural and man-made disaster for officials of Central and state government departments and Public and Private sector undertakings as well as for NGOs and voluntary agencies with a particular aim to make them aware of potential hazards, their control and equip them to conceive and prepare emergency plans and execute them effectively at the right moment in case a crisis arises due to natural disaster or disaster caused by human activities.

Administrative Staff Collage of India, Hyderabad conducts one course each year for senior executives. National Civil Defence College, Nagpur organises training courses with priority to the life saving techniques particularly for civil defence personnel.

Joint Assistance Centre, New Delhi being the premier voluntary agency organises training programmes at headquarters and other places. Most of the courses are designed and organized for voluntary organisations.

A few other voluntary agencies also conduct training programmes at regional level. Some of these agencies are PREPARE, IYDP, CASA, Rama Krishna Mission, etc.

It is perhaps clear from the above discussion that training resources in our country in this areas are still limited in number and scope. We have, therefore, yet to go a long way in developing required infrastructure for training and establishing sound credentials in this field. During IDNDR, coveted efforts should be made by one and all to achieve the same.

A Select Reading

A. Ahmed and Ravi Kumar (1982), "Disaster Management" in Proceedings of National Workshop on Disaster Management held at ASCI, Hyderabad.

Central Water Commission, New Delhi (1989), Proceedings of the Symposium on Preparedness, Mitigation and Management of Natural Disaster, Vols. I, II, held at New Delhi in 1989.

C.N. Ritchine. 1990, Counter Disaster Staff Training. Disaster Management, Vol. 3 No. 1, 1990.

Krishno Nimpuno-1990, The Focussing of Training Material for Disaster Reduction, A paper sent for National Convention on 'Role of Voluntary Agencies in Natural Disaster Reduction' held in August 1990 at New Delhi.

United Nations, New York (1984), Disaster Prevention and Mitigation: A Compendium of Current Knowledge, Vol. 11 Preparedness Aspects.

A SELECT BIBLIOGRAPHY

BOOKS

Bawa, D.S. *New strategy for industrial development of flood and drought prone areas*, New Delhi, The author, 1980.

Biswas, A. *The new educational pattern in India*. Delhi, Vikas, 1976.

Chisholm, Anthoney and Robert Dumsday (eds.). *Land degradation: problems and policies*. Cambridge, Cambridge University Press, 1987.

Cohen, Stephen P. The Andhra cyclone of 977: individual and institutional responses to mass death. New Delhi, Vikas, 1979.

Coleman, Ronny J. and John A. Granito, (eds.) Managing fire services. New York, International City Management Association 1988.

Davis, Ian (eds). *Disasters and the small dwelling*. Oxford, Pergamon Press, 1989.

Dhar, Trilok N. *Education and employment in India*. Calcutta, Minerva Associates, 1976.

Drabek, Thomas E. *Emergency Management: strategies for maintaining organizational strategy*. Springer Verleg, 1990

Ghosh Ratan. (eds) *Education and the process of change*. New Delhi, Sage, 1987.

Gore, M.S. Education and modernization in India, Jaipur, Rawat, 1982

Green Stephen International disaster relief: towards a responsive system. New York, McGraw Hill, 1977

Hirshleifer, Jack. Economic behaviour in adversity. Brighton, Wheatsheaf, 1987.

Joint Assistance Centre. Natural disasters. New Delhi, Adhyatma Sadhana Kendra, 1980.

Kamat, A.R. Education and social change in India. Bombay, Samaiya, 1985.

Kanwar, Sain. The flood problem of India. New Delhi, Biral Institute of Scientific Research, 1979,

Palm, Risa J. Natural hazards: and itegrative framework for reserach and planning. Hopkins University Press, 1990

Ravallion, Nartin. Markets and famines. Oxford, Oxford University Press, 1987.

Raza, Moonis, ed. Educational planning: a long term perspective. New Delhi, Concept, 1986.

Stephen, Lynn H., ed. Disaster assistance: appraisal and new approaches. London, Macmillan, 1980

United Nations. Office of Disaster Relief Coordinator. Disaster rpevention and mitigation a compendium of current knowledge. New York, NY, U.N. 1984

ARTICLES

Amrik Singh. "New Policy on education: two years latter". *Economic and Political Weekly* 23 (45 & 47), Special No. 88, pp. 279-92.

Anisuzzaman, Muhmad. "Managing flood disaster in Bangladesh: implications for public administration." *Asian Review of Public Administration* 2(1-2), Jan.-Dec. 90, pp. 12-28

Ardeknai, Siamak. "Logistics problems in the aftermath of the 1985 Mexico City earthquake." *Transportation Quartertly* (42), Jan. 88, pp. 107-24

Ashton, Basial *et al.* "Famine in China, 1958-61" *Popublation and Development Review* 10 Dec. 84, pp. 613-45.

Banerjee, P.S. "Five service-the fourtharm of defence." *Civic Affairs* 31(5), Dec. 83, pp. 17-26.

Berke, Philip R. "Hurrica vertical shelter policy: the experience fo two states." *Coastal Management* 17(3), 98, pp. 193-217

Bhttaria, P.L. "Fire safety in high rise building." *Civic Affair*, 32(3), Oct. 84, pp. 29-32.

Brett, Jain E. "Crisis public ralations plans." *Journal of Property Management*, 49, Jul. Aug. 84, pp. 17-21.

Britton, Neil R. "Policy development and social crisis administration." *Asian Review of Public Administration*, 2(1-2), Jan.-Dec. 90, pp. 74-91.

Brown, Robert D. and William J. Kockelman. "Geology for decision-makers: protection life property, and resouces." *Public Affairs Report*, 26, Feb. 85, P. 1-11.

Caldwell, John C. and others. Periodic high risk as cause of fetility decline in a changing rural environment: survival strategies in the 1980-1983: South Indian drought." *Economic Development and Cultural Change*, 34, July 86, pp.677-701.

Chang, Semoon "Disasters and fiscal policy: hurricane impact on municipal revenue." *Urban Affairs, Quarterly*, 18 Jun. 83, pp. 511-23.

Dhatwalia, H.R. "Natural calamities and preventive measures." *Journal of Himachal Pradesh Institute of Public Administration* 11(2), Aug.-Dec.87, pp. 29-33

Dregne, H.E. "Soil Erosion: cause and effect." *Land Use Policy*, (4), Oct. 87, pp. 412-18

Engineer, Rusi, "Punishing corporate negligence industrial diasters and criminal law." *Economic and Political Weekly*, 24(14), 8 Apr. 89 pp. 711-13

Ink, Dwight. "Response to the Alaskan earthquake." *Asian Review of Public Administration* 2(1-2), Jan.-Dec. 90, pp.66-73.

Istance, Daivd. "Polices for quality in schooling." *OECD Observer* (154) Oct.-Nov. 88, pp, 15-17

Junwei, Lu. "The earthquake disaster management system and strategy of China." *Asian Review of Public Administration,* 2(1-2), Jan.-Dec. 90, pp. 57-65.

Karetz, Jack D. "Crisis reponse planning: toward a contingent analysis." *American Planning Association Journal,* 50 Winter 84, pp. 9-21.

Khanna, S.S. "Drought mangement," *Yojana,* 33(11), 16 Jun. 89, p. 4-8.

Khous, Martin Stick. "Earthquakes, earth expansion, and the cycles." *Cycles,* (38), Nov. 87, pp. 192-7.

Kouzmin, Alexander and Allan Jarman. "Towards comprehensive planning in Australian crisis management." *Asian Review of Public Administration,* 2(1-2), Jan.-Dec.90, p. 92-113.

Krishna Kumar. "Revived Policy interest in edcuation: issues at primary level in India." *Future,* (26 & 27), Autumn Winter, 89, pp. 27-30.

Lambright, W. Henry and Jane A. Heckely. "Policy-making for emerging technology: the case of earthquake prediction." *Policy Sciences, (Amsterdam)* 18, Nov. 85. pp. 227-40.

McCann, John P. "A stith in time: earthquake preparedness management." *Insurance Review,* 46, Mar.-Apr. 85, pp. 24-30.

Mackenzie, Deborah and Robert Walgate. "Locusts swarm while experts argue." *African Business,* Jan. 88, p. 14-15.

May, Peter J. and Linda L. Noson. "Reducing earthquake risks: sesimic sapty policy," *Wash Public Policy Notes* 14, Autumn 86, pp. 1-6.

Miller, Christopher and Geraldine Bachman. "Planning for hurricanes and other coastal disturbances." *Urban Land,* 43, Jan. 84, pp. 18-23.

Nilson, Linda B., (ed.) "Symposium on natural disasters and public policy, *Policy Studies Review*, 4, May 85, pp. 641-738.

Olshansky, Robert B. and J. David Rogers. "Unstable ground: landslide policy in the United States." *Ecology Law Quarterly*, 13(4), 87, Pp. 939-1006.

Petak, William J., ed. Emergency management: a challenge for public administration. *Public Administration Review*, 45, Jan. 85, p.1-172.

Pilar, Nestor N.
"Crisis/disaster management: the Philippine experience." *Asian Review of Public Administration* 2(1-2), Jan.-Dec. 90, pp. 34-56.

Pittman, Garry L. "Military support to civil authorities during disaster relief operations." *Police Chief*, 51 May 84, pp. 53-4

Rana, Madhukar, S.J.B. "Disaster management in Nepal." *Asian Review of Public Administration*, 2(1-2), Jan.-Dec. 90, pp. 1-11.

Robson, Emma. "Saving the land, serving the people." *World Development* 4(2), pp. 22-4

Rodell, Scoot M. "Where there is fire, three is smoke: most injuries in fires come not from the flames but from the fumes." *Environmental Action*, 15, May 84, p. 23-7.

Rosenthal, Uriel. Beyond disasters: common ground for crisis management." *Asian Review of Public Administration* 2(1-2), Jan,-Dec. 90, p.114-22.

Ross, Lester "Earthquake policy in China. *Asian Survey*," 24, Jul,. 84, pp. 773-87.
PAIS 1985

Ross, Lester. "Flood control policy in China: the policy consequences of natural disasters." *Journal of Public Policy* 3, May 83, pp. 209-31.

Sacks, Stephen R. "Public *vs* private prouction of fire protection service," *North-East Journal of Business and Eonomics,* 13, Fall/Winter 86, pp. 60-71.

Salmon, Jack D. "Vertical Evacuation in hurricanes: an urgent policy problem for coastal managers." *Coastal Zone Management Journal* 12, 84, pp. 287-300.

Samanta, R.K. "Instructional aids for education and training." *Indian Journal of Training and Development,* 18(6), Nov.-Dec. 88, pp 27-32.

Sayee Kumer and S. Gopala-Krishnan "Disaster management: a psycho-social crisis." *Social Welfare,* 36(5), Aug. 89, pp. 33-4.

Singh, S.P. and C. Prased. "Resarch and development coordination for soil conservation." *Productivity,* 30(4), Jan. Mar. 90, pp. 415-19.

Special issue on drought. *Administrator,* 33(4), Oct.-Dec. 88, pp. 1-62.

Special issue on educationl planning. *Journal of Educational Planning and Administration* 2(1-2), Jan.-Apr, 88, pp. 1-219.

Tierney, Kathleen J. "Emergency medical preparedness and response in disaster : the need for interorganisational coordination" *Public Administration Review,* 45, Jan. 85, pp. 77-84.

Toulmin, Camilla. "Drought and the farming sector: loss of farm animals and post-drought rehabilition." *Development Policy Review,* 5, Jun. 87, pp. 125-48

Zhange Zhijin. "Disaster mangement in China." *Asian Reivew of Public Administration,* 2(1-2), Jan.-Dec. 90, pp. 29-33.

